Latin American Lawyers

A Historical Introduction

ROGELIO PÉREZ-PERDOMO

Stanford University Press
Stanford, California
2006

Stanford University Press
Stanford, California

Library of Congress Cataloging-in-Publication Data

Pérez-Perdomo, Rogelio.
Latin American lawyers : a historical introduction / Rogelio Pérez-Perdomo.
p. cm.
Includes bibliographical references and index.
ISBN 0-8047-5126-9 (cloth : alk. paper)
1. Law—Study and teaching—Latin America—History. 2. Practice of law—Latin America—History. I. Title.
KG46.P47 2006
340'.071'18—dc22 2005022699

Original Printing 2006
Last figure below indicates year of this printing:

15 14 13 12 11 10 09 08 07 06

Typeset by Classic Typography in 10.5/12 Bembo

LATIN AMERICAN LAWYERS

Contents

Preface

Lawyers have been present throughout the five-century history of Latin America. But how did lawyers in 1550 differ from lawyers today? Does it mean the same to be a lawyer in Mexico City or in Temuco, in the South of Chile?

Comparative law scholars include Latin America within the civil law tradition (Merryman, 1985; David, 1988; Zweigert and Kötz, 1998; Clark, 1999), implying a basic identity among Latin American lawyers themselves and between European and Latin American lawyers. The tradition of civil law generally reverts to ancient Rome and Roman law. This book will show the problematic aspects of this identity and highlight some of the enormous differences between lawyers in distant epochs and societies, as well as some basic traits that allow them to be wrapped together and compared. We have felt obliged to discuss the meaning of the Roman law tradition for Latin American lawyers.

In the early 1500s, Spanish kings forbade lawyers to travel to the "Indies" without special permission, but by the 1550s they created universities and law schools in the new territories. Only Old Christian white males were eligible to enroll. Portuguese royalty followed a different path: universities and law schools were prohibited in colonial Brazil, forcing wealthy colonists to send their children to Coimbra in order to study law. In spite of all the restrictions, lawyers in Latin America numbered about 1,500 by the early 1800s. Royal officials thought there were too many.

In today's Latin America, lawyers number more than a million and universities are filled with law students. Yet requirements vary from one country to another; in fact, more similarities exist between Brazilian and Mexican lawyers today than between eighteenth-century and present-day Venezuelan lawyers. Education, stratification, and social role have evolved quite similarly in the various countries.

Lawyers are a crucial part of understanding state legal systems and societies. They have special knowledge and skills to operate the legal and political system, and their role is to articulate for the individuals and businesses within the state. Although many lawyers are state functionaries, most are private lawyers paid with private money. Latin American lawyers have played this role in a notorious way: they frequently have been high officials and they primarily have served, and served well, wealthy people.

The first question is why, given their significant role, there have been no previous books on Latin American lawyers. The answer is that lawyers have been key to nation building, and their history and study are thus more related to individual countries. In fact, little has been written on Latin American law per se, and legal scholarship and literature on lawyers remain generally national.

As national studies addressing specific eras abound, the second question is why no previous effort at synthesis has been made. The answer mirrors the first one: there was little interest in thinking of Latin America as a whole in relation to law and lawyers. And that is surprising: whole libraries are devoted to Latin American literature, music, and culture. Law is staunchly national probably because its rules and principles vary so widely from place to place. A book on Latin American lawyers is possible in the measure that scholarship pays more attention to historical trends and the relation to culture and society.

The synthesis is not an easy task. What national studies do exist were written with many different perspectives and tend to center on lawyers' political roles or contribution to the legal field (see Halliday and Karpik, 1997). Other studies focus on legal education. This book proposes to connect occupation, knowledge, and political role while pointing out the contextual elements that allow a better understanding of this relation. But the reader should be aware that this book is possible only because it builds on previous scholarship and, at the same time, that we are limited by this bibliography.

The focus of this book is on the relation of lawyers and politics. Lawyers have been extremely important in Latin American politics from independence to present day, but their role requires a kind of baroque understanding. The political role is far from obvious because in Latin America rule of law has not been a dominant trait of politics. The relation is not a linear one. The present work will explore this complex dynamic, taking into account different times and political circumstances.

Acknowledgments

This book is a much-revised version of four lectures given at Universidad Diego Portales, in Santiago, in August 2000 by invitation of the Fueyo Laneri Foundation. I thank Don Gustavo Serrano, then-president of the foundation, Dean Carlos Peña, and my Chilean colleagues for the occasion to begin work on this book and for the warm reception given at the start of the whole enterprise. In 2002 the Universidad del Externado de Colombia, in

Bogotá, provided the occasion for me to return to the book. I thank Rector Hinestrosa and Director Silva García for that invitation and for the subsequent publication of the Spanish version of this book.

My work was possible because of the previous scholarship on lawyers of different periods and countries of Latin America. It is a varied scholarship, written with different approaches and not always easy to locate. I thank my Latin American friends and colleagues who provided me with information and insights on the history of their countries. I should mention especially María Inés Bergoglio, Eliane Junqueira, Carlos Peña, Edmundo Fuenzalida, Marcelo Montero, Iñigo De la Maza, Fernando de Trazegnies Granda, Gorki González, Renzo Honores, Alfredo Fuentes-Hernández, Germán Silva García, César Rodriguez, Alfredo Chirinos, María del Refugio González, José Antonio Caballero, Héctor Fix-Fierro, Asdrúbal Baptista, Carmen Luisa Roche, Yajaira Freites, Manuel Gómez, and Irene Torres.

During the time I was writing this book, my country was living in turbulence. The Stanford University Law School provided the necessary tranquility and scholarly environment, making the inception of this book possible. The library is any scholar's dream, not only for its wealthy collection but also for the diligent and friendly staff. I am most grateful to all of them, with special mention of Alba Holgado and Sonia Moss. The fellows of the international program were a diverse set and provided a living course in comparative law and lawyers, and the students of my course in Law in Latin American obliged me to explain many aspects of lawyering that usually we take for granted. Two of these excellent students, Kate Unterman and Robert Watson, were the translators of this book. The Library of the Oñati International Institute for the Sociology of Law helped me, too, thanks to the facility of electronic communications. Elvira Muñoz and Sole Aguirre assisted me from across the Atlantic.

My time at Stanford was also one of solitude. My colleagues made this period less difficult with their friendship and spirited conversation. I wish to mention Tom Heller, Bill Gould, Miguel Méndez, Jonathan Greenberg, and Erick Jensen. Kate DeBoer, from the Stanford Program for International Legal Studies, assisted me on all practical and bureaucratic matters.

I am especially grateful to John Henry Merryman and Lawrence Friedman. They are true *sabios maestros*, as we like to say in Spanish, and this book is deeply indebted to their teaching. In addition, Lawrence Friedman revised and edited the English version, a huge job that is a sample of his enormous generosity. I associate this book with lunch on Monday with John Merryman, which became almost a ritual, and with many dinners and conversations with Lawrence and Leah Friedman, even if we talked of many other subjects than lawyers in Latin America.

Los Palos Grandes, Caracas,
and Palo Alto, California

LATIN AMERICAN LAWYERS

CHAPTER 1

Lawyers and the Civil Law Tradition

LATIN AMERICAN lawyers feel that they are the heirs of a grand tradition, Roman law. We study it from the first year of law school and are staunchly taught that the Romans who lived twenty centuries ago formulated our fundamental principles and concepts. But is this really the case?

The Rome that stirs our admiration is *classical Rome*, or Rome in the classical period. This era lasted roughly from the century before the birth of Christ until two centuries after it (100 B.C.–250 A.D.).[1] It was the period when Rome blossomed from a large village headed by a minor king into the capital of a world empire. The city was spectacularly transformed. Great public works were erected in stone and marble, the ruins of which we still admire today. During this period, the city of Rome had one million inhabitants and became an active commercial center where people, cultures, and products converged from all over the known world. It was also a city ravaged by epidemics and fires (Friedländer, 1947). This great capital of the ancient world, seen through the eyes of a modern-day tourist, would seem only a foul-smelling, medium-sized city. So how could it be that these ancient Romans could have framed the law for a continent that was not even known to exist at that time? How is it that we have seemingly not been able to add anything substantial to that law in twenty centuries?

Roman jurists of the classical period made an immense contribution to their society. They had the creativity and intelligence to adapt the law of their day to the enormous social changes resulting from the world's first wave of globalization. But it is not at all certain that today's idea of law is the same as that of ancient Rome, nor that our lawyers resemble such figures as Mucius Scaevola, Papinian, or Cicero in either their daily work or their social role.

The notion of classical Roman law as a set of logical, ordered principles and rules is in large part a modern myth. Moreover, the idea that the Roman jurists created a geometrically ordered system of law in the style of Euclid, as was commonly thought between the sixteenth and eighteenth centuries, has been discredited by historical research. This work will not enter into a discussion of the difference between the law of the Rome of Augustus and the mythic law of classical Rome. Instead, our theme concerns the Roman jurists, those who knew the law and worked with it. It is inevitable, however, that we tackle the question of what was considered law and how it was studied in each era, because that is crucial for understanding the knowledge and work of the jurists. Thus it is important to emphasize from this point forward that the expression *Roman law* actually stands for many very different realities in the more than twenty centuries of its history.

Jurists, Lawyers, and Orators

Who were the Roman jurists and lawyers of the classical period? How were they trained? In fact, two types of jurists had pivotal roles relating to the legal system, both of which correspond to today's notion of lawyers. The *advocati*, or *causadici*, aided others in public courts. The *jurisconsulti*, or *jurisprudenti*, advised judges, functionaries, litigants, and lawyers in legal matters. They answered inquiries about the content of the law and possible actions to take and also could draft lengthy documents. Neither type bore a specialized title or attended an institution charged with transmitting legal knowledge—that is, a law school such as those we know today.

A striking difference separated these two types of jurists: *jurisconsulti* (jurisconsults) were of distinguished social origin, had a deep knowledge of the law, and were at the same time *prudent*, meaning they dealt with the practical, general knowledge needed for conducting both public and private matters (Cicero: *De oratore* 3.133–35). The first jurisconsults held the highest religious positions (pontifex and pontifex maximus). In fact, the opinions that first began to shape the teachings that today we call law came from the pontifices.[2] One characteristic of the classical period, as opposed to the Archaic period, is that people of high social standing, with practical knowledge (or "prudence," in the proper sense of the term) and familiarity with the rituals and complexities of the law, began to issue opinions; and these opinions began to circulate in writing. These possessors of juridical knowledge were the only legitimate jurists of that time. They frequently held high political positions, and their status as jurists aided them in their election. Later, in the imperial period, jurists held even more exalted positions, including that of advisor to the emperor (Schulz, 1946; Bauman, 1983, 1985, 1989).

In contrast to the high-birth qualifications of the jurisconsults, it was easy to become a lawyer. According to Cicero, one could do it in only three days, if desired (Cicero, *Pro Murena*, 28–29). This is probably an exaggeration—Cicero made the statement in a polemic work—but note that advocates, or lawyers (*advocati*), did not need to know law; most had only the most rudimentary legal knowledge and needed to know just enough to be able to pose questions to the jurisconsults. Nor was there any professional body or public entity that examined them. Lawyers did not have high social standing or come from the best families. But occupational divisions in Rome were less marked than in our day. There was a certain continuity between the tasks of the jurisconsult and the lawyer; the former generally advised the latter (as well as the judges) and sometimes assumed some of the lawyer's roles, such as when a matter involved a friend or a prestigious person or case.

It is not easy to get to the bottom of what it meant to be a lawyer in classical Roman days. For example, we consider Cicero a lawyer, but he defined himself as neither jurisconsult nor advocate, but rather as an orator. Today much of his work could be qualified as a lawyer's arguments, but in Cicero's time, Roman law was under the influence of Greek thought, especially in rhetoric. This had the effect of bringing together rhetoric, in the Greek-classical sense (which today we would call argumentation theory; see Perelman and Olbrechts-Tyteca, 1958), and the law. Oration was a stratified occupation, with positions in the hierarchy for very distinguished orators, such as Cicero (106–43 B.C.) and Pliny the Younger (61 or 62–*c.* 113 A.D.), as well as for others of lower class.

Another aspect of Roman law that might be surprising to contemporary lawyers is its rejection of the idea of representation. Litigant parties had to be present at the trial and personally perform in them (Rasi, 1957). This is in stark contrast to today's idea of what it means to be a lawyer.

Undoubtedly, there was legal training in classical Rome, as what distinguished the jurisconsults was their knowledge of the law. In the republican period the training took the form of an apprenticeship. A youth would stay at a jurist's home and share his family life. He would accompany him to the court and hear the cases presented and the jurist's responses. At night they probably discussed the cases that had been presented that day. But formal training was beneath the *dignitas* of a jurist. "Schools" did arise in the imperial period, but we do not know what they were like. We do know that two rival schools of thought prevailed: the *Sabinian* and the *Proculian*. Undoubtedly scholars and students met and discussed texts and cases, but without a fixed locale. A teacher's house or public place could serve as a meeting place (Schulz, 1946). There was also a didactic literature, of which the greatest surviving example from the classical period is Gaius's *Institutes* (Villey, 1964).

No official recognition or title applied to jurists during the imperial period. Augustus granted the distinction of *jus respondendi ex auctoritate principi* to a small number of jurisconsults, the significance of which has been debated. It may have signified his approval, though it did not exclude those without the title from also giving advice. In any case, later emperors did not impart such distinctions and had no known connection to legal education. But there is no doubt that the schools referred to earlier, albeit informal, allowed the number of jurisconsults with important functions in the high bureaucracy to multiply. Jurisconsults reached their peak in the third century.

A highly valued form of knowledge in ancient society was rhetoric, or the art of argumentation and persuasion.[3] The art of rhetoric was developed considerably by the Greek philosophers, including Aristotle, and entered Rome with great force in the last century of the republic, justly called the Hellenistic period of Roman legal science because of its Greek influence (Schulz, 1946).[4] Rhetoric was a skill that was closely associated with law; it was used in pleading on behalf of one party in case of a conflict to be decided by a third party. The teaching of rhetoric in Rome was considered part of a young citizen's education. In fact, legal learning changed during the classical period as a result of the influence of rhetoric. Examples from the law were frequently used in rhetoric, thus allowing citizens to gain a basic legal education.

In *De oratore*, Cicero expressed the desire to establish law as an *ars*, or an ordered, methodical body of knowledge. Gaius's *Institutes* demonstrates that this sort of ordered reasoning had already developed by the second century, though that book hardly resembles a modern legal code or handbook. Roman law is more casuist, or case-centered, and Gaius's *Institutes* is more an orderly presentation of cases than of principles and rules contained in modern civil law books.

The underlying point here is that Roman jurisconsults, advocates, and orators were not the equivalent of lawyers today. They did not constitute a social group with a certified knowledge, nor did their occupation provide them with sufficient income to maintain a particular social level. There was no regulating body that concerned itself with supervising their work and activities, and they lacked an identity within their own collective imagination. In other words, law did not constitute a profession, nor did the elements for the formation of a profession exist.

In the postclassical period, law became a field of knowledge that went beyond general prudence. The opinions of jurisconsults approached a special prestige or *auctoritas* (social legitimacy), and they became the basis of legal knowledge. Law schools arose—in the physical sense that we know them today—in Rome, Constantinople, and Bayreuth. Legal teaching was still unformed, consisting mostly of discussions of the main jurisconsults' opinions, especially Labeo and Papinian. It is generally recognized that a lack of creativity characterized Roman law in this period, which also coincided with Rome's decline. The empire divided in two, and the western part was lost with the fall of Rome in the fifth century.

It was in this period, in the sixth century, that Justinian, Emperor of the Eastern Roman Empire, or Byzantium, made a lasting mark on Roman law. He ordered the opinions of the jurisconsults from the classical period to be compiled into a coherent order. Interpolations, or short explicative texts, were added to facilitate the transitions between different opinions and to aid coherence. The resulting work was the *Digest*, the realization in a tangible volume of the *ars* that Cicero had proposed. Moreover, its importance in the later history of law is incalculable.

Justinian was not only a compiler. In the *Codex* and the *Novels* he gathered legislative acts, including some of his own, subsequent to the initial compilation of the *Digest*. The *Digest*, *Codex*, and *Novels* were accompanied by a didactic work fashioned after Gaius's obsolete version of the *Institutes*, called the *Institutes of Justinian*. These works changed the content of teaching; it no longer centered on the opinions of Labeo and Papinian but began referring to the *Digest* (Archi, 1979). The entire collection of works was known as the *Corpus Juris Civilis*. To a certain extent, it was the grand compilation of Roman legal knowledge, realized in the twilight hours of the ancient world.

Justinian also tried to reunify the empire and managed to control part of modern-day Italy, especially the area called the Exarchate of Ravenna. His other military and political exploits were less successful. The expansion of the Arabs, Scandinavians, and Slavs restricted navigation in the Mediterranean and made land communication in Europe insecure. Commerce and economic activity declined radically during the early Middle Ages. Roman law did not disappear, but it was applied only locally. After the German invasions, as each group preserved its own ethnic law, Roman law survived as the law of the Romanized peoples and the church (Koschaker, 1955). Some Germanic kings promulgated works of Roman law and applied them to their subjects. Alaric published *Breviarium Alaricianum* in the year 506. In Italy, Justinian's work continued to be applied in Ravenna, Rome, Meridionial Italy, and Sicily, though it was not widely known. The understanding of law was rudimentary and was studied as an aspect of rhetoric (Koschaker, 1955: 106; Calasso, 1954). As economic life decayed, the interest in law studies decreased proportionally.

A great change occurred at the end of the eleventh century in Bologna, with the rediscovery of the *Corpus Juris Civilis*. In the ancient world, books had been mere reminders of opinions, thus the medieval reverence of the knowledge contained in books was new in the history of mankind. The most important of all books was the Bible, or the revelation of the truth by God himself. Justinian's works, in particular the *Digest*, came to have a similar role in medieval thought. Law (or justice, as there is no clear difference in Latin between the two words) was believed to be wholly contained in this fundamental work. Law studies began to constitute a crucial part of higher learning. Since its inception in the twelfth century, the university has preserved this fundamentally book-based character. The *Corpus Juris Civilis* was the body of work that contained the true knowledge of law and shaped all legal studies. In contrast to the Anglo-American tradition of *common law*, in which law training was essentially practical, lawyers from the *civil law* tradition received university training in law, primarily through study of Justinian's works.

This characteristic of the legal profession has endured to our own day. Hence we turn our attention to the role of professors and their relations with lawyers when examining the subsequent history of the profession.

Professors and Lawyers

The *Digest* was not an easy work to understand in the twelfth century. First, because it contained consolidated teachings elaborated over centuries. Second, by the time the *Digest* was again at the center of legal studies, the social, economic, and political circumstances had changed so much that many matters referred to had altered greatly. The fact that it was in Latin and was read in Latin in late medieval times made for a very misleading text, as the significance of many words had changed over time. In relative terms, present-day scholars would actually have fewer difficulties reading the *Digest*, despite our even more remote distance in time from the original text. We have the benefit of studies about the Roman economy and society that those reading in the twelfth century did not. Nor do we look to the *Digest* for enforceable rules, as they did then.

These difficulties did not discourage medieval scholars. They believed that the great books contained necessary knowledge and accepted that such works were difficult and required arduous work to interpret. The Gospels and the works of Aristotle were not transparent either, especially if one searches in such books for guidance. A professor was a person who was familiar with these great works and could explain them to others, his students. This was the task of the university at the time of its birth (Calasso, 1954, Stelling-Michaud, 1955).

In the twelfth century, Bologna was the home of the first university to center largely on legal studies. Irnerius and later Ugo, Rogerio, and Azo, among other great instructors, read and explained the *Digest*. Gratian's *Decretum* and other canonical legal works also were read. The *Institutes*, an introductory text of lesser importance than the *Codex*, may have been read and taught by graduate students (*bachilleres*). Of course, before the invention of the printing press instructors could not simply send their students over to the university bookstore to buy books. They probably dictated the text, perhaps stopping after each paragraph for a more careful reading and commentary to aid in comprehension. This was the *lectio*, the origin of the Spanish word *lección* and the English word *lecture*; however, in no way should it be confused with today's classroom-style lecture. The importance of the text and the difficulty of getting copies of it created a tendency to memorize it, a habit that was criticized as early as the mid–thirteenth century by Odofredo (Stelling-Michaud, 1955: 75). The professors also wrote comments in the margins, and these texts became the commented versions that marked the era.

Reading texts generated difficulties, because one text might be contradicted by another that enjoyed the same degree of authority. This converted the subject into a *questio*—in which students argued pro and con—and the teacher's role was to make the *determinatio*, or appropriate interpretation, that would resolve the problem (Stelling-Michaud, 1955). At night, students would discuss cases in *disputationes* determined a week in advance by the professor. The structure was similar to that of the *questio*, but the teacher had a less central role (Cavanna, 1979: 109; Stelling-Michaud, 1955). When we read a *questio* (or a collection of them in a *summa*), we can imagine the atmosphere of the discussion in a medieval university. It is a very different literature from the handbooks and treatises commonly used today in the world of civil law, which do not reflect any discussion.

Who were the law students? Remember that Europe was largely rural and illiterate, with poor means of communication. Those who could read and write in Latin and were able to withdraw from economic activity long enough to dedicate themselves to the interpretation of arcane texts could not have been more than a very limited number. If we think of the enormous costs of moving from one place to another without organized transportation, renting a place to live, buying manuscripts, and paying the professors—we know that the students must have had considerable wealth at their disposal or must have relied on the institutional support of the church. They were frequently nobles, prebendaries, or sons of wealthy merchants (Stelling-Michaud, 1955). Their social status was such that they frequently traveled with a personal servant, and the richest traveled with a secretary.

What did the students who went through this training learn? In the first place, they became very familiar with the *Corpus Juris Civilis* and the fundamental texts of the law canon. They learned the great Roman jurists' language and approaches. In the second place, they received good training in making conceptual distinctions and delimitations, and in analyzing the relevance of arguments about specific interpretive cases or problems. Besides teaching specific knowledge, the universities offered certification in the form of a degree. In a world of nascent bureaucratization, holding such certification was of the greatest importance—not only were those who possessed it accredited, but also those who did not possess it were discredited as ignorant.

In spite of the high cost of moving to and living in Bologna for five years or longer, more than a few students were attracted to the new legal studies. The number of students had already reached one thousand in the time of Azo (1150–1230) at the beginning of the thirteenth century, and fifteen hundred by midcentury (Stelling-Michaud, 1955: 39, 77). Students came from all over Europe and were grouped in "nations," essentially by linguistic affinity.

It comes as no surprise that the graduates who returned from Bologna had knowledge and skills that were highly appreciated at this moment when Europe was flourishing in economic and intellectual terms and political forces were in the process of rearrangement. The university as an institution had achieved great importance. In the politically polycentric world that was the Middle Ages, universities were protected by persons of power, who in turn sought reciprocal benefits. The Pope, the emperor, the kings, and the cities all began to grant privileges to universities, which in turn gained status as important institutions (Stelling-Michaud, 1955). Universities with legal studies flourished in all of Europe. The Bologna model multiplied, and Roman law became a truly European law (Koschaker, 1955; Cavanna, 1979; Calasso, 1954).

The Iberian Peninsula was especially fertile ground for new universities. The University of Salamanca began to function in the 1200s, and by the mid-1400s six universities were in operation in Castile and Aragon. By the late 1500s, some 15,000 university students resided in Castile alone. Note, however, that Spain boasted the highest education rate in all of Europe. This figure allows us to calculate that around 3,000 students were admitted each year, or more than 5 percent of the eighteen-year-old male population, according to Kagan's calculations (1974: 200). Approximately one-third of them studied law, and a smaller number actually graduated. Pelorson (1980: 105ss) estimates the number of graduates with bachelor's degrees in law to be about 500 per year from 1570 to 1610, which allows him to calculate that between 10,000 and 20,000 law graduates lived in Castile around 1610. The lower figure is the more probable because of the emigration of jurists to other regions and to the American colonies, though he does not count the graduates from Bologna, where Spanish students were always numerous.

It is important to observe that not all jurists actually became lawyers or were interested in practicing law, as other career possibilities existed. On the other hand, prior to the sixteenth century, legal studies were not required for the practice of law as a profession. For example, in the era's definitive legislative work, *Siete Partidas* (*Partida* III, *Titulo* VI), a lawyer was described as "todo ome que fuere sabidor de derecho, o del fuero, o de la costumbre de la tierra," or, any man with legal knowledge; and it was up to the judges to decide who could act as lawyers and to keep a registry. Naturally, in court those lawyers with limited intellectual training could not possibly defeat those trained in the universities, who were familiar with the canonical law books and had superior reasoning capacity. Because of this difference, university law studies began to be demanded of lawyers in Spain around 1495 (Kagan, 1981: 63).

The number of lawyers grew rapidly. Kagan (1981: 65) estimates that there were more than a thousand lawyers in Castile in the sixteenth century, but Pelorson (1980) offers much higher numbers. Kagan's figure is based on the registers in the tribunals and consequently does not count judges, notaries, and other personnel with legal training. This does not imply that lawyers had a monopoly over the proceedings in the tribunals. There also existed *procuradores* and *solicitadores*, who generally lacked university law training. Each functioned in some capacity as lawyers, but the former were recognized by the courts and the latter were not. They were in charge of initiating the trials in the labyrinth of slow proceedings and of paying whomever had to be paid. Lawyers, who had superior status, intervened only in the decisive parts of the trial at the moments in which it was necessary to design a strategy or argue in public (Kagan, 1981).

Castilian society was notably litigious in the sixteenth century. Kagan (1981) and Pelorson (1980) have both documented the considerable increase of lawsuits in the various courts from the early 1500s through the mid-1600s. The royal tribunals had the distinction of being the highest court in the land, with sufficient authority to limit the jurisdictions of the lords and to rein in the power of the nobles. The period also corresponds to an era of material prosperity and intellectual production referred to as the *siglo de oro* (golden century). What today is seen as a clear link between prosperity and greater litigiousness was not a consideration at the time. Instead, lawyers were faulted for generating the lawsuits along with the lies and crimes associated with them (Quevedo y Villegas, 1951 [1622]). In the mid-1600s royal power and material prosperity declined in Spain, and the number of law students, lawyers, and lawsuits also fell.

Litigation was not always the principal occupation of those trained in the law. During the Middle Ages, government officials were nobles whose everyday duties involved fighting wars and training for war. In contrast to our modern notion of "nobles," they bore scars on their faces and bodies and their clothes were covered in patches. As the modern state developed and bureaucracies were formed, the rulers were no longer men on horseback, but rather men at desks. They were pale, scrawny men with clothes worn away at the elbow from leaning so much on the desks. Jurists were especially in demand to occupy these positions, as they were able to maneuver easily in that world of rules and written documents (Maravall, 1972). The demand for jurists for government tasks and for the highest judicial positions began weakly in the thirteenth century, but by the sixteenth century they were already a strong, consolidated presence.

If the jurists trained in the universities were socially and politically important, we can well imagine the status of the professors. They were unrivaled as the most learned, those who best knew the arcane texts. Note that the definition of their role did not demand that they produce new ideas or publish, simply that they know flawlessly the books of knowledge. Their preeminence was such that powerful figures solicited their opinions on important matters. Many of those consultations dealt with themes of great political interest and pertinent theoretical problems. Writings by the professors began to circulate as independent works, generally following the literary model of the *questio*, and ultimately became an important source of the law itself. The collection of writings based on Roman law became the European *jus commune* or common law—not to be confused with English common law, which is fundamentally law based on judges' decisions without reference to Roman law.

The importance given to professors is one of the characteristics of the civil law tradition (Merryman, 1985; Van Caenegem, 1987), but it seems to have reached its pinnacle in the 1400s and early 1500s at the final stage of the Middle Ages, or beginning of the modern era (Thieme, 1967; Wieacker, 1957: 112ss). To illustrate the extreme reverence of professors, one can point to the fact that Louis XII of France went to the University of Pavia to listen to a commentary on the *Digest* by Jason del Maino (Gilmore, 1963: 68); and Emperor Charles V sat on the uncomfortable benches of Salamanca to listen to Francisco de Vitoria (Torrubiano Ripoll, 1917[1557]).

The principal source of the *jus commune* were the collected opinions of the doctors of law, as the authors were called. Naturally, in this proliferation of divergent opinions and as the number of published writings multiplied, it often was difficult for readers to prioritize the works. The authors with the most prestige enjoyed the most authority, and sometimes political intervention worked to create a hierarchy of preferred authors' opinions—as Augustus legislated in Rome and the Catholic monarchy decreed in Spain.

The doctrinal construction of law, or interpretation of law through authors' opinions, was controversial. One famous dispute with enormous subsequent relevance arose in the fourteenth century regarding *mos italicus* versus *mos gallicus*—that is, the Italian scholastic method versus the French humanist method. The work of the glossators became more complex with the evolution of commentaries on commentaries. In Orleans and Montpellier, jurists emerged who were interested in deducing principles and rules and applying them to cases (Stelling-Michaud, 1955: 74). The *mos italicus* school was continued by the Italian post-glossators, or commentators, of the fifteenth century (among them Bartolo de Sassoferrato). *Bartolistas*, as they were called, sprung up throughout Europe. In France the most important of these was Pierre Du Moulin. The *mos gallicus* school generated the creation of jurist-humanists, who were outraged by the corruption that Latin and the Latin texts had suffered in the medieval period. Their attacks not only were against Bartolo and the Bartolists but also included Justinian and especially his minister Tribonian, the editor of the *Digest*, whom they accused of corrupting the ancient texts out of lack of understanding. The central idea of the jurist-humanists was to return to or rebuild classical Roman law (Villey, 1968; Piano Mortari, 1980).

One of the new challenges confronting jurists and scholars of the sixteenth century was the "discovery" of America, particularly important in Spain. Were the "Indians" human beings? Would they have the right to keep their republics and their sovereignty? What right did the Spanish sovereigns have to make war against them? Would it be a just war? Could they be justly enslaved if they were defeated? The great jurists were called upon to express their opinions, and the quality of their discussion still amazes us today (Hanke, 1949). In this controversy we see a conflict between two viewpoints: the theories closest to the thought of Aristotle and Roman law as it was understood in the Middle Ages, in the work of Ginés de Sepúlveda (1490–1570; first published in 1951), and a much more individualistic and rationalist theory articulated by Francisco de Vitoria (on Vitoria's thoughts and his polemic with Sepúlveda, see Hanke, 1949). Sepúlveda wrote that Spain had the right to wage war on the barbarian tribes of America. If they were defeated they could be enslaved. In contrast, Vitoria supported the idea that Indians were people and their governments legitimate. Spain had the right to visit them, enter into commerce, and preach the true religion. If they did not recognize these rights, then war was justified, but they could not be enslaved. His theory, which anticipated modern international law, was called *jus gentium*, giving new meaning to the Roman expression for law applied to non-Roman citizens. Vitoria is one of the great names of the *Escolástica Española*, a powerful movement of Spanish theologians, political philosophers, and law scholars in the sixteenth century. His main works—short, written in elegant Latin, and published posthumously—were called *relecciones* (Vitoria, 1917[1557]). The structure and spirit of these works are fundamentally modern, similar to lectures today, yet the medieval *questio* is perceived in the way he treats the arguments.

Among the great jurist-humanists in the sixteenth century were Cujas, Budé, Bodin, and Althusius; and in the seventeenth century, Domat. Their task was to put the civil laws (meaning the legal rules found in the *Digest*) in their natural order, or ordered in a way that conformed to a geometric model of reason. This task was continued by the likes of Grotius, Pufendorf, Heineccius, Thomasius, and Wolf of the *Escuela del Derecho Natural y de Gentes* (School of Natural Law and of Peoples). Its founder, Hugo Grotius, also wrote in Latin but in a style that appears geometric or deductive. In the preface to *De jure belli ac paces [The law of war and peace]*, he declares his debt to the scholars of the *Escolástica Española* (Grotius, 1724). Grotius and the natural law doctrines were incorporated into law schools in the eighteenth century.

Law teaching in Europe and Spanish America continued to be heavily based on Roman and canon law during the 1700s, but greater emphasis was given to Justinian's *Institutes*, which had acquired the content of a rationalist work thanks to the commentaries of Heineccius and later Vinnius. The eighteenth century also incorporated the study of national law as important innovation. Arnaud (1969) carefully studied the doctrinal sources of the French civil code and found it derives from such natural law authors as Samuel Pufendorf and Robert Joseph Pothier. The teaching based on codes was a way to consolidate natural and national law.

Given the preeminence of jurists in the society and politics of sixteenth-century Spain, it is not surprising that universities and legal studies were created in the American colonies quite early. This will be the theme of the next chapter. This book will compare the development of Latin American lawyers and legal education with their parallels in Latin Europe. If we formulate the hypothesis that the ideology of Latin American jurists followed that of their European counterparts, one also could ask just how "Roman" they really are at the beginning of the twenty-first century. Here we can give a tentative answer: the intellectual training based on the study of legal concepts and codes has little to do with that of the jurists and lawyers of ancient Rome or the thirteenth-century Bolognese doctors of law. The modern concept of law in Latin American countries approaches the natural law theories of Vitoria or Grotius but is far from those of the learned Castilian lawyers of the seventeenth century, whose training was always imbued with the *mos italicus* method.

The social position of present Latin American jurists and their use of law also differs from that of their ancient, medieval, and Golden Age Castilian ancestors. These ideas will be developed in the following chapters. This point is stressed in disagreement with the common vision of the history of law that presents the Roman concepts as traveling through the ages without appearing to undergo any modification (for example, Watson, 1977, 1993, 2000). Similarly, we disagree with the idea that different populations—such as medieval Germans and native Latin Americans—adopted or received Roman law because they realized its technical-juridical superiority or because a stronger force imposed it on them (Levaggi, 1994). One cannot receive or transfer a law in the same way that one can receive the books where the legal rules are contained. Identical legal texts are likely to be understood and used in different ways under different circumstances. Castilian law and its jurists acquired a new meaning once they were transplanted to the Americas.

These affirmations are not incompatible with the existence of a civil law tradition (Merryman, 1985) or with the fact that Latin Americans share this heritage. Nor does it necessarily follow that today's law resembles Roman law, but rather that a certain continuity has existed in the training of jurists and in their place in society. In this sense, the roots of Latin American legal tradition lie more in the academically sophisticated Bologna of Irnerius (1050–1130) than in the Rome of Papinian (*c.* 140–212), because law today is studied at the universities, it is mostly a knowledge contained in books, and professors are important legal actors. Papinian's Rome, in contrast, had no universities or law schools, experience and one-to-one learning was paramount, and law was not a bookish knowledge. On the other hand, Roman law, which was practically reinvented in each era, has provided today's lawyers with a basic conceptual design and a system of beliefs that is not historically true but which has undeniable practical value. It can be called an ideology in the sense that it maintains a consistent vision with cognitive support and justifies social action.

The identity of Latin tradition becomes obvious when we look at other traditions, like that of English-speaking countries. Oxford, among the oldest universities in Europe, has taught Roman and canonical law throughout the ages. Yet in the common law tradition, lawyers did not receive university law training, and because of that professors and scholars had limited prestige in the legal system. But that tradition has been transformed. Lawyers in the United States have received university training since the late 1800s—although not in Roman law. In England the trend toward university legal education came about later, in the latter 1900s. The frequency with which Latin American lawyers, and those from the civil law tradition in general, are obtaining postgraduate degrees in the United States and England has produced a mixing of traditions, as noted by Merryman (1981). The frequency of lawyers from different traditions working together in international business and projects leads in the same convergent direction. Legal traditions that started from different premises are today blending together. That will be one theme of this study.

CHAPTER 2

The American Lawyers of the Spanish Monarchy

THE INQUIRY of this chapter covers the period from 1500 to 1830, usually referred to today as the colonial period. This designation is not entirely precise, however, when considering that Spanish Americans in the vast dominions of the royal Spanish empire never fully adopted the stature of second-class citizens expected of colonists. Indeed, one aspect of Spanish colonialism we will analyze are the restrictions imposed by the crown around the mid-1700s that ultimately led to independence.

This chapter talks about Spanish America. Because the Portuguese policy on legal and higher education was quite different from that of Spain, for our purposes here Brazil will be rather a comparative reference. The lawyers to be studied identified themselves as American lawyers of the Spanish crown. They thought of themselves as American Spaniards and as royal functionaries. In accordance with their titles, they were, for example, "lawyers of the Charcas *audiencia*" or "of the royal *consejos*." This denomination not only denoted the territorial limits of their professional practice but also indicated an institutional and political loyalty.

The Spain that "discovered" and conquered the American territories was a country in the process of consolidation as a nation and as an absolute monarchy. Chapter 1 discussed the central role of lawyers in the construction of the bureaucratic order that characterized sixteenth-century Spain. It is only natural that this role would carry over to the conquest and colonization of the new territories.

The explorers and conquerors were required to sign contracts (*capitulaciones*) with the crown of Castile—the most famous ones being those of Christopher Columbus, Hernán Cortés, and Francisco Pizarro, but practically every conqueror signed one. The contract specified the obligations and privileges of the contracting parties in great detail (Zavala, 1988), setting forth their prerogatives and submitting the conquerors to considerable regulation of their actions. Disputes frequently arose over the rights of the conquerors, and the general tendency was for the royal authorities to concede important privileges that would later be limited or rescinded as the conquest was consolidated. The regime that resulted was a "patrimonial bureaucracy," in the sense that the Indies were considered to be directly linked to the king and subject to his will, and authority was expressed by means of a bureaucratic organization (Sarfatti, 1966).

The juridification of the conquest can be perceived not only in the *capitulaciones* but also in the ongoing debates over the legitimacy of the Spanish monarchy's conquest of recently discovered territories and about the rights of the indigenous peoples. The abundant legislation (*Leyes de Indias*, or laws of the Indies) produced by the monarchs in an attempt to regulate the different aspects of the conquest and of life in Spanish America is certainly the best-known and most studied element of this juridification. As Malagón Barceló (1966: 81) has pointed out, it was "a colonization of people of laws."

The ubiquitous presence of legal clerks (*escribanos*)[1] is another indicator. On his first voyage, Columbus was accompanied by the clerk Rodrigo de Torres (Luján and Muñoz, 1982: 30). In fact, clerks regularly accompanied the discoverers and drew up statements regarding the founding of cities and other documents of interest to the crown. Cortés was a law student in Salamanca and later a clerk in Santo Domingo before becoming the conqueror of Mexico (Malagón Barceló, 1966: 88). Frequently clerks did not have a formal legal education, especially in the early period of colonization, but they were subject to examination by established clerks or by the *audiencia* (high court) in their legal knowledge and writing ability. A literature for clerks contained outlines of the more usual documents as well as considerable legal information. Among the books used by the *escribanos* was *Civil and Criminal Practice and the Institution of Clerks*, by Monterroso y Alvarado[2] (Leonard, 1992), which demonstrated a widespread knowledge of practical law. In any case, the clerks of the colonies produced an oceanic quantity of legal documentation that has facilitated the study of Spanish colonization.

This chapter is concerned with clerks and other legal occupations—such as *procuradores* and *tinterillos*[3]—only tangentially and in relation to lawyers. The research aims to describe the intellectual training and social placement of lawyers, those who received a formal legal education and whose knowledge of the law was certified by the universities and the *audiencias* of the era. How did they contribute to the consolidation of the state in the colonies? What were their relations with the colonists, the indigenous peoples, the imported African slaves, and the majority mestizo group that resulted from the mix of all the races?

This chapter starts with a description of the prevailing bureaucracies before turning to the intellectual training and social placement of lawyers.

The Bureaucratic Organization and the Law

The Spain that began the task of conquest in the 1500s also was in the process of configuring itself as a modern state, a bureaucratized absolute monarchy that intensively used the law and jurists to organize and govern society (Maravall, 1972). It is natural that this experience would transfer quickly to the efforts to organize the American territories recently brought under the Spanish crown. In their determination to use the law in the government of the colonies, the Spanish monarchs abundantly used legislation and very quickly established legal courts. A high percentage of jurists served on these courts for jurisdictional tasks and other governmental duties. The role of law and lawyers is at the heart of Latin America's so-called centralist tradition (Véliz, 1980)—that is, the early tradition of bureaucratization of the Spanish empire.

LAW AND LEGISLATION

In the late 1400s, Spain achieved a political and dynastical unity, yet one could not speak of a "Spanish law" or of any unity apart from that imposed by consolidation of the crown into a single dynasty. The crown of Castile had won as much territory through the incorporation of different kingdoms as through the conquest of lands from the Moors. The last of those was Granada, conquered in 1492, which coincided with the year of Columbus's first voyage. The Crown of Aragon reigned over different peoples with distinct legal orders: Aragon, Catalonia, Valencia, and Majorca, in addition to other possessions in the Mediterranean with sovereign law. The manner through which the crown acquired a kingdom in large part determined its legal regime. Kingdoms united *aeque principaliter* (on equal terms) retained their laws, which the monarch had a duty to respect. The kingdoms incorporated by accession—especially by conquest—did not have such prerogative and instead had to submit to the monarch's law, usually that of the principal kingdom (Manzano, 1948).

In 1530, Carlos V ruled that the legislation of Castile would be applied in the colonies, in the order established by the *Leyes de Toro* in 1505. The decree was ratified by Felipe II and by Felipe IV in the *Compilation of Law of the Kingdom of the Indies* (*Recopilación de Leyes de los Reynos de las Indias*, 1681, book 2, heading 1, law 2) and was justified as a matter of conquest deriving from the war against the indigenous peoples of America. This point was not disputed, although the legitimacy of the war and of the Spanish crown's exclusive presence in the new territories were the theme of frequent debates (Hanke, 1949).

Another debate developed over what policy to follow regarding the Indians. Some saw only idolatry and barbarity in the indigenous cultures with which they came into contact. A report by the viceroy of Peru, Francisco Toledo, for example, supported the eradication of all indigenous customs and structures. Others, more tolerant or pragmatic, saw good qualities in the indigenous social organization and in many customs. They also sensed that a relatively small group of Spaniards would not be able to control a much larger indigenous population if the colonizers did not utilize the local structures of power and control. This debate led Carlos V, in August 1555, to order that those indigenous customs and statutes that were not contrary to either the Catholic religion or a royal decree would be respected (*Recopilación de las Leyes de Indias*, book 2, heading 1, law 4).

The coexistence of royal legislation specifically promulgated for the new territories and the existing laws of Castile gave rise to a hierarchy of authority for the application of legislation. The first legislative order to prioritize the application of laws was the *Ordenamiento de Alcalá* of 1348,[4] which emphasized a king's power to legislate and ordered that the application of those laws held highest authority. In the absence of royal legislation, colonists referred to the *fuero real* (royal privilege) and to the municipal *fueros*, when they were in use, and ultimately to the *Siete Partidas*, which was ordered published. Each subsequent compilation rearranged the hierarchy, inevitably placing the author at its head. This is what the *Leyes de Toro* of 1505 did, followed by the *Indiano* legislation (Spanish law applicable to the entire territory of the Indies), which replaced the *Leyes de Toro* at the top of the hierarchy.

The task of arranging the various decrees into a hierarchy is complicated if we are respectful of the texts and the spirit of the age, because the conviction existed in that day that custom was important and that the great interpretations of the Roman texts also had their role. For example, Juan II of Castile ordered in 1427 that authors later than Juan Andrés and Bartolo not be cited, which indicates that the citation of authors was frequent in the disputes of that era. The Catholic monarchy ordered in 1499 that Juan Andrés was preferred in canonical matters and, in his absence, the Abbot of Sicily (Nicola Tudeschi). In civil matters, Baldo followed Bartolo. Indigenous custom also had its role. Consequently, a strict priority of the different orders and legislative bodies was difficult to attain.

An interesting question is why the Spanish monarchs ordered their laws to be enforced, especially their legislative compilations, and even specified the order of authority among the different compilations. This should be surprising to today's jurists, as it is no longer considered necessary to legislate that laws be enforced or to establish express hierarchies of authority. On the contrary, we would repeal the earlier legislation. Without doubt, we are facing a very different concept of the law.

The insistence that legislation be applied in a certain order of preference indicates an important change from the medieval notion of the law as the declaration of the right or just. In a role closer to what we today consider that of a judge or the jurisdictional function, the king was the custodian of the law who declared it but should not innovate (Stein, 1988; Quaglioni, 1988; Maravall, 1972: 405ss). A shift in thinking occurred in the early Middle Ages: the function of legislation began to be seen as establishing the law, giving the king the power to change the legal rules (Maravall, 1972). Yet the marriage of contemporary law and the old notion of law was not automatic. The royal order that imposed the legislation was exerting the desire to be in control, to configure the social rules, but the monarchy was conscious of the fact that it was building on top of knowledge that had been amassed for a millennium. Legislation thus referred to the most prestigious authors and the ancient scholars, as the *Ordenamiento de Alcalá* had expressly done. This perception of the law also explains why Roman law was studied in sixteenth- and seventeenth-century universities, as we saw in Chapter 1, and why attention was paid to the work of jurists such as Bartolo and Baldo as well as to the great canonists (Moccia, 1988).

The legislative technique of medieval times and the first centuries of the Modern Age was very different from that of the nineteenth and twentieth centuries. The borders between legislation, administration, and jurisdiction were not clear, and the language was less precise. The *Siete Partidas* as a work is much more entertaining than the modern Commercial Code or *Law of Intellectual Property*, uniting as it does the expected results, exhortations, advice, recommendations to functionaries, and even small stories. The same phenomenon is present in *Leyes de Indias*, in which the prevailing casuist mentality of that period was reflected in the legislation (Tau Anzoátegui, 1992a, 1992b); thus laws were written with a view to particular cases or concrete situations that the prolix style of legislation generally makes evident.

Monarchs from the fourteenth century on produced copious legislation, the sheer volume of which raised serious difficulties for judges and lawyers. The later compilations attempted to organize the disperse legislation, although the act of compiling imposed further limitations. The compilations organized the laws by topic yet retained many of the tangential elements of the original legislation—resulting in neither the systematic characteristics of a code nor the preservation of a chronological order. Reading them is complicated, even in the later editions in which indexes were added. The *Compilation of Law of the Kingdoms of the Indies* (1681) has these characteristics.

Explanations of *Indiano* law found in most historical law literature are drawn principally from that compilation. Yet jurists of the era did not consider it a code that repealed earlier *Indiano* legislation, nor did the *Consejo de Indias* (Council of the Indies) or the *audiencias* themselves view it as a fixed law that could not be modified. Relatively few editions existed in the 1700s,[5] indicating that it probably was not widely circulated. Published in the second half of the century, many of the decrees were obsolete and probably had more symbolic than practical value. When the early work was sent to Spanish America in the late 1600s, it received a fairly hostile reception in the *audiencia* of Lima (Tau Anzoátegui, 1992b: 235). It was not studied in the universities and was rarely cited in forensic writings. Much more frequent was the citation of the *Siete Partidas*, which appeared in last place in the ranking of Castilian law sources. On the other hand, the panorama of legislation applicable in the colonies was much more complex than the compiled law and included uncompiled Castilian legislation (the *Ordenanzas de Bilbao*, for example) and provincial *Indiano* legislation (the *acuerdos*, or rulings, of the *audiencias*). Thus scholars have recently proposed that *Indiano* law was the law effectively applied in the Indies and that less attention should be paid to the *Recopilación de Leyes de Indias* or to the collected Castilian legislation (Tau Anzoátegui, 1997).

Those who have studied the legal culture of the colonial period through the libraries of jurists and the bibliographic collections of the era present the image of jurists who consulted the principal works of the different currents of the European legal thinking, imbued with the Romanist and canonical tradition (Barrientos Grandón, 1993). The *Recopilación de Leyes de Indias* and the private collections of *Indiano* law seem to have had a lesser presence, according to Barrientos Grandón (1993: 59ss), although unfortunately he does not quantify his analysis. In judicial practice the use of the *Siete Partidas* was constant and continued until the nineteenth century, while the *Recopilación* seems to have been cited much less frequently (Barrientos Grandón, 1993: 235ss). These themes will resurface in a later analysis of legal studies and books used in the practice of law.

For now, it is enough to say that in the colonial period, analysis of legislation was extraordinarily complicated and slow going, given the complexity of the legislation, the relative scarcity of texts, and the paucity of public libraries. Nor was lawyers' knowledge particularly legalistic—an important fact for the analysis of legal knowledge and culture.

BUREAUCRACY AND TRIBUNALS

From the onset of the period of conquest and colonization, the Spanish monarchs declared their interest in exerting complete political and economic control over the American territories. Authority was first exercised by way of the *capitulaciones* or contracts with explorers. Potentially this generated the establishment of an estate system, but clearly this was not the chosen way. The governmental and judicial institutions of Castile (and to a lesser extent, Aragon) were adopted in the colonies; and finally, the absolute monarchy under construction in Spain was extended to the colonies. The monarchs also were concerned with maintaining control over the ecclesiastical authorities by means of patronage.

Despite the distances, communication difficulties, and limited organizational means of the era, the Spanish crown succeeded in holding considerable control over the American territories. Criticism regarding the colonial regimes had more to do with their excessive centralism and the bureaucratic slowness caused by the difficulties in communication, and never with their reluctance to exercise authority. Dominion was maintained without major difficulties. We will later analyze the crisis during which it was lost.

As the occupation of the Spanish American territory advanced, organs of government were slowly established and their functions defined. In the doctrine of the day, the distinction of functions seems to have been clear (García-Gallo, 1972: 661ff). The secular government, the spiritual or ecclesiastical government, the judiciary, and the treasury constituted the principal functional areas of the monarchy. Municipal areas and governments also arose. In practice, the distinctions may have lost clarity (Méndez Calzada, 1944: 47ff).

Specialization among positions also prevailed. Men of "cloak and dagger"—that is, those with military posts and a certain nobility—were called upon for government positions (viceroys, governors) and high military posts (*capitanes generales*). Usually lacking legal training, they generally could rely upon advisors with a legal education. Ecclesiastical positions were reserved for the clergy, a select group of whom had legal training, notably in canonical law. The *letrados*, or those educated in law, enjoyed a monopoly on the high judicial offices and a general importance in all governmental functions, for which they were generally called upon as advisors.

The highest tribunals of the Indies were the *audiencias*. Decisions made by the *audiencias* could be revoked only by the king or by the *Consejo de Indias*. The *audiencias* were presided over by the viceroy, governor, or other political authority that acted as advisor on government decisions (Ruiz Guiñazú, 1916; Polanco Alcántara, 1992). Moreover, the presiding officer was not able to intervene in legal cases. The *audiencia* thus could be defined as a court of law, although with important political and legislative functions generally not found in today's tribunals. For the majority of civil and criminal cases, the *audiencia* served as an appeals court. It also could hear cases of those who claimed that an act by a political authority had caused them injury (*daño en contra del derecho*). Today we would call this jurisdiction administrative litigation.

The chronology of the creation of the *audiencias* reflects the early interest of the crown in providing the new colonies with such tribunals. The *audiencia* of Santo Domingo (Dominican Republic) was created in 1511, that of Mexico in 1527, Panama in 1538 (eliminated in 1543 and reestablished in 1563),

Lima (Peru) in 1542, Los Confines (Guatemala) in 1543, Santa Fé (Colombia) in 1547, Guadalajara (Mexico) in 1556, Charcas (Bolivia) in 1559, Quito (Ecuador) and Chile in 1565 (the latter eliminated in 1574 and reestablished in 1609), Buenos Aires (Argentina) in 1661 (eliminated in 1671 and reestablished in 1783), and Caracas (Venezuela) and Cuzco (Peru) in 1786 (Polanco Alcántara, 1992). Notice that most of the *audiencias* were established in the sixteenth century and that difficulties in communication or political problems led to some eliminations and reestablishments. Few were established in the seventeenth century and only three in the eighteenth century, during which the *audiencias* were reorganized to include the position of regent. The *Royal Instruction of Regents*, an instructive for managing the *audiencias* in the Indies, also went into effect during the eighteenth century.

Audiencias were composed of learned lawyers who held the position of *oidor* (judge) or *fiscal* (representing the crown's interests). *Oidores* numbered between three and eight, according to the importance of the *audiencia*, and generally there were one or two *fiscales*. "Supernumerary" judges also might be present, in excess of the established number but also with the function and rank of judge. The position of regent was created in 1776 to preside over the *audiencia* in the capacity of judge. The typical staff was composed of *relatores* (court reporters who also were lawyers) and *escribanos* (clerks without formal legal training) (Gálvez Montero, 1990). The regents and judges constituted an elite in the government and judiciary of Spanish America and as such have triggered the interest of historians. Thus we have considerably detailed knowledge about their social origin, intellectual training, career, and many other aspects of their lives (López Bohórquez, 1984; Lohmann Villena, 1974; Burkholder and Chandler, 1977).

The responsibility for appointing judges lay with the king, although the purchase of positions was a frequent practice in that age, and from the 1600s until 1750 judgeships could be bought. The requirements of intellectual preparation were not necessarily swept aside in these transactions, although probably little attention was paid to the details. The relative disproportion between the price paid for such a position and the reliable income it generated has produced suspicion among some historians of corruption by some judges (Lohmann Villena, 1974), although others seem convinced that the ideal of honest, learned, modest, and impartial magistrates, as reflected in legislation, was realized in practice "more than one might think" (Polanco Alcántara, 1992: 70).[6]

A biography of 693 judges in the colonies (Burkholder and Chandler, 1977) shows that approximately 60 percent were born in Spain and the rest were criollos (whites of Spanish descent born in Spanish America). The latter were frequently sons of high officials born in Spain. Criollos could hold appointments during the 1600s and first half of the 1700s. From 1750 to 1808, however, only 23 percent of appointees were criollos (Ibid: 145). Consequently, criollos were the sole purchasers of judgeships before the practice was prohibited in 1750.

Other considerably strict prohibitions also went into effect at that time—such as against marrying women from the *audiencia*'s district, owning property in it, and attending parties and funerals, except in an official capacity—with the purpose of improving political control over the colonial territories and promoting impartiality among the *audiencia* judges by cutting any ties they might have with the local society.

These means of control included the rule that prohibited "sons of the country" from rising to the position of judge; that is, natives of the *audiencia*'s jurisdiction could not aspire to be judges there. In practice, these policies increased the crown's control and actually achieved a more impartial justice, but it effectively impeded the sons of long-established colonial families from becoming judges. The enormous cost of performing the necessary steps in Spain to present a candidate for a high post in the colonies was outside the reach of most criollo families. As Burkholder and Chandler (1977) show, there was a tendency to prefer graduates of certain universities in Spain (Salamanca, Valladolid, Alcalá). In turn, the sons of Spanish officers were favored for admission and as scholarship recipients in those universities. Thus informal local networks tended to exclude de facto those who were born in Spanish America and graduated from American universities. Criollo lawyers began to sense, correctly, that they were being excluded from judgeships and other important political positions starting around the mid-1700s.

Below the *audiencia* there sometimes existed special courts such as the *sala del crimen* and provincial officials such as *justicias mayores, corregidores*, or *alcaldes mayores*. In the municipal or local sphere, justice was carried out by the *alcaldes ordinarios*, designated by the municipal governments.[7] In general these positions were filled by *honoratiores*, people of social prestige and political importance in the community who did not receive a salary (though they could charge certain fees). Frequently they were not lawyers, but if any existed in the community they were generally consulted as advisors. Nor did the advisors receive any significant or regular remuneration.

Besides the ordinary courts of justice, many special tribunals existed: ecclesiastical (including the *Santo Oficio de la Inquisición*, or Holy Office of the Inquisition), commercial, maritime, property of the deceased, royal treasury, land, mining, and postal (Soberanes Fernández, 1980; Ferrés, 1944). General Indian courts operated in Mexico and Peru (Borah, 1970, 1983), and the *Tribunal de la Acordada* (MacLachlan, 1974) in Mexico. Disciplinary bodies, or bodies of conflict resolution, also existed in the guilds. The presence of lawyers was prohibited in some tribunals, such as those for commercial and mining matters, but they were generally consulted as advisors by the judges (Molina Martínez, 1986).

In general the judiciary in the colonies presented a varied, complex scene. The courts tended to consist of unpaid community members, and lawyers participated as advisors to the judges and surely to some of the parties. As we will see later, the lawyer's position carried honor but brought little profit. First, however, we will look at who aspired to this honor and what their merits and knowledge were.

Social Origin and Intellectual Training

The first lawyers in the Spanish American territories came from Spain, and this migratory current continued throughout the colonial period. Our primary interest in this study is in lawyers of American origin who were trained in the colonies. This section focuses on the study of law in Spanish American universities, because except for a short period in Mexico, university studies were required in order to become a lawyer in the colonies.

The Spanish monarchs had a sustained interest in the creation of universities and legal studies in America. The University of Santo Domingo, the region's first institute of higher education, was created in 1538. In 1551 the University of San Marcos (Lima, Peru) and the University of Mexico were founded. Other universities included Quito (1586); Bogotá (1594); Cuzco (Peru, 1598); San Francisco Javier of Chuquisaca (or Charcas, today Sucre, Bolivia, 1622); San Carlos of Guatemala (1681); Caracas (1721); Havana (Cuba, 1728); San Felipe (Chile, 1738); Córdoba (Argentina, 1761); and Guadalajara (Mexico, 1791). The literature does not always coincide with the actual year of foundation, since generally an institution was first created as a seminary and later became a university; or a university was created but there was a delay before it began to function (García-Gallo, 1977, 1997: 242; Rodríguez Cruz, 1973; Lanning, 1940).[8] All of the universities mentioned had at least two professorships in the legal area, concerning Roman law (or civil law, as it was then called) and canonical law. Other institutions, such as the seminaries (or, in the 1700s, the academies of royal and practical law) could provide legal education. Law was taught in Caracas in 1715–16 even before the university opened in 1724 (Pérez-Perdomo, 1981). This characteristic distinguishes the Spanish colonization from the Portuguese: in Brazil neither universities nor legal studies were created, as part of an express policy to maintain colonial ties. The Brazilian elite sent their sons to study in Coimbra (Venâncio Filho, 1977; Bastos, 2000).

Who were the students? The constitutions or statutes of each university were explicit: only white Old Christians, "clean of blood" could be admitted—that is, free of miscegenation with "bad" races such as the Moors, Jews, blacks, or *pardos* (people of mixed race). Also excluded were illegitimate children and the children of those who held low-class or mechanical posts (Silva, 1992; Leal, 1963)[9]. Each student had to propitiate a small proceeding in which witnesses testified under oath regarding the candidate's family ancestry and antecedents. The university authorities took great care over the quality of students and applied the same standards to peninsular Spaniards. For example, the Spanish cleric Alberto Benito de Soto was rejected from the *Colegio del Rosario* in Bogotá in 1687 "for not having in the city people of Puerto de San Lucar to testify concerning knowledge of the parental antecedents." He was later admitted under the condition that he would bring all his parental filiations within two years (Silva, 1992: 205). This proceeding was not a mere formality: university authorities paid attention to the quality of the witnesses and the tenor of their testimony.

As is well known, miscegenation was common in Spanish America, thus the requirement of "purity of blood" was not always easy to fulfill—although racial definitions of that time were not equivalent to those of today. Depending on the era, a "pure" paternal branch could outweigh the presence of an indigenous mother or grandmother and might not diminish one's quality of whiteness—though one's skin color might reflect something else. This gave rise to more than a few disputes, because indigenous antecedents could be a stubborn obstacle to one's ambitions. In the same *Colegio del Rosario*, a witness reported in 1720 that Nicolás Betancur had "blood of the earth" (indigenous ancestry), for which the faculty decided "to investigate for the information of the official record and with witnesses of all exception, the purity of blood, nobility, and legitimacy . . . with testimony of the highest grade" (Silva, 1992: 205).

University authorities could be stricter than even the king. In the 1700s light-skinned *pardos* could purchase the status of whiteness. In 1803 the University of Caracas denied admission to Lorenzo Mexías Bejarano, whose father had been "relieved" of the condition of *pardo*. The king was obligated to issue an official order demanding his admission and prohibiting his abuse under pretext of different color (Leal, 1963: 323). Similar situations occurred in New Granada (Colombia) to Cristóbal Polo in 1755, and to José Ponceano Ayarza in 1794[10] (Uribe-Uran, 2000: 23).

In Mexico in 1761 one young man was prevented from taking exams because he was the son of a mulatta. He ultimately won his case against the university because his father was a well-known Spaniard and because he was not a mulatto but a *cuarterón:* only one of his grandparents was nonwhite

(Chocano Mena, 1999; 2000: 211). In seventeenth-century Lima, the León Pinelo brothers, of Jewish blood, became distinguished lawyers (Trazegnies Granda, personal communication). These cases reveal that the universities were not always strict.

An important indicator of the social position of students was their father's occupation. Silva (1992: 209) notes that among 219 candidates admitted to the *Colegio del Rosario* (Bogotá) between 1660 and 1800, 20 percent were the sons of military personnel, 20 percent sons of officials of the Royal *audiencia* or Royal Treasury, 16 percent sons of mayors, and 10 percent sons of members of the town council. Minor occupations such as clerks and pharmacists were very weakly represented. In Caracas 31 percent of the students' fathers were landowners (Leal, 1963: 338).

The colonial university education, including legal education, was thus reserved for families of Spanish origin with deep roots in the colony and for the sons of high colonial officials, generally of Spanish peninsular origin. The "bad" races and the *blancos de orilla* (whites of the shore)—that is, poor immigrants who had recently arrived from Spain in search of fortune and lived in the outskirts of the cities along with the *pardos*—were excluded.

The academic requirements to begin legal studies were a constant during the colonial period, requiring basic study in Latin grammar and rhetoric, followed by general studies (or study of the arts), which included philosophy and mathematics. These studies resulted in the degree of "bachelor of arts," which was required for graduate studies and legal studies. Once admitted to this higher category, students spent five more years in the classrooms of law in order to obtain the degree of "bachelor of law." They could later aspire to the titles of "*licenciado*" and "*doctor*." The time requirement might be waived, but an exam was always demanded.

Little information has survived regarding student population figures. Available statistics for Bogotá and Caracas show fairly small numbers. Enrollment records for law classes in Caracas, 1789–1811, list between 35 and 83 students (Pérez-Perdomo, 1981: 62). In Bogotá the total is more difficult to pin down because students were divided into colleges, and figures exist for only some of them. Between 1778 and 1795, the number varied between 8 and 33 in one of the colleges, the *Colegio del Rosario* (Silva, 1992: 151). The number of graduates confirms relatively low figures. In the University Santo Tomás de Aquino in Bogotá, 76 students graduated with a bachelor's degree in law and 302 in canonical law between 1768 and 1808 (Silva, 1992: 155). As it was possible to get a degree in both, the number of graduates probably is fewer than 378. This makes an average of about 8 or 9 graduates per year.[11] The equivalent numbers in Caracas for the period 1760–1810 are 109 and 145, which totals 254, or approximately 5 graduates per year (Pérez-Perdomo,

1981: 64). Certainly the numbers must have been higher in Mexico and Lima, but the extreme social selectivity nevertheless guaranteed low figures in those places as well.

We have relatively more information about what they studied, teaching methods, exams, and the degree ceremonies (see, for example, Mendieta y Núñez, 1956; González Echenique, 1954; Tau Anzoátegui, 1992; Barrientos Grandón, 1993; Leal, 1963; Pérez-Perdomo, 1981). Basically, students were trained in Roman and canonical law. Some significant differences prevailed among universities according to the school's importance and the historical period. The biggest universities had six legal chairs: three for each type of law. The professors of Roman law dealt with the four works of Justinian's *Corpus Juris Civilis: the Institutes*, *Codex*, *Digest*, and *Novels*. The professors of canonical law dealt with the great canonical texts of the *Decreto* and the *Decretales*. The less-endowed universities had only two chairs, one for each type of law.

We also know the teaching method relatively well. Fundamentally, it centered on a text or a section of a larger book, involving a close reading and dictation and accompanied by explanations for the difficulties in comprehension that arose. Secondarily, debates (*disputas*) were held in which a student would support certain conclusions after explaining the controversy. Other students were invited to participate in the exercise, arguing for or against the sustained conclusion, and the student submitting the conclusion would have to defend his position. At the end, the professor would make the *determinatio*. The time for arguments was carefully regulated, and the ability to recite long texts in Latin by memory was highly esteemed as knowledge of the law (Mendieta y Núñez, 1956; Pérez-Perdomo, 1981).

The exams were very formal, with public attendance and following the structure of a debate in which graduates participated in reverse order of their time of graduation. Once they passed their exams, the degree ceremony was the next step. The ceremony for the bachelor's degree was relatively simple, with a formal act in the *aula magna* of the university and a speech by each of the graduates (González Echenique, 1954: 112ss). That of the *licenciado* was much more formal, with parades through the city, dressed in special attire on saddled horses, accompanied by music. All of this involved considerable expenditures by the graduate's family (see Mendieta y Núñez, 1956; Leal, 1963; González Echenique, 1954: 113ss).

Changes to the instructional content during the 1700s included greater emphasis on the *Institutes* and on royal law, although no chair was established for royal law. Justinian's *Institutes* was originally used as a simple introductory text. Its character lent itself to use as a rationalized explanation of the law, using the edition by Vinnius with comments by Heineccius—two authors of the so-called "school of natural law and of peoples."[12] The *Institutes* was originally a didactic work, fairly well ordered, which due to its brevity and structure could be given a rationalized interpretation, highlighting its general principles and assumptions. In contrast, the *Digest* and the *Codex*, casuist works that were not especially well ordered, fell into relative disfavor.

Another tendency of the Enlightenment was attention to royal or national legislation. The study of royal law was seen as an explanation of the principles that inspired royal legislation—not of the legislation itself—using the legislative rules as examples of the application of those principles (Tau Anzoátegui, 1992). The *Siete Partidas* was favored as the great work of royal law, admired because of its order and relative conciseness, although it was last in the formal order of legislative priority.

Royal law was frequently taught as a complement to the rules of Roman law—both in academies separate from the university and at the universities. The academies were created by the *audiencias* and afforded experience that partially substituted the requirement of an apprenticeship in a lawyer's training. Starting in 1776 they were established in Charcas, Santiago, Caracas, Lima, Mexico, and Guatemala, following the model of Madrid (Tau Anzoátegui, 1992: 255). The explanation of principles was emphasized from a methodological point of view at the academies, and the discussion of the classical cases diminished but did not disappear altogether.

A report presented in 1803 by Juan Germán Roscio, professor of the *Institutes* in Caracas (García Chuecos, 1937: 96–97) describes the teaching of law. By that time, Roman law was the center of attention and the key book was Justinian's *Institutes* in the Vinnius edition. References were made to the *Digest* and *Codex* and to royal law, especially the *Siete Partidas*.[13]

In Roscio's description of his teacher's instruction, he mentions "the public disputes," which still existed in the early 1800s but probably were not given the same importance as in earlier centuries. The preference of the *system* over the *case* created greater emphasis on the professor's analysis. This orientation toward the system and the professor's analysis also seems to have been dominant in the academies of jurisprudence (or of "royal law and practice," as they were called at that time).

Finally, it is relevant to point out the perception of law as knowledge in colonial society. Law was linked to justice and political virtue. The status-conscious society of colonial times occupied itself with defining the position and limits on power of society members—especially officials. Knowledge of the law carried the prestige of ancient Rome. It implied familiarity with the great Roman texts and with the legislation of the kings, councils, and popes. A person educated in law had a superior knowledge that was of enormous relevance to collective life but inaccessible to the majority because it was expressed in limited editions of great books, mostly in Latin. A virtuous conduct could be expected of possessors of this superior knowledge, since knowledge and conduct were intimately associated in the mind-set of the era.

In summary, law graduates belonged to the highest strata of society; they were able to cite by memory great texts in Latin, an incomprehensible language for the majority of the population, and they could argue eloquently about specific cases. Their membership in the world of knowledge was periodically exhibited in sumptuous parades or public acts. In a clearly stratified and largely illiterate society, these exterior signs of knowledge and respect gave a privileged place to university graduates. The rituals of exams and graduation ceremonies reinforced the perception of a superior, arcane knowledge that was so valued by society.

Who Were the Lawyers and How Many Were There?

The *Siete Partidas* laid out certain general prohibitions. Women,[14] the insane, the absent-minded, the blind "of both eyes," the deaf "who do not hear anything," the prodigal, and those indicted for adultery, treason, homicide, or another offense of similar gravity could not be lawyers. Those who fought wild beasts for a price could not be lawyers either. The Catholic kings also had prohibited heretics, their children, and their grandchildren from the practice of law. This included "reconciled" heretics, or those who were reaccepted into the church (González Echenique, 1954: 223). Naturally, the strict qualifications for lawyers applied to candidates for the study of law as well.

A university degree in law was necessary but not sufficient to acquire the title of lawyer. The only known exception to this requirement was the short period in which the *audiencia* of New Spain had not yet established legal studies (Mendieta y Núñez, 1956). Titles were granted by the *audiencia* to those graduates in law (secular or canonical) who served as an apprentice for four years (or two in some periods and places) with a known lawyer and who took a formal exam in the audiencia, in which candidates argued in an assigned trial. Arguments referring to the facts had to be made in Spanish, and the parts referring to the law, in Latin. In the late 1700s, participation in the work of the academies of royal law and practice in those cities where they existed also was a requirement, partially substituting that of the apprenticeship. Once the requirements were completed before the *audiencia* and the tax of *media anata* (half an annual salary; typically higher for lawyers than for other posts) was paid, candidates were admitted into the *colegio de abogados* (bar association), which functioned as a professional guild. The bar required new demonstrations of purity of blood. After that, new lawyers had to sit in courtrooms in lawyer's dress for a number of days, so that colleagues and the public could meet them in their new position. Who took on these additional troubles and what did the position of lawyer mean?

Not all graduates in law had an interest in becoming lawyers. In the first place, there were those who belonged to religious orders or were ordained *in sacris*, who had severe limits on practicing law. A significant portion of law students and law graduates belonged to this category because a degree in law facilitated ascent within the ecclesiastical bureaucracy and church administration. Second, as we will later analyze, people of high nobility generally exempted themselves from becoming lawyers.

The question of who the lawyers were has two subthemes: the motivation behind choosing that career, and the number of people who did so. We will consider these questions in reverse order.

Testimonies quantifying lawyers of the period are quite contradictory. At certain historical moments the profession fell out of favor or was thought to be overpopulated. At other moments, sometimes on the heels of the previous ones, a dearth or complete lack of lawyers was perceived. The idea of scarcity or excess seems to have derived from the perception of lawyers' usefulness or harmfulness and not from actual numbers.

Concern about the injuries that could be caused by lawyers seems to have much precedent. In 1509, lawyers were prohibited from travelling to the colonies without a special license, and in 1521 their number was regulated in Cuba (Uribe-Uran, 2000: 21; Ruíz Guiñazú, 1916: 330ss). The prohibitions did not come only from the crown: in 1526 the town council of Mexico ordered "that attorneys do not plead nor advise, with punishment for the first time of 50 gold pesos for the chambers and the public treasury of [His Majesty]; and for the second 1,000, applied in the same way and the complete prohibition from the trials of the legal profession; and for the third, they lose all their property and are banished from New Spain" (cited in Ruíz Guiñazú, 1916: 333). Given that there were no law schools in the colonies in the early 1500s, the number of lawyers who had traveled there—under the limitations of the prohibition of 1509—surely were not many. In 1613 there were no lawyers in Buenos Aires, but when the city council learned that three were on their way, it ordered that they not be allowed to enter, for fear that they would promote conflict and lawsuits. As one city council member pointed out, with attorneys "there is no lack of lawsuits, tricks, and messes, and other strife that results in expenses and the loss of homes for the poor neighbors and carefree dwellers" (cited in Ruíz Guiñazú, 1916: 333).

Ruíz Guiñazú (1916: 332) attributes the early restrictions to the insistence of the conquerors, who saw their abusive conduct and excessive rapaciousness limited by lawyers who demanded the rights of the affected. This argument is not too convincing, as lawyers acted on behalf of numerous parties, including such conquerors as Cortés (Ruíz Guiñazú, 1916: 334). But it is certain that relations between certain lawyers and the conquerors were more than tense. In the first years of the conquest of Chile, Francisco de

Aguirre ordered that the attorney Antonio de las Peñas get his nose cut off and be given whips and stabs for having decided to his detriment in an arbitration (González Echenique, 1954: 71, 311ss). García Hurtado de Mendoza attacked his lieutenant and legal advisor, the attorney Ortiz, with his sword in the streets of Concepción and ordered that the staff of justice be taken from him—that is, that he be dismissed as judge (Ibid).

Along with concern over litigation provoked by lawyers, the opposite worry also arose regarding disorder in lawsuits and lack of justice due to the absence of lawyers to handle the cases. From there, the town councils and other colonial authorities petitioned for the creation of universities with legal studies (Ruíz Guiñazú, 1916: 330). In practice, the absolute number of lawyers was probably quite low in the 1500s, and most of them seem to have occupied positions in the *audiencias*, the councils, and other bodies of the colonial administration. At that time, judges and official were not completely exempt from practicing law.

The life of lawyers in this period seems full of conflict and danger. The biography of Gabriel Sánchez de Ojeda, the first criollo lawyer to practice in Buenos Aires (Cutolo, 1964), demonstrates those difficulties. The *Santo Oficio* persecuted him for having supported royalist, heretical theories and for being an enemy of the church, for which he was exiled to Tucumán in 1608. In 1622 he was accused of having served as a judge and as a party in a proceeding against a clerk. He was condemned once again to exile and was fined one thousand silver pesos. Finally, his belongings were seized and he lost all of his property, including his valuable library and two black slaves. Years later, he confessed to his friends that he committed the offense to please Juan de Vergara, whose acquiescence was necessary to live in Buenos Aires at that time.

In this first stage of colonialism, an ambiguity or tension arose from the conflicting forces wrought by the occupation of new territories, formation of new political organizations, and the lack of structure. Lawyers were perceived as educated people who could resolve these conflicts, but because of the lack of a political backing for their decisions, the harmed parties tended not to accept the decisions and to accuse the lawyer of ignorance or dishonesty.[15] A need surfaced to legitimize and make available educated lawyers, to create legal studies, and to set limits in order to attract lawyers to the colonies.

With respect to the seventeenth and early eighteenth centuries, information is scarce.[16] In the colonies for which we have figures, the number of lawyers was quite small. In 1694 the *audiencia* of Bogotá signaled the city's need for lawyers, as there were very few (Uribe-Uran, 2000: 21). There were no lawyers at all in Caracas until the early 1700s, and by 1733, only one trained judge and four lawyers (Pérez-Perdomo, 1981: 47). Until 1760 only nine lawyers practiced in Buenos Aires, including Baltazar Maziel, a clergyman who enjoyed practising the profession despite the limitations imposed by his status (Mariluz Urquijo, 1988: 176). It is likely that the figures were somewhat higher in Mexico, Lima, and Santo Domingo, where legal education was installed in the mid-1500s, though this assertion is not supported statistically.

The prevailing impression is that lawyers were few in number and tended to occupy important posts or positions of relative importance in the colonial bureaucracy. The only group we know of that has been analyzed are the students of San Bartolomé, in Santa Fé de Bogotá, between 1605 and 1719. Of 52 graduates whose occupations are known, 4 became judges; 5, governors; 15, mayors; 15, officials of the treasury or of the *audiencia* without specification of rank; and 8 became lawyers (Silva, 1992). We do not know if all these people were law graduates or lawyers, but note the high number of officials, including high officials. Apparently those who wished to practice law in the early 1700s had access to sufficient business and earnings. For example, the biography of Maziel (Mariluz Urquijo, 1988) describes an active, busy lawyer in mid-eighteenth-century Buenos Aires, despite being a clergyman. His annual income was around two thousand pesos, a high sum in that day.

As the colonial period advanced, the life of a lawyer tended to be calmer, judging by the biographies of a few distinguished lawyers (Levene, 1941; Halperin Donghi, 1994) and the biographies of lawyers admitted to the Colegio de Abogados of Caracas from its inception in 1788 through the early 1800s (Parra Márquez, 1952, 1973). By the end of that period, practicing law became dangerous again: the Caracas lawyer Miguel José Sanz was expelled to Puerto Rico in 1809 because of a suit between his son-in-law—to whom he gave legal advice—and the Marquis de Toro (Parra Márquez, 1952: 266; Pérez Vila, 1997). The wars of independence once again launched lawyers into grave conflicts and misfortunes.

At the end of the eighteenth century and beginning of the nineteenth, there was concern again about the excess of lawyers. This worry was expressed in the decision handed down by the *Consejo de Indias* on December 12, 1802, in which it determined that in order to avoid the consequences that "with grave injury to the public, good government, and administration of justice the multitude of lawyers in the dominion of the Indies stirs up," the American *audiencias* were ordered to report the number of lawyers in their respective districts and assess how suitable this number was (Levene, 1959; González Echenique, 1954: 74). Thanks to this decree and the responses of the *audiencias*, we can ascertain the number of lawyers in the early nineteenth century.

Analysis of the *audiencias* for which we have data reflects relatively similar figures. In 1802 the *audiencias* of Mexico and Guadalajara had a total of 432 lawyers, but only 243 were active in the profession. Mexico City had 123 and Guadalajara had 18 who practiced law (Tanck de Estrada, 1982: 23). The population of New Spain (later Mexico) at that time was around 6 million, which makes 7 lawyers per 100,000 inhabitants (4 if we count only active lawyers). In Santiago in 1797, there were 77 lawyers, of which 33 practiced law (González Echenique, 1954: 74), or 11 lawyers per 100,000 inhabitants (4 active). Lima had 91 lawyers in 1790 and apparently not many more in the rest of Peru (Burkholder and Chandler, 1977). This last affirmation does not seem valid for Arequipa, which had 57 lawyers in 1800 (Ramos Núñez, 1993: 30).[17] In Havana around 1792, there were 85 lawyers (Del Arenal Fenochio, 1980: 541). Assuming that these were all the lawyers in Cuba, and estimating the population at half a million, that makes 17 lawyers per 100,000 inhabitants.[18] In Buenos Aires 98 lawyers were admitted since the establishment of the *audiencia* in 1785 until 1802 (Levene, 1959: 11). As the population of the viceroyalty of Río de la Plata was around 1.3 million, we can estimate about 8 lawyers per 100,000 inhabitants.[19] From 1802 to 1810, 54 more lawyers were admitted. In New Granada (Colombia) in 1806, Uribe-Uran (2000: 25) calculates that between 130 and 150 lawyers. With a population slightly under two million, the indicator is 7 lawyers per 100,000 inhabitants. In Venezuela in 1805 there were 105 lawyers, of whom 56 resided in Caracas, according to the report. As Venezuela had a population of one million, the indicator is 10 lawyers per 100,000 inhabitants (Pérez-Perdomo, 1981: 72–74). Puerto Rico had 3 or 4 lawyers in 1790, and 12 when the bar association was founded in 1840 (Delgado Cintrón, 1970: 7–8).

We do not know whether the figures for Argentina, Colombia, and Venezuela include all the lawyers, or only those who were active. The former seems more probable. In any case, one can make a rough calculation of an average of 8 or 9 lawyers (perhaps 4 or 5 of whom were active) for every 100,000 inhabitants of Spanish America around 1800. This calculation matches that of Burkholder and Chandler (1977: 117), who estimate that about one thousand lawyers existed in Spanish America in 1808. Estimating the total population at around 12.5 million (Lockhart and Schwartz, 1983), this comes to 8 lawyers per 100,000 inhabitants. Table 2.1 presents a summary of these figures.

Was the number of lawyers in different jurisdictions considered sufficient? The assessments on this topic vary. For instance, in 1784 Mexico City judge Vicente Herrera asked the king to limit the number of lawyers because the 227 already in the city was excessive. The reports of the *audiencias* of Mexico City and Guadalajara, however, found the number in 1802 not to be excessive nor in need of reduction. Guadalajara had 18 lawyers, and the *audiencia* estimated that there should be 24. In many cities of "such a vast kingdom" there were no lawyers at all (Tanck de Estrada, 1982: 23; Del Arenal

TABLE 2.1.
Lawyers in Spanish America, Late–Colonial Period

Country and Year	Number of Lawyers	Number per 100,000 Inhabitants
Cuba 1792	85	17
Chile 1797	77 (33)	11 (4)
New Spain (Mexico) 1802	432 (243)	7 (4)
Río de la Plata (Argentina) 1802	98	8
Venezuela 1805	105	10
New Granada (Colombia) 1806	140	7
Peru 1813	177	14

NOTE: Figures in parentheses are active lawyers.
SOURCES: *Cuba*: Del Arenal Fenochio, 1980. *Chile*: González Echenique, 1954. *Mexico*: Tanck de Estrada, 1982. *Argentina*: Levene, 1959. *Venezuela*: Pérez-Perdomo, 1981. *Colombia*: Uribe-Uran, 2000. *Peru*: Uribe, 1999.

Fenochio, 1980). In Puerto Rico in the 1790 exposition of Prbo. Ruíz Peña to Carlos IV, requesting the establishment of law schools on the island, he indicated that the lack of lawyers caused grave damages, since the lay litigators with "a thousand errors and ignorances confuse the justice of the parties" (Delgado Cintrón, 1970: 7). On the contrary, according to the councilmen of the municipal government of San Juan, the city was quite well supplied with lawyers.[20] In Río de la Plata the *audiencia* reached the conclusion that the appropriate number for the city of Buenos Aires was 24; in the provincial capitals, 8; and in the other cities, 6 (Levene, 1959: 10). Unfortunately, Levene does not say what the total figure would be according to this calculation, or if the number already in existence was considered adequate. Tau Anzoátegui (1987: 16) estimates the number of lawyers in Buenos Aires to be 71 in 1810. The number in other *audiencias* was considered excessive. In 1767 the viceroy of Peru wrote to the king complaining of "the multitude of lawyers of uncertain birth and bad habits" (Del Arenal Fenochio, 1980: 539), but unfortunately we do not know the number in this "multitude," nor do we have better information about their habits and birth. The governor of the island of Cuba reported 85 lawyers in Havana around 1792, when in his opinion 15 or 20 would be sufficient (Del Arenal Fenochio, 1980: 541).[21] Caracas in 1796 had 59 lawyers and another group prepared to join them. This worried the head of the bar, who proposed that the number of lawyers authorized to practice in Caracas be limited to 50. The *audiencia* prohibited the admission of new lawyers in 1802 and 1803 but continued to admit lawyers who indicated that they would not live in Caracas (Pérez-Perdomo, 1981).

The concern about the excess ("multitude") of lawyers does not seem to have had a direct relation with large numbers of them, and it is possible that the *Consejo de Indias* was reflecting more a peninsular than American reality,[22] although the opinions of viceroys, judges, and other *Indiano* authorities also could be influential. From a modern-day perspective, the numbers are sufficiently low that the outcries about an excess of lawyers in Spanish America call for reflection. In the same vein were the opinions of those who thought the number of lawyers inadequate, but close to being reached. A comparison with other professions can better illustrate the point: at the beginning of the nineteenth century in New Granada, there were 3,504 priests, 485 military officials (with a total of 11,500 soldiers and militiamen), and between 130 and 150 lawyers (Uribe-Uran, 2000: 25). The *Consejo de Indias* did not seem to have been worried about the abundance of priests or soldiers, but rather about lawyers.

The question to investigate is why the perception existed of an excess of lawyers, or why the number considered sufficient was not much higher than that which existed. It also is relevant to ask what were the social evils that were feared from the excess.

Occupation, Honor, and Remuneration

Uribe-Uran's (2000: 26) description of colonial lawyers' occupation varies little from what a lawyer today does: they prepared documents, wrote the wills of wealthy clients, prepared commercial contracts for local and foreign businesspeople, and handled financial conflicts as well as criminal cases and litigation over dowries, primogenitures, inheritances, gifts, property, and matters of honor. The Catholic church, an institution with numerous properties and businesses in colonial society (Bauer, 1995), required lawyers for its transactions. Even the clergymen needed lawyers to ascend in the ecclesiastical hierarchy and to help them manage fortunes that were sometimes quite considerable (Uribe-Uran, 2000: 27).

Yet lawyers complained about their lack of income. For example, one of the worries of the head of the bar association of Caracas in 1796 was that the number of lawyers would reach 100 in 1800 and 200 by 1820. According to him, this would mean that three-quarters of them would end up beggars, even though the population of the city would grow fivefold during that time (Parra Márquez, 1973: 109). Pedro Domingo Gil, in Caracas in 1790, opposed the obligatory bar association membership fee of six pesos, arguing that "there has not been a lawyer in this country who with only his occupation could maintain himself decently" (cited in Parra Márquez, 1952: 202). Actually, the practice of the profession was not seen as a possible source of wealth; on the contrary, it could cause personal fortunes to dwindle. That was the case of Pedro García, residing in Coro, Venezuela, who in 1798 requested to retire from the profession because after having practiced it with success and honor for twenty-four years, in which he had worked with the greatest unselfishness (economically, one would suppose), his estate had diminished "to less than a third of what he inherited from his predecessors because his lawyerly duties had not permitted him to attend to it and administrate it personally" (Archivo General de la Nación, 1958: 43). The lack of economic success was seen as a sign of having exercised the profession well. The lawyers of New Granada had similar complaints, like those expressed by Camilo Torres and Joaquín Camacho (Uribe-Uran, 2000: 27). The Caracas lawyer Miguel José Sanz had only the modest sum of three thousand pesos in his possession when he married (McKinley, 1993: 134).

In fact, most lawyers were not really poor. They dedicated themselves to agriculture or other economic activities as a way of earning income, sometimes of a very substantial amount (Kicza, 1984; Uribe-Uran, 2000). Of the 70 members of the bar association of Caracas in 1802, 10 came from important families in the provinces (McKinley, 1993: 134). The biggest employer was the bureaucracy. Of the 258 members who constituted Mexico's bar association, 71 were in the royal or municipal bureaucracy, 42 were clergymen, 12 had curacies, 5 were university professors, 8 had jobs in which they earned incidental income, and 5 were retired (Kicza, 1984: 143–44). Roughly half of this group had earnings from the royal, municipal, or ecclesiastical bureaucracy. Remember that many lawyers came from distinguished families and that generally they could rely on the family's estate or enter into a convenient marriage. The wife of lawyer Miguel José Sanz inherited a cocoa estate, and Juan José Mora, another Caracas lawyer, also inherited a land estate (McKinley, 1993: 133–34).

The premise of this work is that relatively few matters required the intervention of lawyers and that other social actors could substitute for them in their functions. In other words, colonial society had little demand for lawyers. Certainly, this bold assertion will require some justification.

The first thing to point out is that previous studies are scarce, such as those that analyze the caseload of the *audiencias*, what kinds of matters were debated in trial, which were the cases of economic significance, and what was the role of lawyers in the handling of cases. Despite the fact that research on these topics might provide valuable information for social history and the history of law, and although the documentation produced by the *audiencias* exists and is generally well conserved in the different capitals of the various countries or in Seville, the application of the social sciences to law is a recent phenomenon with few representatives in Latin America. Among the few studies that exist are those of Malagón Barceló (1966: 169–218) regarding cases in the *audiencia* of Santo Domingo, whose archive seems to have suffered grave calamities. In view of the scarcity of data, we can formulate only conjectures and hypotheses.

The economic structure of colonial society is one guide in the formulation of these conjectures. The principal assets of the era were real estate—land and houses. These constituted the family estate, and in theory it was not expected that they would be sold or bought except in exceptional circumstances. There existed relatively little important personal property, and commercial exchanges were moderate. Financial transactions involving capital were equally scarce. In fact, once colonial society was consolidated, there was little if any demand for the elaboration of complex contracts. Little dispute surfaced over the economic content of contracts, and litigation over such content was even more scarce. Besides, commercial conflicts were resolved in the tribunal of the consulate, and mining conflicts were resolved in another special tribunal. In both types of tribunals the presence of lawyers was prohibited. Documents that even hinted of being written by a lawyer were rejected. In other words, much of the work that occupies business lawyers today was practically nonexistent in Latin America in the eighteenth century.

Other types of conflict generated some court activity. Colonial society was far from a sea of tranquility, and although banditry and rebellions were frequent (Taylor, 1979; Haslip-Viera, 1999; Walker, 2001, Whigham, 1994), the tendency was to favor negotiation or pure and simple repression for such conflicts. Only the most serious rebellions, especially those against the king, were formally processed and received severe punishments. Homicides, robberies, and other crimes, though processed by the judicial system, generated relatively little work for lawyers. In general, lawyers were used more as advisors to judges than as representatives or advisors to the parties.

On the other hand, certain conflicts uncommon in today's society merit attention: those that derive from matters of privilege, status, or honor. For example, the denial of a particular place in the church or other public act to someone believing himself the rightful occupant of that place; denial of admission into the university or the bar association; or even the misuse of a wig or sword could produce lawsuits that sometimes became inflamed. In cases like these, people could turn to lawyers and the conflict could reach the *audiencia* or the *Consejo de Indias* (for a particular case, see Castro Leiva, 1994: 29ss). Although these cases attract our attention today because of what they reveal about a different society, it is doubtful that they were sufficiently frequent to produce a constant flow of work for lawyers.

A myth sometimes prevails about the high propensity for litigation in colonial society. Although some historians have echoed such perceptions (Honores González, 1993; Uribe-Uran, 2000: 27), this work maintains that affirmations not based on studies quantifying the activity of the *audiencias* and other courts are unsustainable. Small increases in litigation during a particular time period, or the concentration of cases of a particular nature, do not indicate a historical trend.[23] When the appraisal comes from present-day historians, the supposed litigiousness of the colonial era may be attributed to the perception that matters were litigated then that today we consider trivial, such as questions of social preeminence.

Apart from the perhaps insignificant number of cases to be processed in the tribunals or complex documents to be prepared, those that did exist did not necessarily produce work for lawyers. Theoretically, lawyers had a monopoly on representation of parties before the *audiencias* and other tribunals, but this may have meant little in practice. Parties were expected to appear in court and present documents themselves, whereupon legal representation was not really necessary. In other tribunals, as we have already seen, the appearance of lawyers in court and outside representation by lawyers was prohibited. In fact, lawyers had very fierce competitors in the procurators, clerks, and petitioners of the era.

Procuradores (procurators) were functionaries who performed judicial duties in the *audiencias*—an official position with a limited number of openings. They had the day-to-day responsibility over the cases, performing the necessary procedural steps. Generally, they did not have a formal legal education or the status of lawyers, but they knew the ordinary matters of the *audiencia* well. It was not considered appropriate for a lawyer, who was a figure of greater rank and prestige, to perform these low-status tasks.

The public clerks (*escribanos*) were the equivalent of notaries. The first institutions to train clerks were created in the eighteenth century. Clerks gave legal authority to documents and had a practical knowledge of the law, especially in document writing. They were doubtless a source of competition for lawyers.

The petitioners (*tinterillos* or *pica-pleitos*) were true substitutes for lawyers in any of their activities. They did not have a formal legal education but demonstrated a practical knowledge of the law. Being of modest social origin, their fees must likewise have been modest, although by reputation they were always ready to exploit indigenous people and the poor.[24] Their low fees and greater cultural proximity with the majority of the population may have made them a fearful challenge to the more socially distant lawyer.

It is noteworthy that even with a full caseload, lawyers did not always receive sufficient remuneration. Among the moral obligations of lawyers was to serve the poor for free, something they did not always do willingly. The preference was not to serve them at all, leaving the poor and indigenous to be attended by *tinterillos*.

This helps explain the paradox that for a clearly small number of lawyers the perception of excess prevailed. But not all lawyers felt underemployed or without sufficient income. Some who were appointed to advise various organizations received money and distinction through posts that were considered honorable.[25] Others, generally the younger lawyers who graduated closer to 1800, or those with fewer social and political connections, began to have serious difficulties earning money from the profession, leading some who were not independently wealthy to quite reduced or dire circumstances. Some even resigned from the legal profession in order to search for income in occupations in which lawyers were not allowed. Thus the topic of honor and its relation to remuneration is pertinent to our discussion.

To be a lawyer was an honor, an idea not readily comprehended in today's society (Maravall, 1979). Colonial society, like Spanish society of that period, was stratified, the core idea being that people are inherently unequal and earn status according to their position in society. Membership in a social group is determined by birth, and each group has specific privileges and obligations. Higher learning was reserved for white Old Christians, because other groups did not have the capacity or ethical wherewithal to make good use of it—in other words, other groups would use education perversely to upset the social order. Thus admission to the university and the bar association was an effective divider that excluded the inferior groups.

Although nobility was inherited, certain activities could increase it, such as military exploits and the fulfillment of high positions in the service of the king. The occupation of lawyer was a noble function in that lawyers were in the service of the common good. The profession carried a stamp of quality that guaranteed knowledge and ethics and made lawyers eligible for the high positions in the service of the king or the community. The royal decree of Carlos IV (November 17, 1795) declared that lawyers should be treated as nobles and gentlemen—an idea with firm roots since the late Middle Ages throughout Europe and the colonies.

Furthermore, a person of the highest nobility might obtain a law degree, but the title of *abogado* (lawyer) did not add to his already exalted status (Kicza, 1984), and he probably wouldn't want to be subject to certain obligations. Later we will analyze these obligations. Among the examples, one can cite Francisco Rodríguez de Toro (the Marquis of Toro), who graduated in Caracas as a bachelor of law in 1783. It is unthinkable to see him being subjected to the discipline of the bar association. On the other extreme, the position of lawyer could be an inconvenient burden for someone without a family fortune, in the sense that it restricted the types of activities that were permitted to persons of status.

Lawyers were obliged to be at the service of the king and thus had an ideological link to power. Regulations on the profession and on personal behavior may be difficult to understand in the context of today's ethics. A lawyer pertained to an *audiencia* and filled the important public function of "pre-judge" of claims and actions of those who asked him to advise or defend them.[26] Lawyers were not obligated to defend unjust causes. In fact, it was extremely difficult for those who had rebelled against the crown, for example, to find a defense lawyer, even among their relatives—as Antonio Nariño and his co-conspirators in New Granada experienced in 1795 (Uribe-Uran, 2000). Nor would lawyers of that era be well evaluated in the context of today's ethics if considering the defense of human rights or access to justice—concepts that would be totally anachronistic in that period—as that was never considered to be the mission of a lawyer.

The *colegio de abogados* was the profession's guardian of honor and took great care, above all, over who was admitted to the group. In addition to the academic requirement and the requirement of professional practice that the *audiencia* inspected, the bar again demanded a demonstration of purity of blood. Proof previously obtained by the university was not considered sufficient. There had to be new testimony, and the bar could take its role very seriously—as was experienced by Juan Germán Roscio, doctor in both civil and canon law and professor of civil law in the university, who was not admitted to the Caracas bar in 1799 because of an indigenous ancestor on the maternal side. Roscio took his dispute to the *Consejo de Indias* in order to be admitted[27] (Parra Márquez, 1952, 1973; Pérez-Perdomo, 1981).

Besides being highly selective about who could enter the body, the bar also had powers that today we would find intolerable. The head of the bar association had the obligation "to be attentive to the life and habits of lawyers of the bar, ensuring that all behave Christianly and orderly with moderation and decorum . . . and have the necessary education and diligence" (statutes of the bar association of Caracas, cited in Parra Márquez, 1952: 342). In the exercise of this authority, for example, the dean had to authorize the marriage of any bar member, the implicit rationale behind these rules being that any behavior that lessened the honor of a lawyer would mean a reduction in the honor of the group.

Lawyers could be reprimanded for conduct contrary to the honor that pertained to them, even when such deviations occurred in private spaces. A good example is the case of the punishment of Pedro Domingo Gil, of Caracas. In December 1791 he attended the festivities of a mulatto wedding, and at night he played cards with three mulattos. The incident was considered by the bar association to be extremely peculiar and offensive to his rank, to the class to which he belonged by birth, and to the noble and honorable occupation that he exercised. According to the bar, Gil was well aware that conforming to the laws of the state was necessary "to conserve the distinction and total separation of castes, not only as to occupations and public positions, but also as for public manner in word, style, dwellings, familiar communication, and everything else that good police demands" (Archivo General de la Nación, 1958: 233). It is important to note that the bar did not cite the specific "laws of the state" referred to and that in his defense Gil did not dispute the rule but instead argued that he had been condemned without being heard. This reveals that neither the bar nor Gil questioned this abiding social norm.[28]

Lawyers' personal distinction was displayed in their special attire, the importance of which is discussed by Ruiz Guiñazú (1916: 326). In the courtroom they wore "*golilla y manteo*," a robe with a closed skirt and loose, round sleeves and a silk-lined, short-brimmed hat. For ceremonies outside the tribunals, they wore robes and hats embroidered with silk. In 1787 lawyers made a formal petition to be granted the "privilege of the cuffs," that is, cuffs of crepe. The emphasis on matters of dress had the purpose of marking their special place in society as well as their distance from less noble occupations.

The importance of honor for lawyers has been emphasized by Uribe-Uran (2000) in the very title of his work (*Honorable Lives*) with respect to the lawyers of New Granada in the late colonial and early republican periods, but it also is valid for the rest of Spanish America. This work recognizes that the very honor of the occupation in effect diminished and extremely limited employment opportunities. The more modest functions, including that of procurator in the *audiencia*, were off-limits to the *nobleza del oficio*, or nobility of the profession of lawyer. Nor were they able to charge the Indians and the poor for their services. Additionally, in the latter 1700s the American-born "sons of the country" were practically prohibited from the high official positions, such as *oidor* (judge) or *intendente* (administrative official), because of the Bourbon policy of exclusion—preference was given to peninsular Spaniards who had graduated from certain universities in Spain (Burkholder and Chandler, 1977).

These customs prevailed in times of relative economic growth in which the local artisans (who practiced *oficios viles*, or lowly professions) had greater incomes than the low officials of the bureaucracy (Socolow, 1987: 107). Still more serious was the situation of many lawyers with incomes that were less secure and often lower than even the bureaucrats (Uribe-Uran, 2000: 27). This turned upside down the order perceived as natural, since nobles who served the king and the public good often lived in greater poverty than many *pardos* with mechanical jobs.

It is useful to have an idea of the differences in income at the end of the colonial period. An *oidor* had an annual salary of four thousand to five thousand pesos, depending on the cases, and received various benefits through special proceedings involving confiscated goods or through paid official capacities such as witnessing cockfights or lottery drawings (Lohmann Villena, 1974: XLII, LXXVIII; Arnold, 1988: 59ss). A porter and an office clerk had salaries of four hundred pesos (Arnold, 1988: 149), and the remuneration of a judge or university law professor was not much better. A court reporter for the *audiencia*, one of the highest positions attainable by a criollo lawyer, frequently earned one thousand pesos. Another indicator is the fixed remuneration of one hundred pesos for lawyers who were designated to defend Indians and the poor.[29] Only in a situation of complete lack of income, and perhaps in the hopes of achieving a better position in the future, would a lawyer deign to accept such a position and poor remuneration. We have already mentioned the lawyer who considered an obligatory contribution of six pesos to be excessive, given the paltry incomes of lawyers.

This is, therefore, the "damage to the public" generated by "the multitude of lawyers." We are accustomed to reasoning in market terms: we think that the increase of lawyers, especially in a society where there were not many, could make justice more accessible and eventually improve the administration of justice, as it could lead to the appointment of more judges. This was not the perception at the time. The reality was that the "nobility of the profession" extraordinarily limited the possible sources of employment or occupation, and the lack of income severely limited the growth of the bureaucracy. Without a doubt, many lawyers occupied positions that produced a certain economic benefit, but a growing number found themselves in a trap in which maintaining honor and social consideration seemed incompatible with earning a sufficient living. The situation was no doubt worrisome to the authorities in the *Consejo de Indias* as much as in the colonies themselves. The effort to limit the number of lawyers seemed the easiest solution but in practice probably only increased the pressure in a society and political system already exhibiting dangerous winds of change.

The high incomes of the *oidores*, not always accompanied by great ability for the job nor by irreproachable conduct,[30] probably caused even more feelings of frustration among the criollo elite. This introduces a very controversial theme: that of the causes of independence. Some point to the discontent of criollos—and especially criollo lawyers—at being excluded from high positions as being among the causes of the various independence movements. This position is supported by many testimonies from the time, like that of Ignacio Herrera y Vergara (Uribe-Uran, 2000: 52–53), or the well-known one by Bolívar (1970[1815]) in the "Letter from Jamaica." On the other hand, a strong trend by historians (Eyzaguirre, 1957; Lohmann Villena, 1974; Uribe-Uran, 2000; Torrente, 1829) is to point out that criollos managed to attain high positions in the imperial and ecclesiastical bureaucracy. This work maintains that such a tendency ignores the policy change in this matter that made it extremely difficult for criollos to attain high positions after the second half of the eighteenth century. Nor does it take regional differences into account: while the Peruvians had a relatively high rate of participation in royal jobs, this was not the case of the Mexicans, the Argentineans, or the Venezuelans. On the other hand, although some lawyers were able to reach high positions in the bureaucracy, this possibility seemed forbidden to the majority, who felt to be without any political or economic future despite the recognition of their preparation and high distinction.

This introduces the theme of the next section: the role of lawyers in the independence movement.

The Betrayal of the Lawyers?

By the end of the eighteenth century, colonial society had reached a considerable social and economic maturity and had begun to experience a series of political agitations that led to the rupture of the colonial link in the early 1800s. Spanish dominion extended to the end of the century only on the islands of Cuba and Puerto Rico. In chronological terms, the four decades between 1790 and 1830 become the next focus of this chapter. At the beginning of that period, the dominion of the Spanish monarchy appeared completely consolidated. Four decades later, Spain had lost its immense empire on the American continent. It is therefore appropriate to speak of a grave and final crisis of colonial society (Halperin Donghi, 1985; Domínguez, 1980; Guerra, 1992; Lynch, 1973; Rodríguez, 1996).

Lawyers had their role in the breaking of colonial ties. As we will see later, they provided the justification for independence: lawyers had leadership in the town councils and the congresses, where they acted as promoters of independence, and they prepared the documents in which the purposes and the constitutions and fundamental laws of the new states were explained. In 1811, Lima lawyer López Aldana pointed to the fundamental role that lawyers had played in the liberty of various South American countries and invited his Peruvian colleagues to continue the example by posing a question: "Would you be less victorious in your pleas than the immortal lawyers from Buenos Aires, Bogotá, Quito, Chile, Caracas, and Cartagena, who have already won the great battle for their countries' freedom?"[31]

The fight for liberty and independence could be presented as a form of treason against the monarchy, as reflected by the realist author Mariano Torrente (1829: I, 93–94), who wrote at a time when the independence movement of the Spanish American republics was not yet consolidated. His perception was that these republics were going to fall into the hands of the inferior castes and into anarchy if they separated from the Spanish monarchy.[32]

From today's perspective, one can distinguish two subperiods. Between 1790 and 1808 several attempts to rupture the colonial link ended in severe repression, with the clear use of the law and the tribunals against the *independistas*, or promoters of independence. Lawyers, as a group and with very few exceptions, clearly favored the continuation of the Spanish monarchy in America. After 1808, the events in Europe—especially the imprisonment in that year of Fernando VII, the Spanish war of independence against Napoleonic dominion, and the fight between liberals and conservatives in Spain—made the independence of the Latin American countries appear more like a crisis of the monarchy than a war against Spain, as many history books in Latin American countries still present the events. In fact, Spain sent only one substantial military expedition (with 15,000 soldiers in 1815). From the Latin American perspective, the struggle signified a civil war between the supporters of the continuation of the Spanish monarchy and the promoters of independent nation-states (Vallenilla Lanz, 1929). From the perspective of this work, it interests us to analyze why the majority of lawyers (but not all) changed their position and, to use the language of Torrente, ultimately "betrayed" the cause of the monarchy.

The comparison with Brazil is very pertinent here. Because of the Napoleonic threat in Europe, the Portuguese royal family moved to Rio de Janeiro. Thus Brazil lost its colonial status while still remaining loyal to the monarchy. When in 1821 Portugal tried to recover its supremacy and João VI returned to Portugal, his son Pedro I stayed in Brazil as emperor, declaring independence in 1822. Brazil remained a monarchy until 1889, when Pedro II abdicated in favor of the new republic. In the Spanish empire, independence was wrought with serious social and political disruption, in contrast to the relatively trauma-free experience of Brazil. Also important is the comparison with countries that opted to remain under the Spanish monarchy, especially Cuba, a key colony in the period, or those countries where independence came late or by external circumstances, such as Peru (Domínguez, 1980).

The conspiracies and rebellions at the turn of the century were discovered early, defeated easily, and punished harshly. It is notable that few lawyers were among the conspirators, and on the contrary, many assumed the personal defense of the regime, pursuing and capturing the conspirators, or refusing to defend them.

An example is the conspiracy of Nariño in New Granada (today Colombia) in 1794. Antonio Nariño was a criollo with a good economic position and social connections, who carried out average bureaucratic functions and owned a printing house. He translated and published the *Declaration of the Rights of Man* that emerged from the French Revolution. Implicated in the conspiracy were the lawyers Ignacio Sandino, Pedro Pradilla, Enrique Rodríguez, and five law graduates who were preparing to be lawyers. José Antonio Ricaurte was the first lawyer who tried to defend Nariño and was jailed for the contents of one of the documents that he planned to present in court. Later, almost all the lawyers, including those designated by the *audiencia* to defend Nariño, excused themselves from doing so (Uribe-Uran, 2000: 40ss). Uribe-Uran explains that several of the lawyers who recused themselves were related to Nariño or the other conspirators, and that it might have been supposed that they would be willing to assume the defense out of family, friendship, and associational solidarity. The resistance to defending Nariño is explained not only out of fear of repeating Ricaurte's fate but also because it could derail a bureaucratic career or block the road to beginning one (Uribe-Uran, 2000: 42ss). This seems probable, but the overriding sentiment among lawyers against defending unjust causes is an equally valid explanation: after all, conspiracy against the king was a crime against His Majesty. In other words, the conflict was not only between moral principles and opportunistic behavior; an ethical dilemma prevailed as well. Of course, opportunism and fear of blemishing one's career cannot be excluded from the lawyers' real attitudes and motivations.

Another example was the so-called conspiracy of Gual y España in 1797 (Grases, 1978), well known as one of the important antecedents of Venezuelan independence. A lawyer, Luis Tomás Peraza y Ayala, was implicated in the conspiracy. In the court prosecution and capture of the conspirators, the lawyers José Bernabé Días, Juan Ambrosio F. Borges, Antonio Martínez Fuentes, Carlos Garay, Francisco Espejo, and Francisco García de Quintana, among others, were very active defenders of the king and repressors of the rebellion. The *audiencia* requested honors and rewards for all of them from the king. Peraza y Ayala was sentenced to six years imprisonment in the fortress of Havana, monetary fines, and exile for life for his association with the conspiracy. The bar association of Caracas agreed to erase his name from all books. Among those who signed the decision was the head of the bar, Miguel J. Sanz. He was later one of the promoters of independence and died in a battle in 1814. Espejo was a member of the first triumvirate who exercised executive power in Venezuela (Parra Márquez, 1973: 193ss).

The second subperiod to be examined began around 1809, when many lawyers became leaders of the independence movements that arose in almost all of the Latin American capitals. Historians have traditionally noted that the independence leaders were the criollos, whites of Spanish descent born in America, and that the institutions they used for their purposes were the town councils, of which they had complete control. Because lawyers were criollo intellectuals who were closely associated with the town councils, it is not surprising to see them as pro-independence civic leaders. This simplified vision has the severe shortcoming of failing to explain why lawyers did not demonstrate their revolutionary calling earlier, why some criollo lawyers remained loyal to the monarchy, and why the independence of some countries was delayed beyond that of others. This compels us to move ahead with more thoroughness and care, to look at the levels of political participation by group, and to examine the motivations of the participants.

The tendency between 1808 and 1818 in most of the *audiencias* was the establishment of boards with the active participation of the town councils and distinguished citizens. *Juntas supremas gubernativas* (supreme governing boards) were established, which initially governed in the name of Fernando VII, the Spanish king being held prisoner by Napoleon. Between 1811 and 1820, most of today's Latin American countries made formal declarations of independence. The wars of independence took place between 1812 and 1826, with differing duration and intensity according to the country.[33] This was the most intensely studied period in the history of each Latin American country, which allows us to know who had the top-ranking roles in the process of independence. We know who had positions of leadership, who formed juntas and governments, who signed the proclamation or act of independence, and who signed the first constitution on behalf of the first congress or constituent congress. The history of independence in the different countries sheds light on the role of lawyers—who, as we know, were distinguished members of the intellectual and political elite.

The participation of lawyers in the independence movement has been well documented in numerous studies. For example, in the famous open town council of Buenos Aires on May 22, 1810, twenty-one lawyers voted for the sacking of the viceroy, and none voted for his continuation. This made them the most resolute and tight group among all the professions represented[34] (Levene, 1959: 11–12). In the governing board of Bogotá that was established on June 27, 1810, with 35 members, 14 were lawyers (Uribe-Uran, 2000: 47). Of the 42 signatories of the act of independence of Venezuela on July 5, 1811, 17 were lawyers (López Bohórquez, 1984: 148–49). In the political elite that led Mexican independence, 12 lawyers made up the third-largest occupational group behind the clergy (22) and the military (14)[35] (Domínguez, 1980). The numbers do not reveal all of the law graduates or people with legal training who could have appeared in the category of clerics or in other categories.

Nor does the quantitative analysis reflect lawyers' enormous qualitative impact. For example, among the principal ideologues of Venezuelan independence were Miguel José Sanz, Juan Germán Roscio, and Francisco Javier Yanes—without a doubt the early intellectual leaders of the movement and writers of the principal documents such as the act of independence and the constitution of 1811 (the first in the Spanish American world). Mariano Moreno, one of the intellectual leaders of Argentinean independence, was among the writers of the principal documents of that country (Levene, 1959: 12). In Chile the lawyers Juan Martínez de Rozas, Juan Egaña, Mariano Egaña, Bernardo de Vera y Pintado, José Gregorio Argomedo, Gaspar Marí, and Fernando Ezárrazuriz had important roles in the independence movement[36] (González Echenique, 1954: 78). In Colombia, Manuel Bernardo Alvarez y Casal, Francisco Caicedo de la Llera, Felipe Caicedo y Cuero, José Gutiérrez Moreno, and José María Lombana Cuervo were among the twenty-eight lawyers executed, particularly in 1816, by the antirevolutionary terror as leaders of the independence movement (Uribe-Uran, 2000: 69). Note that the executed comprised close to a third of the *audiencia*'s total number of lawyers. In Mexico, Juan Francisco Azcárate, Francisco Primo de Verdad, Manuel de Alderete y Soria, Carlos María Bustamante, Andrés Quintana Roo, and José Manuel de Herrera were among the early autonomists and writers of the constitutional decree for the liberty of Northern America.[37] Generally when the impact of the ideas of the Enlightenment is studied, the importance of legal learning is especially emphasized (Rodríguez, 1996; Edwards Vives, 1936: 24). However, not all lawyers declared themselves in favor of independence. There were those who opposed it and those who wavered and underwent radical changes in allegiance. Thus it does not fit to attribute the ideas about independence to legal learning, although that education turned out to be useful for the justification of independence and for a certain preeminence of lawyers in leading the process (De la Maza, 2001: 39ss). Nor is it possible to understand one position or another solely in terms of material interests, of a greater or lesser degree of opportunism, or of the lawyers' maturity. In Venezuela the criollo nobility was in favor of independence, yet no young people were represented among the early leaders of independence. The argument about the exclusion of the criollos from the highest positions possibly has more weight as a motive. It at least explains the lack of force of the rebellion in Peru, where criollo lawyers did occupy many influential positions (Lohmann Villena, 1974), and it explains the force of the rebellions in colonies where criollos were treated inequitably.

This chapter has emphasized that independence was a profound political crisis that turned even more serious with the forced abdication of Carlos IV and his son Fernando VII in favor of José Bonaparte, and the imprisonment of Fernando from 1808 to 1814. In Latin America there was little certainty about the direction events were taking in Spain, whose political elite were divided between the *afrancesados* (proclaiming allegiance to the French), who saw in Bonaparte a catalyst for political reform, and the *legitimistas*, who did not accept the change in dynasty. The mass of the population was in the latter category, and a popular resistance movement formed against the new king (Napoleon, called the *tyrant*). The rebellion was carried out in the name of Fernando VII, and juntas or governing boards were established in almost all the important Latin American cities. Later, a "*Junta Central*" was established in Seville, which the Spanish American provinces were invited to participate in, although with fewer representational powers than the other participants.

The Latin American *juntista* movement was not viewed kindly by the royal authorities and peninsular Spaniards, who feared it would become a movement for autonomy and finally independence. By 1809 the French had occupied practically the entire peninsula, and the *Junta Central* had to dissolve itself. A *Consejo de Regencia* (Council of the Regents) was established in Cádiz with nine members of dubious legitimacy. Under those circumstances, it is not surprising that in Spanish America the autonomist movements strengthened enormously. The repression of those movements in several of the American capitals by Spanish authorities radicalized the autonomists and produced the enormous division between the peninsular Spaniards and the Spanish Americans, leading finally to independence (Rodríguez O, 1989, 1996; Jocelyn-Holt Letelier, 1999). On the other hand, in Cuba the rulers better accommodated the desires of the criollos, in the process alienating a portion of the peninsular Spaniards (Domínguez, 1980).

The avatars of politics on the peninsula—first with the predominance of the liberals in the courts of Cádiz, who wrote the constitution of 1812; later with the reactionary and repressive policies of Fernando VII after 1814; and finally with the new liberal turn in 1820—were an important element that once and for all strengthened the advocates of independence. However, the recounting of history centered in these conflicts and events generally underestimates the fact that they occurred in the context of a modernization of political thought generally accepted by the elites (a critical view in Guerra, 1992; Jocelyn-Holt Letelier, 1999) and that the modernizers were mostly the elite who were well educated in the law.

The historical process is naturally complex, since entering into the picture were rivalries between provinces and the participation of the feared socially subordinate groups (*pardos*, Indians, and slaves). In Peru, where an important indigenous rebellion (that of Tupac Amarú) had occurred in the late 1700s, the autonomist movement was not strong in Lima but had more resonance in the provinces (Aljovín de Losada, 2000). However, the thought and action of a lawyer like Baquijano Carrillo shows the legalist and autonomist consciousness at the same moment in which Tupac Amarú's rebellion was being repressed (Burkholder, 1980). Other judges of the Lima *audiencia* also showed sympathy for autonomy or independence and later collaborated with the republican state (Gálvez Montero, 1990).

One can thus explain why relatively few lawyers were implicated from the start of the independence movements until the close of the eighteenth century—such as in the conspiracies of Nariño and Gual y España—and why they instead positioned themselves on the side of the crown. Still easier to explain is the absence of lawyers in the indigenous revolt of Tupac Amarú. The combination of a crisis of the Spanish monarchy at the dawn of the nineteenth century with the diffusion of modern thought served to align most lawyers with autonomist aims. The ideas of independence were in fact strengthened as a reaction to the highly repressive policies of Fernando VII and of those who favored maintaining the link with the Spanish monarchy.

When the intellectual production and biographies of lawyers of the period are analyzed, we see differing degrees of agreement with the ideas of autonomy and independence and how changes came about. Most certainly, lawyers such as Azcárate in Mexico, Roscio in Caracas, Funes in Buenos Aires, Camilo Torres in Bogotá, Juan Martínez Rozas in Chile, and López Aldana in Lima were early advocates of separation. Other prominent names had a slower conversion. For example, Manuel Antonio de Castro, closely linked to the viceroy and other colonial authorities in Río de la Plata, was initially suspected of being unsympathetic to the idea of autonomy and independence, but later played an outstanding role when the process advanced (Levene, 1941). In Mexico and Lima several judges were integrated without difficulty into the new states.

From this perspective it does not make sense to establish the idea of lawyers as traitors to the monarchy or as early champions of liberty or republican patriotism. They were the men of legal and political knowledge. It is understandable that it fell to them to justify independence, to emphasize the mistakes of Fernando VII and of colonial policy, to design the political and legal structures, and to write the constitutional documents for the new states. It also is understandable that other lawyers had reservations or clearly opposed aligning themselves with a movement that could unleash serious, socially disruptive forces. In fact, in each country the independence process affected differently the social structure and economic base of what were later the distinct independent states, but in none did it merely substitute the traditional legitimacy of the monarchy with a legalist legitimacy. The establishment of the nation states turned out to be a much more complicated task than was imagined by those writers of constitutions, declarations of rights, acts of independence, and other notable legal documents that today we are proud to display as relics of the birth of our nations. This will be the theme of analysis in the next chapter.

CHAPTER 3

Lawyers and the Construction of Nations

LET US LOOK AT two moments in the history of Latin America: 1830 and 1950. These will be the beginning and ending points of the period we propose to analyze in this chapter. At the first point, we see groups of people writing constitutions and attempting to configure independent nations from the remains of Iberian empires that collapsed at the beginning of the nineteenth century. One hundred years later, those nations exist. The majority of the inhabitants of Brazil, Chile, or Venezuela no longer identify themselves as "Portuguese in America," "American Spaniards," or *pardos* but rather as Brazilians, Mexicans, Chileans, Venezuelans, and so on. The organs of the state have control over the national territory, and there is no doubt that there are functioning nation-states. The nation-building project can thus be considered more or less complete.

If the analysis becomes somewhat more detailed, the view contains many variations and much unevenness. In 1950 not all of the citizens of these nations felt equally like citizens. That was the case for indigenous groups, who were especially numerous in Bolivia, Ecuador, Guatemala, Mexico, and Peru. Their national identity and integration into national life were weak. An important part of the population, even in countries without an "indigenous problem," was marginalized from mainstream political and economic operations. Their rural isolation or poverty and illiteracy made it difficult to consider them citizens. In fact, the elite, the army, and the police did not treat these sectors of the population as citizens, even though its members had achieved the right to vote or had participated in political life by way of war, riots, or revolts. The principles and rights declared in the constitutions for more than a century had not taken root. Frequently, the functioning of the state did not follow constitutional guidelines. In many cases these features still exist today, testifying to the ongoing and incomplete task of nation building.

When independent life began, it was thought that liberation from the colonial noose would be enough for the Latin American countries to blossom economically and to reach the same level of well-being as Europe and the United States, which at that time were not very distant in terms of per capita income. Economic progress turned out to be more elusive during the nineteenth century than hoped for. At the end of the century, and more so in the first half of the twentieth century, economic failure was evident: Europe and the United States had reached levels of development that cast Latin American countries in a "backward" or underdeveloped hue. Only Argentina and Uruguay enjoyed a period of great prosperity in the first half of the twentieth century, which later proved to be short-lived (Bulmer-Thomas, 1994). The lack of economic success can be linked to the difficulties in achieving an adequately functioning political and legal system.

This chapter deals with the role of lawyers and of the law as an academic discipline in the construction of nation-states. Chapter 2 has shown that lawyers were part of the intellectual and political elite in the colonial period and that they played a formative role in the process leading to independence. In this chapter the first hypothesis is that lawyers remained part of this elite; and the second, that the political life of those independent states did not flow through the channels laid out by the constitutions and laws—in other words, the *estado de derecho* (rule of law) was not established. Although seemingly contradictory, this chapter will argue that these two hypotheses are reconcilable. The problem is to determine the political role of the lawyers. A related research question is how the political role and the professional ideology and activity of lawyers were related during the period in question.

The period presents serious difficulties for its study, principally of the independence and diversity of those nation-states. Each one faced specific problems that stemmed from its own social and political arrangement and from its place in the world system. Each state in turn reacted as an independent political unit, tried to organize itself in its own way, and developed its own policies. With regard to the themes of this book, legal education and the legal profession of each state followed completely divergent paths independent of the others. Our analysis must therefore accommodate considerable diversity.

Nevertheless, the colonial empires and resulting independent Latin American states had been shaped by two absolute Catholic monarchies. The metropolitan cultures of the entire region were quite similar during the three hundred years of colonization. After independence the various countries joined the world system whose axis was Europe, thus they shared the same commercial and political restrictions and received similar intellectual influences. In the legal arena, the civil law tradition continued to be based on knowledge that was presented as scientific and universal, leading one to reasonably expect that the study of law in the various countries had similar content and that many of the textbooks were the same. A plausible conjecture is that there existed a cultural unity among lawyers, despite belonging to independent countries with distinct legal systems.

This chapter builds on previous studies about lawyers, legal education, and legal history. The research literature is characterized by its national focus and usually diverges in methodological approaches and themes. Information is scattered among many sources. The enterprise is like the task of creating a picture of a landscape using pieces of photographs from different places, taken by various photographers at different times and from different angles. This picture likewise depends on the fragments we have found and our ability to make them coherent. The analysis will focus on only those countries that have produced relevant literature: Argentina, Brazil, Chile, Colombia, Mexico, Peru, and Venezuela along with mention of other countries for which limited information was found.

The first section describes the institutional and political context in which the life of lawyers developed; the second section analyzes their intellectual formation—the production and transmission of legal knowledge; the third presents background on demographics and employment history; and the fourth addresses lawyers' involvement in political and legal roles.

The Institutional and Political Context

The colonial order was based on a rigid distinction among groups using, fundamentally, racial criteria. Europeans and their descendants had political and economic control. The population of indigenous and African origin worked predominantly in agriculture and was clearly subordinate. Those of mixed blood (*mestizos*) and recent immigrants (*blancos de orilla*) held a more ambiguous position: they were the unskilled workers, masons, craftsmen, and small businessmen; they supplied manual labor which did not bring them honor, but some of them could accumulate a certain amount of wealth. The Catholic church had many functions, among them providing ideological support for maintaining order.

Independence upset that social order. The traditional legitimacy of the king disappeared (with the exception of Brazil) in the nineteenth century and required the creation of a new political order, ostensibly founded on the principle of equality for individuals. In theory, the citizens of the new countries became sovereign and the government became their representative. Yet political organization, distribution of power, and the definition of church-state relations were difficult and controversial tasks. The leaders of the new nation-states attempted to organize the social and political system—much like trying to maneuver in a minefield. For the most part these leaders were the white criollos, and among their tasks was deciding how to incorporate the indigenous population, slaves of African origin, and the great diversity of free, mixed-race people. A large part of these groups had been mobilized in the cause of independence, and they would not easily return to the traditional forms of social ordering. The task turned out to be especially difficult in those countries where pro-independence mobilization was greatest and the independence battles most intense. The internal conflicts often led to civil war, and mobilization continued even after independence was achieved. Thus an order-disorder, civilization-barbarism dynamic was created, placing enormous obstacles in the path of economic progress and the creation of the rule of law.

The law's relationship with this process is rather obvious. Legal documents such as constitutions, international treaties, statutes, and works of legal doctrine tried to establish the channels of order. One tends to see in lawyers the imaginary figures of parents instilling order, or architects of civility. The counterfigures are the *caudillos* and dictators, who with their charisma or astute use of force were able to dominate the uncivilized masses. They were able to achieve this only by manipulating or bending legal channels, imposing barbarity. These characters that exercised arbitrary power have fascinated Latin American novelists, and typically in the "dictator novels," lawyers either have no role at all or appear in negative roles. For example, in *Fiesta del Chivo* by Mario Vargas Llosa (2000), lawyers perform all sorts of legal gymnastics to provide legal cover for the arbitrary acts of Dominican Republic's President Rafael Trujillo, and one even goes so far as to offer his young daughter in order to satisfy the boundless sexual appetite of the dictator and regain his favor. Only one widely published novel reverses the roles. In Rómulo Gallegos's *Doña Bárbara* (1929), Santos Luzardo, a lawyer born in the plains but educated in the capital city of Caracas, is able to defeat, using the weapons of law, the powerful female character who gives the work its name and, in a happy ending, ends up with her daughter. This chapter will discuss the relationship between lawyers and *caudillos* outside of the novelists' imaginations, trying to decipher their role in the effort to construct national order.

The next part of this chapter analyzes the relationship between law and Latin American societies in the examined period (1830–1950). The law that attempted to order social relations experienced significant change by virtue of political independence. New tendencies in legal thinking appeared. Legislation became centrally important to law (Pérez-Perdomo, 1987), especially constitutions and civil codes. Discussion of the constitutions and their relationship to politics will be followed by a look at the civil codes and their relationship to civil society and, finally, by the general social meaning of this change in law.

CONSTITUTIONS AND THE POLITICAL (DIS)ORDER

The history of Latin America in the nineteenth century was undeniably turbulent (Halperin Donghi, 1993). Each country's national history presents a series of civil wars, rebellions, riots, fights in congress or the press, *caudillos*, and dictators. Simultaneously are found elections, congresses, laws, courts, law schools, and the production of legal literature. These processes were not completely independent of one another, except perhaps in the minds of those who study them: political historians see only political conflicts where legal historians see the evolution of legal ideas. Here, there is an attempt to analyze the interrelationship of the processes involved.

Following independence the great task was to organize the state. From 1811 on, Latin America became a great producer of constitutions—a new and rare product in human history until that time (Pérez-Perdomo, 1987). Each newly independent country wrote at least one, and frequently several in succession, continuing throughout the century. The political science of the time determined the approximate content of the constitutions: organization of the various branches of public power, distribution of power among central organs and the rest of the country, relationship between church and state, and declarations of citizens' rights. There were prêt-à-porter models in the United States and France, products of their respective revolutions at the end of the eighteenth century. The Spanish constitution of 1812 also served as a model and was irregularly in force in Spanish American countries during the independence period. Latin American legal and political figures were familiar with the contemporary writings and hesitated neither to use them nor to innovate. In the enormous collection of constitutions from the region, we have all types of models: monarchies, republics, presidential systems, parliamentary systems, lifelong presidents with great power, weak executives, shared executive power, strong central governments, federal systems, confederate systems, central-federal systems, and extensive or very brief declarations of rights. The great variety illustrates that different political regimes were tried out and that stability in a political system was elusive. The political task was complicated and looked to the constitutions to lead the fight against the opposing threats of despotism and anarchy[1] and to establish viable political structures.

Each country has a constitutional history that reflects a particular relationship with political change, though political change does not necessarily always imply constitutional change. Nineteenth-century Brazil seems the exception because of its relatively tranquil political history. The Portuguese royal family took refuge in Brazil in 1808, making Rio de Janeiro the capital of the empire. Brazil declared independence in 1822, following the return of João VI to Portugal, and formed its own empire headed by Pedro I, the former crown prince of the Portuguese throne and Brazil's first emperor. Brazilian independence can be interpreted as the prince's refusal to submit to the ups and downs of the politics of Portugal, but in reality the monarch perceived that either he was going to lead the independence movement or it would take place at his expense. In 1823, Pedro I delivered the first—and quite conservative—constitution after dissolving the constituent assembly. Political developments in both Portugal and Brazil led him to abdicate in 1831 in favor of his young son, Pedro II, and to return to Portugal.

Gradually, Brazil became a constitutional, parliamentary monarchy, with considerable autonomy for the country's provinces, all of which was reflected in constitutional reforms (Wehling, 2000). In 1889 a military coup removed the emperor and installed a federated, presidential republic with a new constitution. In 1922 and the years following, military rebellions led to periods of agitation and authoritarian governments. In 1930, Getulio Vargas came to power. A populist politician, he created the interventionist state before being overthrown in a 1945 military coup. New elections were called, and in 1946 a new federal, democratic constitution was drawn up. Vargas returned to power through elections in 1950 and committed suicide in 1954 (Faoro, 1975). We see that imperial Brazil was very different from the rest of the Latin American countries, but its political problems during the 1900s had considerable similarity. One aspect that interests us about Brazil is its permanence as a single nation-state, despite its organization during the colonial period into two units that were separated geographically by the immense Amazon jungle. The contrast with the Spanish empire is noteworthy, for the latter evolved into eighteen independent countries (see Carvalho, 1980, 1995).

The viceroyalty of New Spain became an independent country in 1821—after battles, difficulties, and a first constitution in 1814, known as the Apatzingán, which was ineffective. The independence plan of 1821 was expressed in a document, the Iguala Plan, that envisioned the establishment of a constitutional monarchy. When the plan failed, General Augustín de Iturbide declared himself emperor in 1822. The empire included all of the territory of the viceroyalty, which quickly collapsed and gave way to the republics of Mexico, Guatemala, Honduras, Costa Rica, Nicaragua, and El Salvador—all of which, except for Mexico, had been controlled by the *audiencia* of Guatemala during the colonial period.

Our attention turns next to Mexico. The 1824 federal constitution of the United Mexican States was a serious attempt to establish order in the republic. The centralist (or unitary, to use the term of that time) constitution of 1836 replaced it. In practice, until 1855 the country experienced extreme political chaos and waged wars with Spain, France, and the United States of America. In the process, Mexico lost its northern territory, which was annexed by the United States and became Arizona, California, New Mexico, and Texas. General Antonio López Santa Anna was the dominant political figure. A period of liberal reform began in 1855, reducing the power of the Catholic church and establishing a federal system. The constitution of 1857 and the so-called "reform laws" expressed the new situation and characterized this period (*período de las reformas*) until 1864. The civil war continued and led to new Spanish and French military intervention. The conservative solution was to import a European monarch, Maximilian Hapsburg. The liberals, led by Benito Pablo Juárez, rejected such a solution. The outcome was the defeat of the conservatives and Maximilian's death by firing squad in 1867. In 1876, control passed into the hands of the liberal general, Porfirio Díaz, who in fact established a dictatorship (known as *el Porfiriato*) that protected landholders, the newly forming bourgeois, and foreign investment. It was a period of considerable material progress.

A reaction against the regime began in 1910 and led to new civil wars and to substantial changes in land-use policy (agrarian reform). This reaction is known as the revolutionary period and led to the 1917 constitution (González, 1998, 2000). A new period of stability began, this time under the control of the Institutional Revolutionary Party, which governed Mexico for the rest of the twentieth century.[2]

The viceroyalty of New Granada and the general captaincy of Venezuela united to become Colombia in 1821, encompassing the present-day countries of Colombia, Ecuador, Venezuela, and Panama and led principally by Bolívar. The 1821 constitution organizing this republic is called the Constitution of Cúcuta, and a parallel effort to complete Latin American independence induced intense legislation changes. Severe political conflicts led to the dissolution of the union in 1830.

Beginning in 1830, Colombia (with approximately the same borders as today, though with several different names) entered a period dominated by conservatives and experienced both conflict and compromise with the liberals. The constitution of 1833 was federal, with two legislative chambers and a single-term executive. In 1843 the state was centralized, and this was reflected in a rather conservative new constitution. Liberal dominance began in 1849, leading to freedom of worship and separation of church and state as well as a marked federalism. The constitution of 1853 was the expression of this new liberal and federal political project. It provided for popular election of the president and vice-presidents, supreme court justices, attorney general, and governors. During the presidency of conservative Ospina Rodríguez

(1857–61), the country endured a bloody civil war. Alternating periods of peace and worsening conflict and civil war endured from 1861 forward. The clearly liberal and anticlerical constitution of 1863 was an important turning point. Rafael Núñez, considered liberal during his first term (1882–84) and conservative during his second (1884–88), presided over a period called *la regeneración* (regeneration). The constitution of 1886 was centralist and conservative, and it remained in force—with some amendments—until 1991. A new civil war, called the "thousand days' war," shook the country again from 1889 to 1903, during which Panama broke off from Colombia with the open participation of the United States. The conservatives had the upper hand until 1930. López Pumarejo (1934–38) was a populist leader who initiated the interventionist state. Political conflict was relatively restrained until 1948, when the assassination of liberal leader Jorge Eliécer Gaitán set off a new cycle of violence.[3]

Venezuela achieved some stability under the leadership of José Antonio Páez and the so-called "conservative oligarchy" (1830–48). The central-federal constitution of 1830, in force until 1858, reflected the conservative order, with the vote restricted to men with some wealth and privileges retained for the church. A riot fueled by President Monagas attacked Congress in 1848, which led to a rebellion by Páez. The period that follows is marked by administrative disorganization and, beginning in 1857, more frequent rebellions leading to the particularly extensive "federal war." The liberals, supporting a federation, triumphed. The constitution of 1864 reflected the liberal-federal project, tried to regulate armed conflict within the republic, and prohibited the stationing of federal troops in the states. The central government retained various symbolic powers, among them codification of law. Universal suffrage was established, including the vote for women, although they were barred from elective office. Under the leadership of Guzmán Blanco (president three times from 1870 to 1890), the country enjoyed relative peace and prosperity. Civil wars intensified in the 1890s and early 1900s, and in 1904 Venezuela was blockaded by the European powers.

The structural problem lay in the lack of resources necessary to finance a true state: in a geographically large country with poor means of communication, the "state" comprised a small number of people without the ability to control the territory (Pérez-Perdomo, 1990). Under Juan Vincente Gómez (in power from 1909 to 1935), who considered himself a federalist and a liberal, the country was tamed and centralized, though formally it remained federal. Oil provided the resources to consolidate the state, and the constitution was reformed frequently to reflect the political mood. The constitution of 1936 was a key part of an effort to submit the country to a rule of law, and political life progressively liberalized. The 1945 coup produced a new cycle of political agitation, instability, and dictatorship that lasted until 1958 (Carrera Damas, 1980; Pérez-Perdomo, 1983).[4]

The viceroy of Peru was overthrown in 1826, forming the republics of Peru and Bolivia. In 1836 the two nations joined together in the so-called Peru-Bolivia Confederation, under the leadership of General Andrés Santa Cruz. The confederation had a short and troubled life. War broke out between Peru and Bolivia over territorial issues in 1841, and in 1889 the War of the Pacific matched Chile (supported by England) against Peru and Bolivia. The result was the loss of territory from Peru and the northward extension of Chile.

The histories of Peru and Bolivia are intertwined yet highly divergent. Peru's turbulent political life gave way to frequent civil wars and a profusion of constitutional texts. The first, in 1821, was never put into effect but was quite liberal and granted a marked predominance to congress over the executive branch. The Bolivian constitution of 1826, in contrast, was conservative and ratified a life term for the presidency. The Peruvian 1828 text also was liberal, and that of 1834 more conservative, consolidating links with the Catholic church. In 1836, Peru separated into two independent countries, North Peru and South Peru, each with its own constitution. Both countries, along with Bolivia, formed a short-lived confederation (constitution of 1837). When General Santa Cruz was overthrown, the quite conservative constitution of 1839 was put into effect. Political chaos, civil war, and fragmentation of power followed in Peru, with periods of relative stability under the influence of liberal Ramón Castilla (1845–62). In 1856 a liberal constitution was promulgated, followed in 1860 by one considered moderate, which—with interruptions in 1867 and 1879 and strong modifications in the 1880s—remained in force until 1920. At the beginning of the twentieth century, Augusto Leguía established an autocratic government (1908–12; 1919–30). The constitution of 1920 was pro-socialist but had little practical effect. In 1931, Leguía was overthrown in a military coup that began a series of military interventions, alternating with elected civilian governments that lasted beyond the period of this study and characterizing the 1933 constitution as having a very turbulent life (Pareja Paz-Soldán, 1954; Trazegnies Granda, 1979; García Belaúnde, 1993).

Chile became independent in 1818 and began its political history with strong clashes between liberals and conservatives. The liberals produced the constitutions of 1822, 1823, 1826, and 1828. Following the conservative triumph in the 1830 civil war, the political system was stabilized under the leadership of Diego Portales, who did not, however, become president. Under the conservatives, the 1833 centralist constitution was written and remained in force until 1925. The government was conservative until 1861, and power was concentrated in the presidency. Between 1861 and 1925, congress and political parties became increasingly important. At different times, particularly in 1851 and 1859, failed attempts were made to change the political system by force. In 1891, congress and President José Manuel Balmaceda faced off in a civil war, which ended with the president's suicide on the last day of his term in office. From that moment on, the system became strongly parliamentary, and cabinet ministers did not last long. Conflict sharpened during the Arturo Alessandri administration (1920–25), and military intervention was necessary to return the ousted president to power in early 1925. The 1925 constitution redefined the distribution of power, with strong executive control. The political system remained considerably stable until beyond the period on which we are focusing (Collier and Sater, 1996; Eyzaguirre, 1966).

The viceroyalty of Río de la Plata became Argentina, Uruguay, and Paraguay. Argentina began its independent life with confrontations among the various provinces and political disorganization that lasted until 1835. Between 1835 and 1852, the conservative *caudillos*—exemplified notably by Juan Manuel de Rosas, known as one of the most ferocious dictators of the time—established a federation amid a bloody regime. Rosas did not find it convenient to create either a constitution or modern legislation, believing that peace should be attained first. Rosas's defeat led to a predominantly civilian and oligarchic government whose legal expression was the 1853 constitution. Nonetheless, the civil wars continued until 1880. Massive immigration in the latter 1800s transformed society, and Argentina became the most prosperous country in the region, with a per capita income close to that of developed countries. But political tensions did not cease. During a severe economic crisis in 1930, the elderly president Hipólito Irigoyen was toppled by an alliance of conservatives, socialists, and soldiers that led the country to instability and military rule—personified by General Juan Perón (president 1946–55 and 1973–74), an archetype of the populist, authoritarian Latin American leader. Perón succeeded in changing the constitution in 1949, but upon his fall from power and following several de facto regimes, the constitution of 1853 was reestablished, although its application remained uneven. The period of instability and dictatorships has lasted beyond the period we analyze here (Levene, 1957; Romero, 1978).

Paraguay is an especially interesting case for its attempt in 1813 to replicate a Roman-style republic with two consuls. The next year, congress named Dr. Francia (José Gaspar Rodrígues de Francia) dictator for five years, and in 1816, perpetual dictator, which he effectively was until his death in 1840 (Catalano, 1983, 1986). A constitution was finally adopted in 1844.

Constitutions reflect political conflicts and political proposals. The most important conflicts were those between liberals and conservatives. The latter believed, for example, that maintaining a strong Catholic church was necessary to uphold social order. The conflict between federalists and centralists (or unitarians, as they were known) concerned the dominance of one region over another. Frequently the liberals were federalists, but not in every case (Pérez-Perdomo, 1991).

The constitutions also reflect a certain social consensus. For example, the political economy was not a center of controversy in the nineteenth century when the liberal economic vision predominated; but it did become a cause of division between the left and right in the twentieth century. The left favored social rights and state intervention in the economy; the right, free markets and a modest role for the state. The right to vote and to be elected to office also were issues. The first constitutions, in the early 1800s, generally reserved these rights for citizens with a certain amount of property. Relatively few could vote. Later constitutions eliminated this requirement but established others, such as the express exclusion of women or the uneducated. Suffrage became universal toward the mid-1900s, the only requirements being citizenship and majority age. Yet the constitutional texts reflected actual political participation. The socially excluded (the indigenous, slaves, peasants, or the urban proletariat—depending on the period) frequently participated politically in the form of revolts, riots, or later, public demonstrations. Vote buying and electoral fraud were common. Many thought that the lower social orders did not have the civil education required to participate intelligently in government. Whatever its tendency, the government's task was to maintain a minimum of social order.

Political conflict led to the suspension of constitutions for certain periods, in which all power was concentrated in one person expected to lead and command in an effort to save the country. In the benign Roman style, such leaders were referred to as *dictators* in the nineteenth century (Miranda in Venezuela, 1812; Bolívar in Colombia, 1828; Páez in Venezuela, 1861). Paraguay's Francia distorted this concept of dictatorship by proclaiming himself perpetual dictator, and his conduct was more in line with the pejorative meaning that the term acquired in the twentieth century. *Dictatorship* became a word to designate an authoritarian government created by force that maintained power by force, as well as one in which all political power is exercised by a single person or a small group that prohibits political opposition or countervailing power. The word became synonymous with tyranny and despotism. Leaders no longer adopted it themselves, rather government critics applied it pejoratively to authoritarian regimes (Rouquié, 1986; Rey, 1989: 39). The tendency of the late nineteenth century and twentieth century was not to declare a dictatorship, but rather to suspend the constitution or its guarantees by declaring a national emergency, state of siege, state of war, or the like (Loveman, 1993). Popularly elected leaders also were guilty of distorting democratic rule in the twentieth century. Perón, popularly elected in 1946 and reelected in 1951, was considered a dictator of this sort.

The terms *caudillo* and *caudillismo*, applied to the nineteenth century and the beginning of the twentieth in Latin America, refer to regional leaders that had controlling power in their area. A caudillist political system was pluralist (Urbaneja, 1975) because power was not centralized, but it was clearly not democratic and impeded the rule of law. Thus Soriano de García Pelayo (1996, 2000) prefers to lump together *caudillos* and dictators with the general term "political personalism": charismatic leaders who distort constitutional and other legal rules in their exercise of power. Soriano de García Pelayo highlights as well that these leaders play with the "dyschronism" of Latin American societies,[5] or the coexistence of elements that correspond to distinct historical structures.

If we look back at the constitutional history of the Latin American countries, one sees that the constitutions tried to perform four functions that can at times be contradictory. First, they defined the rules of the political game, determining who the actors were and how leaders were to be elected. Second, they expressed a political project, be it conservative, liberal, socialist, federalist, or centralist. Third, they organized public power, limited its exercise, and established relationships among the branches of government. And fourth, they declared the rights of the citizens.

Perhaps the constitutions were most successful at expressing the different political projects, although this task could be contrary to that of defining the rules of the game, for it tended to leave out those who did not conform to a particular ideology. The function of declaring citizens' rights also was problematic, as the stated principle was the equality of all citizens and their rights, when in fact the underlying desire was to keep at bay the *pardos* and those who did not share in the political project, or to exclude the slaves and the indigenous. In a society based on exclusion, the significance of the constitution differed from that which today's lawyers attribute to it. It was in essence a political document of fundamentally ideological importance.

The intensity of conflict that caused violence and overflowed legal channels probably requires an explanation outside of the political system. Control of the state apparatus carried such social and economic meaning that conflict was seen as truly vital—a source of honor and income in times of scarce resources and not simply a way to determine public policy or social position. Survival itself was at stake, and political actors could not fail to use every weapon at their disposal, including violence. It would be simplistic to believe that lawyers represented only law, legality, order, and civilization while the *caudillos* and dictators represented only the dark forces of disorder, arbitrariness, and barbarism. Lawyers, after all, were eminent members of the political elite. This is a topic that we will explore later on, but first we will focus on that part of the lawyers' task that is not expressly political: the organization of civil society and criminal justice.

CIVIL CODE, CIVIL SOCIETY

The constitutional task was urgent and primary in the early stages of independent life, for the state had to be organized and the rules of the political game defined. In addition to constitutions, numerous laws regarding the organization of the state (for example, the judicial hierarchy) and public finance were produced (Pérez-Perdomo, 1987). But independence was not just a political change; modernization of society was the desired goal. Thus after every new constitution came legislation regarding central aspects of the new political economy, such as freeing property from limitations like *censos* and *mayorazgos* (ground rent and entailed estates), establishing freedom of contract, and dealing with the situation of the slaves and indigenous. In the first decades and for most laws, the prevailing Spanish legislation generally remained in force unless it was repealed by new legislation in the newly independent states. Modern codes, which were the most complete expression of a new theory of legislation, replaced the old laws over the course of the nineteenth century.

The codes exemplified a new rationalization of law in the civil law tradition (Tau Anzoátegui, 1977, 1992; Guzmán Brito, 2000). In Spain and its colonies there were proposals to substitute the complex body of old-regime law with modern, concise, and simple codes. The old way of arranging legislation in enormous compilations that listed past provisions and their dates tended to omit many of the existing laws. On the contrary, the new codes expressed and organized legal rules succinctly and systematically. They were considered complete in and of themselves and carried the authority to revoke all prior law. Besides being a decidedly modern expression, linked to modern natural law and the Enlightenment, the codes had a national character; they fixed the law in a particular national sphere.

The modern form of the code did not dismantle the underlying ideological differences between conservatives and liberals. The most conservative position was not to codify at all. Moderate conservatives proposed to codify traditional law, without trying to change its content. The liberal position was to change legal rules in order to adopt them to the liberal idea of a modern society. The elaboration of new codes presented the opportunity to change the rules or, on the contrary, reaffirm traditional rules in modern dress.

The best-known model of the time was the French civil code (1804), better known as the Napoleonic Code or *Code Civil des Français*. It began with some fundamental rules about the application and interpretation of law and then set rules to regulate the individual, the family, property, and contracts. The difficulty was that it encroached on a sphere occupied in great measure by the Catholic church. The church controlled birth (baptism), marriage, and death certificates. Its tribunals decided individual disputes and family law matters. It also was the largest property owner and financer. Its properties were generally off the market. Thus the adoption of a civil code had huge political connotations and great potential for controversy.

Modern legal scholars may have difficulty understanding that polemic character, in part because many of the societal problems at the beginning of independence ceased to exist as such by the end of the century, though some have returned to life in new forms. For example, the struggle over the status of indigenous people and slaves was paramount. The results tended to be liberal: treat individuals as legal subjects, in effect superseding prior law about indigenous people. Slavery was generally abolished after the promulgation of the first codes. Indigenous people were declared equal, although in practice they were denied suffrage through various regulations and social practices. Indigenous property ceased being communal and became marketable. In practice, the purchase of these lands by neighboring large landholders was facilitated. Freedom of contract, which in the first half of the nineteenth century usually meant unregulated interest rates and more easily collectable debts, was an important modification of the colonial regulations and tended to be controversial.[6]

The most controversial aspect in the new lawmaking era was the relationship with the Catholic church, which did not look favorably on the state's taking from its sphere of competency the regulation of issues it had traditionally managed. The liberalization of the property regime also affected the enormous property holdings of the church.

Table 3.1 lists the Latin American civil codes by year of promulgation and includes the year of the code currently in force. Next, we will analyze how ideological problems were resolved.

Although the task of civil codification began early, it did not have the same impulse and urgency as the constitutional activity. First there developed a consensus that Spanish and Spanish American legislation was not adequate due to its bulk and disorder. Criticism of Spanish legislation was commonplace from the time of independence until codification (Tau Anzoátegui, 1977; González, 1981; Pérez-Perdomo, 1987; Guzmán Brito, 2000). This criticism was accompanied by efforts to make the law more accessible through compilations (for example, the *Recompilación de Leyes de la Nueva Granada* in 1845; or Del Castillo's *Teatro de la Legislación Colombiana y Venezolana* in 1852) or in works that adopted a modern code style (Teixeira de Freitas's *Consolidação das Leis Civis*, 1855–58).

TABLE 3.1.
Civil Codes of Latin America

First Code: Year of Publication	Country	Present Code: Year of Publication
1825	Haiti	*
1827	Mexico, Oaxaca	1928[3]
1830	Bolivia	1975
1836	Peru	1984
1845	Dominican Republic	1884
1855	Chile	*
1857	Colombia, Magdalena	1887
1858	Ecuador	*
1859	El Salvador	*
1860	Panama[1]	1916
1862	Venezuela	1873
1867	Nicaragua	1904
1868	Uruguay	*
1869	Argentina	*
1876	Paraguay	1985
1877	Guatemala	1963
1880	Honduras	1906
1886	Costa Rica	*
1889	Cuba[2]	1987
1916	Brazil	*

NOTES: * First code still in force in 2000. [1]At the time, part of Colombia. [2]Extension of the Spanish code to its colony for that time. [3]Applicable to the Federal District and federal territories.
SOURCE: Guzmán Brito, 2000: Annexes 1 and 5.

Codes are laws, documents enacted by the legislature. Their content is a synthesis of the law, and the true authors of the codes were legal thinkers who have entered the pantheon of Latin American jurists. Yet they did not act alone, and generally these jurists enjoyed the cooperation or the polemic criticism (which is another form of cooperation) of other jurists. The work of codification was significant: from 1816 to 1916, seventy-one civil codes were promulgated. Some of them are still the national codes; others correspond to states within a federal country or to substantial reforms of previous codes (Guzmán Brito, 2000: annex 1). Still others were drafts that never became codes—such as those of Peru's Vidaurre, Venezuela's Viso, and Uruguay's Acevedo. All of these codifiers shared a universal formation in Roman law, lending a certain unity to the Latin American codes (Schipani, 1992). Today it is unclear why some drafts were not enacted into codes.

Some scholars attribute the failure to political upheaval (Parra Aranguren, 1966, 1974), when in fact a code's content may have been ideologically and irreparably controversial.

In this work our task is to analyze in what way the codes contributed to the creation of national law and of the nation itself. This is related to the topic of influences from other codes, especially the French code. Legal thinkers saw a valuable resource in the previously published codes or drafts and rejected the idea of innovating new rules of law. The codes were not regarded as literary or academic works that were supposed to be original or distinct. In fact, the decision to use a certain code as a model was a weighty intellectual and political choice. With that starting point, they made the necessary changes. The circulation and borrowing of those models does not take away from the national character of the work, but rather reinforces the cultural unity of the region.

It also stands out that the codes have tended to be more stable than the constitutions. Half of the Latin American countries have codes that date from the nineteenth century, something that is not true for any of the constitutions. This stability is naturally relative, in the sense that there have been modifications of content. Guzmán Brito (2000), an excellent guide on this point, considers a code to be unchanged when its structure is maintained, even when a significant portion of its content is modified. For example, the 1873 Venezuelan code was modified in 1880, 1896, 1904, 1916, 1922, 1942, and 1982. Those changes have altered its content considerably. Nonetheless, its structure and certainly the majority of its articles still come from the 1873 version.

The first civil code in Latin America was an adoption of the French civil code. This was the case of Haiti, which also was the first country to gain independence (1804). Haiti adopted the French code in 1825 in its 1804 version—without the conservative revision in force in France after 1816. In 1845 the Dominican Republic also adopted the *Code Civil des Français*. It did so in French, without translation. And even though Spanish translations existed, none was officially adopted until forty years later (Guzmán Brito, 2000; Vega, 1986).

Mexico's history of early civil codification also is interwoven with political transformations. The state of Oaxaca published a civil code piecemeal between 1827 and 1829, expressing its sovereignty. It was a translation of the French code, reducing the number of articles (from 2,281 to 1,415) and modifying other provisions to comply with canon law and the traditional realm of church domain. In 1837 the code was repealed. Thus Mexican codification really began only with the 1870 code, approved initially for the Federal District and Baja California but later adopted with modifications by the majority of Mexican states (González, 1988). A much larger code (3,044 articles), which incorporated much of the 1870 code and added subsequent legislation on divorce and other family law matters, was adopted in 1928.

Bolivia had a very early code, in great measure due to the efforts of General Santa Cruz (Guardia, 2000). In 1830 he presented a draft that was not considered ready by the commission that created it. Several successive publications amended it. In July 1831 the National Constituent Assembly of Bolivia ratified the code and ordered that it be referred to as the Santa Cruz Code. It was a fairly well elaborated adaptation of the French code—briefer (1,556 articles), and one-third of the articles were non-French in origin. Except for a short interruption in 1845–46, the code was in force until 1976 (Guzmán Brito, 2000: 313–15). The code declared citizens equal and, unlike the French code, provided true equality to foreigners. Nonetheless, equality does not appear to have extended to slaves and the indigenous population. Santa Cruz himself—a very French-influenced *mestizo* with indigenous physical features—did not undertake initiatives to free the slaves or worry about true equality for the indigenous. Husbands had complete legal dominion over their wives, and the family model included the extended family as well as servants. The economic model was not liberal, either. Despite a definition of absolute property taken from the French code, the Santa Cruz code restricted the alienation of real property.[7]

Costa Rica in 1841 published a general codification divided into three parts under the name *Código General de la República de Costa Rica*. The first part, entitled "Civil Matters," was an adaptation of the Santa Cruz code in its North Peruvian version (1836) (Gutiérrez, 1969; Guzmán Brito, 2000: 320). It was replaced in 1888.

The 1836 Peruvian civil code, which was an extension of the Santa Cruz code, was repealed before entering into force upon the fall of General Santa Cruz (Trazegnies Granda, 1979: 160; Ramos Núñez, 2001). In 1852 the country was given another, quite traditionalist code, which influenced the Guatemalan civil code (1877). The preparatory work of the Peruvian code, especially the 1847 draft, influenced the so-called *Arosemena* draft that became the 1857 civil code of Magdalena. This latter was the first civil code approved in Colombia (Guzmán Brito, 2000: 338ss).

Without a doubt, the code that had the greatest impact in all of Latin America was that of Chile (1855), usually known as the Bello code. It was named for its principal drafter, Andrés Bello,[8] who conducted a thorough study of the available codes of the day and no doubt gave most attention to the French code. He was influenced by Spanish literature and did not present himself as an innovator (Guzmán Brito, 2000: 368ss). The Chilean code was adopted in 1858 by Ecuador, by different states of the then-Colombian federation between 1858 and 1862, and later by a centralized Colombia in 1873. Panama adopted the code in 1860 when it was still part of Colombia and ratified it after independence in 1903. El Salvador adopted it with notable changes in 1859. Venezuela adopted it in 1862 while under the dictatorship of Páez, but upon his fall from power the code was immediately revoked. Nicaragua adopted the code in 1867, and in 1880, Honduras. One of the code's virtues that was appreciated during this period was its clear and careful language. It was a conservative code, not only due to its link with the Spanish legal tradition but also because its brief regulation of marriage left this subject to canon law, and the regulation of the civil registry was relegated to special laws. Regarding property rights—a controversial topic in Chile—it deferred to a special law that was later approved.[9] Thus when countries with liberal leaders adopted this code, sections dealing with the more controversial areas were adjusted.

Argentina promulgated its first code in 1869. The project was prepared over an extended period of time and was not free from controversy. The principal drafter was Dalmacio Vélez Sarsfield. It was extraordinarily long (4,908 articles) and was influenced by the work of Brazil's Teixeira de Freitas, by the Bello code, by German Romanists, and directly or indirectly by the Spanish tradition. The code accepted the Catholic canon law regulation of marriage, gave clear power to the father in family matters, and set up a portion of states to be excluded from the freedom to bequeath. These characteristics made it very controversial in its day and especially so after its adoption (Tau Anzoátegui, 1977; Levaggi, 1992; Zimmermann, 1999). It was adopted with changes by Paraguay in 1876 (Guzmán Brito, 2000).

It is interesting that the Argentinean code was the first to arouse controversy because of its conservative nature. In fact, most of the codes were conservative, though in different ways. For example, the Santa Cruz code did not regulate slavery, in effect leaving it as it was.[10] The Vélez code preferred deference to canon law and the express submission of women, although in Argentina such provisions seemed excessively conservative for the time.

Brazil presents an atypical case in the sense that Augusto Teixeira de Freitas prepared a compilation of civil laws (*Consolidação das Leis Civis*), published in 1858. Its form is identical to that of a modern code, although its name reflects the intention not to innovate but to consolidate prior law.[11] It was not promulgated as a code. Freitas later prepared *Esboço de Código Civil [Draft of a civil code]* (published in installments between 1860 and 1867), with a total of 4,908 articles. This work influenced not only the Brazilian code that eventually was adopted in 1917 but also the Argentinean civil code (1869) (Guzmán Brito, 2000; Wolkmer, 1998). Compared to the other Latin American countries, the Brazilian civil code was much delayed. This is generally explained by the fact that Teixeira de Freitas's consolidation had practical effects similar to those of a civil code; it was put into use even if it never became formal legislation.

Our analysis of the colonial period legislation shows its enormous complexity. Various bodies of law were in effect simultaneously. Compilation did not repeal the uncompiled laws, and publication only added to the amount of legislation. For these reasons, it is likely that lawyers did not rely heavily on the compilations, nor did the population at large. Lawyers and the legal community relied on handbooks and other works for the day-to-day practice of law. In effect, what the codes replaced was not the vast compilation of prior law but the secondary literature actually in use.

LEGISLATION AND LEGAL KNOWLEDGE

The constitutions and civil codes were prominent pieces of legislation, but they were not the only laws in existence nor the only ones referred to. The penal code also was important: it contained the principles and chief rules related to punishment of crimes and misdemeanors, a list of these, and an indication of the penalty for each. The codes of civil procedure and criminal procedure regulated these respective processes. Commercial codes regulated commercial activity, business transactions, and business associations. These five codes (civil, criminal, commercial, civil procedure, and criminal procedure) were considered the core of law. Other significant legislation regulated specific economic and social activity (such as mining and labor), some of which were called codes in some countries.

Each country's national legislation repealed Spanish or Portuguese legislation that had been in effect during the colonial period, although the old legislation often lasted for several decades beyond independence, depending on the country and the branch of law, as we have seen in relation to the civil code. The new legislation, or national legislation, reconfigured the existing law but did not simply replace it.

In fact, there was a new way to think about law and legislation (Pérez-Perdomo, 1987). Legislation was (or it aimed to be) an expression of reason and, at the same time, an act of will by the political power, which infused it with the force of political authority. Law, as an expression of reason, was to be phrased in general terms (particularism or casuism was considered a grave defect), in short sentences, and with clear meaning. Clear and synthetic expression was considered the legislative virtue par excellence. The codes were models of legislation.

In practice, the social role of legislation changed, involving a transformation in the thinking of legal practitioners and scholars. Traditional Spanish and Portuguese legislation was casuist, complex, and disordered. It was contained in enormous volumes—the *recopilaciones*—which primarily gathered together previous legislation. Consulting the compilations was complicated and difficult.[12] Only a few lawyers and the highest-level judges had those enormous volumes available to them, and it is doubtful whether even they used them intensively, in the way today's lawyers and judges tend to consult modern codes. The books actually used were shorter, practical works that mentioned the legislation (usually in the margins or footnotes) when a rule was explained.

An example is seen in Juan de Sala's book: *Ilustraciones del Derecho Real de España [Illustrations of Spanish Royal Law]*. It was a practical work in which the rules were expressed succinctly and in a well-ordered way, following the known plan of Justinian's *Institutes*. In footnotes one found the location of the rules from *Siete Partidas* or other legal texts. Published originally in Valencia, Spain, in 1803, it became a much-referenced book of knowledge of Spanish law. The second edition, from Madrid in 1820, was "corrected and expanded by its author,"[13] incorporating citations from the *Novíssima Recopilación* (1805). The work was a true publishing success, reprinted in Madrid in 1832, 1834, and 1839 and in La Coruña in 1837. Other editions were adapted to the new legislation of Spanish America. Thus there was a *Sala Hispano-Mexicano* in 1831–33 (Mexico) and 1844 (Paris); and a *Sala Hispano-Chileno* and a *Sala Hispano-Venezolano*, both printed in Paris in 1845. None of the legislative compilations had such a widespread distribution, which makes clear which books were actually used before codification. Sala also was a commonly used textbook by students of national law.

The common legal books had a more extensive public than today, when they are generally read only by lawyers. Pérez-Perdomo (1987) observes that a work such as the *Diccionario Razonado de Legislación Civil, Penal, Comercial y Forense*, by Joaquín de Escriche (1840), was published in Caracas for subscription and sold 919 copies, at a time when Venezuela had only 140 lawyers. One supposes that the majority of lawyers and a good number of educated people were reading and using the common legal books. Citations of legislation from the compilations were generally made only indirectly.

The codified law replaced this literature. It had a great advantage as a work of reason with a basis of political power and universal appeal. Its promulgation by political authority made it national and enforceable. Law—not only the constitution but also the comprehensive laws called codes—had meaning and validity as an expression of the nation.

Legislation supposedly regulated all aspects of social life. Nothing escaped it. Given its rational, systematic character, in cases unforeseen or not provided for (legal lacunae), the person interpreting the law needed only refer to an analogous rule or to general legal principles. Law and legislation became one and the same thing. Thus the legalistic legal culture was born (Squella, 1988).

The legislator was omnipotent in the sense that he could modify legislation (or "the law," conceptually the same thing in the thinking of the latter

1800s), unconstrained by the actual content or the material to be converted into law. As the legislator was definitively the political power, lawyers attached themselves to him, whether for making or interpreting law. Two consequences emerged: first, the law became linked more to political power than to citizens' rights; second, the problem of effectiveness was ignored. Law was obligatory and assumed to shape social conduct. If it did not address a given problem, the law had no contingency plan and the problem had to be swept under the rug or declared nonexistent. *Legalism* implied a lack of attention to the values at stake and to the actual behavior of citizens. Despite receiving criticism since the late nineteenth century—and increasingly in the twentieth century—legalism was dominant in the thinking that underlay legal education from the time of codification to a point beyond the time frame of this chapter.[14] Such thinking is still deeply rooted in Latin American legal culture.

Even though the law was binding on everybody, and in fact was read and understood by many, lawyers were especially adept at interpreting the legislation. After codification, it became clear that the codes were not the answer to all questions of legal knowledge. They required an interpretive apparatus and case-bound knowledge that lawyers could claim as their domain. They continued to be men of books and were expected to know the principles of the legal system rooted in Roman law. Lawyers developed an equal capacity for oral and written expression,[15] and their knowledge and abilities made them the best prepared for the tasks of government and the role of "public men" par excellence. Bravo Lira (1998a: 98) shows that this knowledge all but relegated others, those ignorant of the law, to second-class-citizen status. Legal training was thus an essential credential for acceptance into the political elite.

This situation of privilege lasted throughout the period that we are analyzing. We will see later that the number of law graduates increased slowly and new social strata began to have access to power, which meant important upward social mobility for those who studied law. Only at the end of the period did cracks in the foundation begin to show, in the form of less prestige for the profession.

What did this broad knowledge embrace? Where and how was it acquired? These are the questions that we will try to answer in the next section.

Legal Education and Lawyers' Knowledge

ORGANIZATION OF STUDIES

Independence profoundly affected the colonial universities in Spanish America. War and political conflict caused many young men to abandon their studies, and university enrollment fell drastically. The new countries entered into freer contact with the rest of the world and were open to new ideas. As independence produced more diffusion of modern thinking, modern thought influenced universities' organization and curricula. The need for change was especially clear in the case of legal studies, which constituted the highest standard of political knowledge at that time. The countries' need for people prepared to lead the new political organization demanded that special attention be paid to the teaching of law.

These issues were even more pronounced for Brazil because it lacked law schools. Portugal's policy of prohibiting university studies in its colony was a way of maintaining colonial subjection. This situation was obviously not acceptable to an independent nation. Consequently, the very constituent assembly that drafted the constitution took up the topic of legal studies. Due to the interruptions and priorities of parliamentary life and politics, and because the topic was controversial, it took until 1826 to bring legal studies to Brazil. Two law faculties were created, one in the northeast, in Olinda (Recife), the other in the south, in São Paulo. It was a deliberate choice not to locate the schools in Rio de Janeiro, capital of the empire.

As Falcão (1978: 90) has indicated, the establishment of legal education is tied up with the creation of the nation-state. The political elite understood that law school was the avenue for training state staff and the political leadership of the country. Discussions about the selection of law courses have been compiled and analyzed in two volumes (Bastos, 1977, 1978). A clear consciousness existed about the dangers that teaching certain topics, and certain authors, could pose to the state and its political system. The Viscount of Cairu stated as much in a question that called for an obvious answer, but that he preferred to answer expressly and emphatically:

> Can any government tolerate that in any classrooms be taught, for example, the doctrines of the *Social Contract*, of the philosopher of Geneva, of the *System of Nature* and of *Natural Philosophy*, of ungodly writers, that have corrupted the youth that are the hope of the nation to be its legislators, magistrates, teachers in the church and of the State? Never, never, never [cited in Bastos, 1978: 30–31].

This debate took place in other Latin American countries as well. In Chile the liberals and moderate conservatives such as Bello saw the importance of legal studies for the formation of active citizens that would make up the political and bureaucratic staff. The most conservative feared that such an aim could be destabilizing and preferred studies concentrated on Roman, canon, and Spanish law (Serrano, 1994b). Similar disagreements were seen in Colombia and Venezuela (Gaitán Bohorquez, 2002; Uribe, 1995; Pérez-Perdomo, 1981).

Let us see how this controversy was reflected in the approved plans of study. Table 3.2 shows a synthesis of law school curricula obtained for the first half of the nineteenth century.

TABLE 3.2.
Law School Curricula in Five Latin American Countries, Post-Independence

Colombia 1826	Brazil 1827	Venezuela 1827	Mexico 1834	Chile 1844
Universal Legislation	Natural Law 1	Justinian Institutes	Natural Law	Natural Law
Constitutional Law	International Law 1	Religion & Church History	Public Law	Universal Legislation
Administration Science & Statistics	Natural Law 2	National Law	Principles of Legislation	Political Economy
Roman & National Civil Law 1	International Law 2	Church History	Roman Law	International Law
Church Public Law	National Civil Law 1	Constitution & Administration Science	Civil Law 1	Roman Law
Roman & National Civil Law 2	National Criminal Law	Canon Law	Criminal Law 1	National & Constitutional Law
Political Economy & Col Statistics 1	National Civil Law 2	International Law	Canon Law 1	Canon Law
International Law 1	Church Public Law	Principles of Universal Legislation	Civil Law 2	
Political Economy & Col Statistics 2	Public Law	Civil & Criminal Practice	Criminal Law 2	
International Law 2	Imperial Constitution 1	Political Economy	Canon Law 2	
	Imperial Constitution 2	Legal Medicine	Academia	
	Commercial Law			
	Procedural Theory & Practice			

SOURCES: *Colombia and Venezuela*: Pérez-Perdomo, 1981: 107, 281. *Brazil*: Bastos, 1978. *Mexico*: Mendieta y Núñez, 1956. *Chile*: Serrano, 1994b: 169.

In Brazil, a five-year study plan was approved in substantial detail that specified which authors professors could consult. The plan consisted of three courses per year for the first three years, and two courses per year in the final two years. *First-year courses*: natural law (Grotius was mentioned, along with other authors from that genre); public law; and Justinian's *Institutes* in the Heineccius edition. *Second-year courses*: diplomatic and international law (Grotius, Pufendorf, Watel, and others), public maritime law, and commercial law. *Third-year courses*: public national law, public ecclesiastic law, and national criminal law (part one). *Fourth-year courses:* political economy and national criminal law (part two). *Fifth-year courses:* legal hermeneutics and the practice of law. Note the enormous weight of public law, broadly considered. The first year of study covered the great principles of political organizations—what today we would call comparative constitutional law. Public national law presented a history of Portuguese public law, judicial organization, and elements of tax law. Public ecclesiastic law referred to the rules of government of the Catholic church (Bastos, 1978; Falcão, 1978).

Public education in Great Colombia, including the university level, was organized under the 1826 Law on Organization and Arrangement of Public Instruction. A decree the same year (*Plan de Estudios*) regulated legal education in more detail, and regulations for universities differed considerably from those for general education. According to colonial tradition, a bachelor's degree in philosophy was required for entrance to law school. This was modified to include, among other topics, natural law—a discipline clearly connected to the rationalistic thought of the era, though in its Catholic version (Pérez-Perdomo, 1968).

Three universities were created soon after independence in Colombia. They were in fact transformations of universities and *colegios*[16] of the colonial period: Central University in Bogotá, Cauca University in Popayan, and Magdalena and Istmo University in Cartagena. In Bogotá the old *colegios* (San Bartolomé and Nuestra Señora del Rosario) survived and continued functioning with relative autonomy compared to the universities. Instruction—especially legal education—was considered to be of the greatest public and political interest. Consequently, the government controlled it closely (Uribe, 1995; Gaitán Bohorquez, 2002).

The Colombian study plan for law in 1826 called for a six-year program. It included the traditional subjects of Roman and canon law and added constitutional, political, and international law; political economy; principles of universal legislation and administrative science; and principles of statistics. This plan was applicable throughout the territory of Great Colombia. The government-approved textbooks included the controversial Jeremy Bentham (especially for principles of universal legislation). After several law students were involved in a conspiracy to assassinate then-President Bolívar in 1828, the government banned the Bentham text and reverted to a traditional curriculum until after Bolívar's death in 1830. In 1840 the study plan and Bentham were again prohibited, and professors José Duque Gómez and Florentino González were put on trial and imprisoned (Uribe-Uran, 2000: 111; McKennan, 1978). A new study plan (1842) eliminated the dangerous instruction of general topics such as universal principles of legislation, administrative science, and constitutional law and focused on more practical subjects such as commercial law, civil procedure, and criminal procedure.

Roman law and political economy were retained, as they were considered useful and politically secure disciplines (Uribe-Uran, 2000: 112).

In Venezuela, on the other hand, the 1826 Great Colombian study plan was not directly applicable. The Central University of Venezuela in Caracas obtained a special statute in 1827 to divide instruction into twelve annual courses, two per year. Courses related to religion and canon law retained importance. *First-year courses*: religious fundamentals and religious apologia, and Justinian's *Institutes. Second-year courses*: ecclesiastic history and national law (consisting of Spanish and Colombian legislation). *Third-year courses*: canon law and constitutional law, political law, and administrative science. *Fourth-year courses*: canon law and international law. *Fifth-year courses*: universal principles of legislation and civil and criminal practice. *Sixth-year courses*: political economy and legal medicine (Pérez-Perdomo, 1981: 107). It was therefore considerably more conservative than the general study plan for Great Colombia, with great emphasis on canon law and religion. The plan started out with traditional education and added new subjects in the last years of study. In the 1843 Code of Public Instruction, the study plan was reorganized into two-year periods. It may be that innovations were hidden in the list of courses. For example, civil and criminal practices disappear, but "practical law, governmental administration, and municipal regime" all appear in the listing of one course in the third two-year block. An annual "literature or language criticism" course also appears (Pérez-Perdomo, 1981: 283–84).

In Mexico in 1823 the constituent congress issued a decree enabling universities to establish chairs in natural, civil, and canon law and to grant lesser degrees (bachelor of arts). In 1833 the University of Mexico was suppressed, and the *Dirección General de Instrucción Pública* (Board of Public Instruction) took charge of instruction in the Federal District and the federal territories. The university was reestablished in 1834 and its study plan regulated. The decree itself was modernized. In 1835 other decrees prescribed the instructional texts: Berardi and Murillo for canon law, Juan Sala for national (Spanish and Mexican) law, Wattel for public law. As was normal at the time, it was recommended that instructors accommodate doctrine to the customs and political structure of the country; that they illustrate the maxims with ancient and modern classic authors; and that they omit those points on which the adopted authors were not in consonance with the religion, usages, and politics of the country (Mendieta y Núñez, 1956). In other words, the policy was to adopt moderated modern tendencies.

In 1843 President Santa Anna reorganized Mexico's legal education. This change was more conservative than the 1835 plan: the bachelor's degree required four years focused on Roman law, national law, and canon law, with one introductory law course and one in natural law. Two English courses were included. The law degree required three additional years and included procedural law, public speaking skills, the law of nations, private international law, public and administrative law, commercial law, political economy, and two courses in forensic eloquence. The doctorate required an eighth year of study that included philosophy of law, comparative legislation, and history of treaties.

In Chile the Real Universidad de San Felipe fell into decline around 1810. Instruction moved to the Instituto Nacional, while exams and conferring of degrees continued to occur at the university. Even that privilege was lost in 1823, and its library was absorbed into the National Library. Formal termination of the university was decreed in 1839 (Mellafe et al., 1993: 63ss), along with its Academy of Jurisprudence. Legal studies had moved to the National Institute in 1819 and undergone some modifications. Roman law was eliminated, and two courses were established: (1) natural law, the law of nations, and political economy; and (2) national law, canon law, and speaking skills. Law began to be taught at the Liceo de Chile and the Colegio de Santiago. In the former, constitutional law, Roman law, and national (Spanish) law were taught. In the Colegio de Santiago, Andrés Bello taught universal legislation (which included the fundamentals of civil, criminal, and constitutional law), law of nations, and Roman law. Both schools disappeared in 1830, and beginning in 1832 the Instituto Nacional established its study plan: humanities or rhetoric, Roman and civil law, universal legislation and law of nations, and canon law (Serrano, 1994b: 169). In 1843 the University of Chile opened provisionally and began to administer exams to students from the Instituto Nacional. Some instructors of law also taught privately (Mellafe et al., 1993: 88). The scenario was thus one of a precarious learning environment in which schools tended to operate at a limited capacity, whether because they were too old or too new, and where students often were obliged to take classes at one location and exams at another. Table 3.2 shows the study plan demanded by the 1844 Regulation of Degrees (*Reglamento de Grados*), which established a fairly difficult examination regimen in Chile (Serrano, 1994b: 169). Note that several modern courses appear: natural law, universal legislation, principles of legislation, and national and constitutional law, together with the traditional instruction in Roman and canon law.

By the mid-nineteenth century, legal studies became the object of great controversy due to clashing views of liberals and conservatives over what should be taught, and further disagreement among the conservative factions. In 1852 the ultraconservative Dean Meneses proposed a program oriented entirely toward professional practice that would eliminate the courses on universal legislation—whose text (Bentham) "instilled unhealthy ideas in the youth"—and political economy "for being unnecessary to professional practice" (Serrano, 1994b: 171). Andrés Bello, a moderate conservative, supported maintaining both courses. For Bello, the function of legal education was not merely to form lawyers but rather to form men capable of performing high administrative and legislative functions as well as shaping public opinion (Serrano, 1994b: 171). The compromise solution was, in 1852, to eliminate universal legislation and to retain political economy.

Not included in Table 3.2 are countries for which study plans could not be located. But their tendencies seem to have been the same. For example, the University of Buenos Aires, created in 1822, by 1834 had chairs in natural law and law of nations, civil law, political economy, and canon law. Political economy later disappeared. Córdoba, in accord with the 1815 plan, had chairs in Roman or civil law, canon law, natural law and law of nations, and national (Spanish) legislation. In Buenos Aires as well as in Córdoba some legal academies offered complementary training to those who aspired to the law degree (Tau Anzoátegui and Martiré, 1967: 546).

In summary, in the Latin American countries analyzed, there existed clear awareness that legal studies should be oriented toward forming the political elite. Great attention was thus paid to the study plans and selection of texts. The reform largely followed the program of the Enlightenment, which was to pay more attention to national and natural law. National law presented difficulties in countries that had recently gained independence and where national law was still confused with that of the colonizing country. Yet knowledge that was considered important for political formation had to be taught. Among the new courses, some turned out to be accepted without much difficulty, as in the case of political economy. The most-assigned text for this subject was the *Treaty of Political Economy* by J. B. Say.[17] Other courses turned out to be much more controversial, such as the principles of universal legislation, for which the assigned text was the book by Jeremy Bentham, an author considered ungodly and subversive by conservatives.[18]

Analysis of the curricula shows that the principal task of legal education was to provide the economic and political preparation required to administer the state, as is shown explicitly in the parliamentary debate on the creation of legal courses in Brazil (Bastos, 1978; Falcão, 1978). This was the tendency of most of the countries studied. As a secondary purpose, it was thought useful to develop lawyers who could defend causes before the justice tribunals.

Legal instruction was clearly not legalistic, for the tendency in that age was to criticize the disorder of the legislation inherited from Spain or Portugal. As Tau Anzoátegui (1987: 92) has well observed for Argentina, the result was that the legal practitioners of the day did not stick to the letter of the law, being instead willing to take advantage of different elements within their reach and to widen their horizons.

Less apparent are the transformations in legal education in the course of the nineteenth century and the beginning of the twentieth. As the student population grew, new universities and law schools were created, but slowly. The controversy surrounding legal education appears to have faded by that time. With the consolidation of codification, legal education focused mainly on the codes. In many countries, courses were named simply "civil code" or "criminal code." Instruction centered on the five fundamental codes: civil, penal, commercial, civil procedure, and criminal procedure. The liberal reform that almost every country in the region experienced in the latter 1900s, and the relative loss of importance of the Catholic church, diminished the presence of canon law in all countries where liberals were predominant. In some cases, such as Mexico in 1869, courses on canon law were eliminated altogether (Bazant, 1982: 154).

The tendency to secularize university instruction produced dissatisfaction in Catholic circles and led to the creation of private Catholic universities in several Latin American capitals (Santiago[19], 1888; Lima, 1917; Rio de Janeiro, 1938). The history of Colombian universities was especially conflict ridden and led Catholic groups early on to create private universities, especially the Javeriana and the Colegio Mayor del Rosario, based on the colonial *colegios*. When the Universidad Nacional was under control of the conservatives in 1886, the liberals created the Externado de Colombia. In 1923 another liberal group created the Universidad Libre (Silva García, 2001: 26ss). And in Mexico, the independent Escuela Libre de Derecho was formed in 1912, arising out of a political conflict between students and the government (Arce Gurza, 1982: 232). These private schools and universities were created for various political or ideological reasons. In Brazil by 1907, five private law schools already figured among the ten law schools in the country (Brazil, 1927).

It is noteworthy that the ideological disputes and the creation of schools did not generally involve innovation or differentiation in the study plans, which retained considerable national uniformity and a positivist-legalistic orientation throughout the continent. In the Colombian case, where the conflict between liberals and conservatives was especially intense, the regulations of 1895, 1934, and 1936 made the study plan of the Universidad Nacional mandatory for all the law schools (Martínez Peñaranda, 1981: 41).

Despite the creation of the Catholic universities, teaching of canon law weakened considerably, in large part because the transformation of state and society decreased interest in this area of law. In the absence of a detailed comparative study of a Catholic university curriculum, it is nonetheless assumed that the Catholic character in these schools was reflected solely in the existence of courses related to religion and of religious activities within the universities.

We see in Table 3.3 five examples of curricula from the early 1900s. They are easy to compare, inasmuch as the courses were annual and the curriculum did not allow elective courses.

TABLE 3.3.
Law School Curricula in Five Latin American Countries, Early 1900s

Argentina 1905	Venezuela 1905	Mexico 1907	Brazil 1911	Chile 1912
Introduction to Law	Roman Law 1	Principles of Sociology	General Introduction or Encyclopedia	Philosophy of Law
Sociology of Law	Public Church Law	Political Economy 1	Public & Constitutional Law	Roman Law
Ancient & Roman Law	Natural Law & Sociology	Civil Law 1	Public & Private International Law	Political & Social Economy
Civil Law 1	Roman Law 2	Political Economy 2	Administrative Law	Constitutional Law
Penal Law	Spanish Law	Civil Law 2	Political Economy & Finances	Civil Law 1
Civil Law 2	Political Economy	Civil Procedure 1	Roman Law	General History of Law
Commercial Law 1	Civil Law 1	Civil Law 3	Criminal Law 1	Civil Law 2
Public International Law	Political & Administrative Law	Civil Procedure 2	Civil Law, Family	International Law
Agrarian Legislation	Penal Law & Military Code	Penal Law & Penal Procedure 1	Criminal Law 2	Penal Law
Civil Law 3	Civil Law 2	Commercial Law	Civil Law, Real State	Agrarian & Industrial Law
Commercial Law 2	Public International Law	Civil Procedure 3	Commercial Law 1	Civil Law 3
Provincial & Municipal Public Law	Commercial Law	Penal Law & Penal Procedure 2	Civil Law, Inheritance	Procedural Law 1
Civil & Commercial Procedures	Private International Law 1	Constitutional Law	Commercial Law 2	Commercial Law
Civil Law 4	Civil & Commercial Procedure	Administrative Law	Public Medicine	Mining Law
Private International Law	Private International Law 2	Selected Cases, Practice	Civil & Commercial Theory of Procedure	Administrative Law
Federal Constitution & Administrative Law	Criminal Procedure	Synthesis of Law	Criminal Procedure Theory & Practice	Procedural Law 2
Penal Procedure	Legal Medicine			Public Treasury
Eloquence & Forensic Litt				Legal Medicine

SOURCES: *Argentina*: Tau Anzoátegui and Martiré, 1967: 751. *Venezuela*: Pérez-Perdomo, 1981: 285. *Mexico*: Mendieta y Núñez, 1956: 122. *Brazil*: Bastos, 2000. *Chile*: República de Chile, 1912, Vol. 5, *Instrucción*.

The 1902 Chilean reform was inspired and led by Valentín Letelier, a prestigious author on state theory and innovator of his time. The reform replaced courses named "civil code" and "criminal code" with ones called "civil law" and "criminal law." The subtle change in name reveals a larger shift in methodology away from comments on the code and toward the building of general concepts and insistence on the construction of systematic concepts (from the French *école de l'exégèse* to the German *Begriffjurisprudenz*). In the former method, the professor's role had been to comment on the code; in the latter method, it was to explain the discipline and underlying principles of the code and to present the legal rules and concepts in their logical or systematic order. The reform also brought in modern courses, more related to social development, such as labor law, public finance, and industrial and agriculture law (Lowenstein, 1970; De la Maza, 2001). Chile's study plan of 1912 was similar to the 1902 reform, probably with some later changes. The reform did not achieve a diminishing of legalism in instruction, which has remained a characteristic of the Chilean legal culture (Squella, 1998; Peña, 1994).

The Venezuelan study plan was similar but even more conservative than Chile's. It maintained canon law (or public ecclesiastical law, in this case), which was dropped from all other study plans. It did not introduce new subjects such as agricultural and industrial law, as in Chile, or agrarian law, as in Argentina. One innovation that should be noted, however, is that the course on private international law incorporated comparative legislation (a discipline known today as comparative law), which was a new concept at that time and received substantial attention.

The 1911 Brazilian reform not only affected the curriculum but also established the basic principles for running the schools and the examination system (Bastos, 2000: 170). The general introductory law course was known also as "legal encyclopedia," and the text for it in Brazil and several other countries was Ahrens.[20]

The Mexican study plan made explicit that the ultimate purpose of all courses was theoretical and practical knowledge of current Mexican legislation. Nonetheless, professors were not to follow the literal order of the code, but instead be more in accord with its pedagogy. The plan indicated, as well, that although the courses did not seek to teach scientific principles or general theories, "the way in which those principles and theories have been applied by national legislation" historically would be studied (Mendieta y Núñez, 1956: 124). The Mexican approach was legal positivism in the extreme, with some influence from legal dogmatism. The plan reproduced in Table 3.3 belonged to the Escuela Nacional de Jurisprudencia (later Facultad de Derecho de la Universidad Nacional Autónoma de México). Other Mexican schools had a similar orientation, as shown in the summary charts appearing in Mendieta y Núñez's study plans for all Mexican universities (1956: 165).

The Argentinean study plan in Table 3.3 is from the Universidad de la Plata, established in 1897. The plan was the first one for that university and was considered highly innovative in its day. It expressed the view that even in courses dealing with codes, study should not be limited to memorizing the letter of the code but also should include commentary based on contemporary science, social change, jurisprudence, and the future of society (Tau Anzoátegui and Martiré, 1967: 752).

In all of these statements, one sees that extreme legalism had opposition, but the choice that was made—which was to explain the principles of law and the rules rationally derived from those principles—ended up reinforcing formalism.

The study plans from the mid–twentieth century that we have been able to locate show an increase in the number of courses when compared to the beginning of the century. In Mexico, the number of required courses went from 16 to 30, in addition to a number of electives (Mendieta y Núñez, 1956: 328), and in Venezuela, from 17 to 26 (Pérez-Perdomo, 1981: 293). This increase was largely due to the division of the courses (especially civil, commercial, and administrative law) into segments and the appearance of new branches of law such as labor law.

Controversy over legal studies in the nineteenth century was not limited to the curriculum. Discussion also centered on whether to restrict legal studies—and university studies in general. Two basic arguments prevailed. The first was the lack of employment for university-formed professionals (mostly in law and medicine at the beginning of the period, and later also engineering), who ended up seeking political positions and promoting revolutions. An anonymous Mexican article from mid-1835 states it this way:

> Decreasing, then, the number of schools where such careers are taught, will thereby decrease the number of students who enroll there and receive little fruit for their efforts, to become later—due to the lack of jobs in their profession—the swarm of pretending office seekers that surrounds the Government, and which is always lying in wait for the favorable moment to form revolutions that create opportunities to thrive [cited in Rodríguez de San Miguel, 1981: 389].

The second argument was the lack of usefulness of the professions, especially law. Thus priority had to be given to technical studies that were directly useful. Alberdi, one of the great midcentury intellectual figures of Argentina, expressed it eloquently:

> What have our South American institutions and universities been, if not factories of verbosity, of idleness, of demagoguery, and of accredited presumption? . . . Instruction,

to be productive, must concentrate on the sciences and applicable arts, on practical things, on living languages, on immediately and materially useful knowledge [cited in Zimmermann, 1999: 109].

Such opinions did not go unanswered. Thus the climate of controversy in university policy in general (Safford, 1976), and on the legal profession in particular, continued. In practice, the predominant need in relation to legal studies was to fill judicial offices and other high-ranking state positions. Whether due to the impact on university policies of opinions against the legal profession and studies or, more probably, because there was no clear occupational goal for law students, the number of students and lawyers remained limited. Later we will analyze the number of students and lawyers and the occupations pursued by the latter.

These disputes seemed to abate in the first half of the twentieth century, probably because universities made room for the growing number of students and because the occupation of lawyer became a viable path to stable income.

Informal knowledge was acquired extracurricularly in casual conversations with classmates and professors, at work sites such as the courts, and in other meeting places. This parallel learning culture is more difficult to reconstruct, but we should keep in mind its existence and discount any belief that legal knowledge derived solely from law school classes and their official curriculum.

PRODUCTION AND DISSEMINATION OF LEGAL KNOWLEDGE

Each Latin American country had its own law schools. Colonial-period universities gradually gave way to large national universities, as was the case of the Universidad de Mexico; the Universidad de San Marcos in Lima; and the Universidad Central de Venezuela, to name just a few. In contrast, the Universidad de Buenos Aires, created in 1822, quickly gained primacy in the latter 1800s at the expense of the University of Córdoba, which was predominant in the colonial period and in the decades immediately following independence. The Universidad de Buenos Aires grew to be the country's largest university and shaper of the political elite. Grand buildings were erected throughout Latin America in the first half of the twentieth century in testimony to the importance placed on public universities. The divergent case is probably Colombia, where intense political rivalry in the early 1800s created the incentive to build private universities. The state-run Universidad Nacional lost its central role by the end of that century.

Because the law school mission was to teach national law, none of the Latin American law schools attracted many students from other countries. The national elites were thus formed domestically, and a country's borders tended to be the limits of a school's influence.[21] Law was considered national knowledge in spite of its universal base. This characteristic of legal education clearly shows how law was perceived as an instrument of nation building.

As we have already seen, national authorities in the 1800s handled the politically sensitive task of selecting textbooks, and the professor's role was to explain the selected material. He was not expected to add to that knowledge with research and published findings. On the contrary, he was more frequently a "public man," one who held public office and participated in politics, sometimes at the risk of losing his teaching position. Toward the end of the nineteenth century and more so in the twentieth, responsibility for selecting textbooks shifted to the universities and the professors. The trend toward research among law professors came much later. Such was the case of legal studies reform at the Universidad de Chile in 1935, with the creation of seminars, greater attention to a thesis, and in 1945, the creation of the Editorial Jurídica (legal press) de Chile (Mellafe et al., 1993: 167). Mendieta y Núñez (1956) cites as a novelty of mid–twentieth century the abundant production by law professors of the University of Mexico.

In the nineteenth century some professors translated and adapted known works. Adaptation was necessary in order to customize the works to the situation of the recently independent countries and to eliminate any teaching that could be understood to contradict Catholic orthodoxy. Andrés Bello adapted the work of Heineccius as the text for his Roman law course and the work of Vattel for his international law (or law of nations) course, as indicated in the prefaces to those works. To look for an original contribution in these works or to consider them the product of personal scholarship is to misunderstand what was expected of a professor in that time (Pérez-Perdomo, 1982). These works were very successful and ran through many editions in various Latin American countries during the nineteenth century.[22] The need to meticulously follow religious orthodoxy disappeared with time, and a few authors undertook to create works directed at the student population. Some of these books were of an elevated academic level. At the end of the nineteenth century and in the twentieth, the need was to adapt the didactic literature to national legislation, or to better explain the *system* of a branch of the law; that is, the principles and the rules that derive from them.

Toward the mid–twentieth century, some more general literature for teaching law emerged. The increased facility of communications helped spread these works. One example was *La Ley y el Delito* (*Law and Crime*) by Jiménez de Asúa (1945), which became the textbook for criminal law for all of Hispanic America. The author was a Spanish exile in Buenos Aires, who gave a series of talks in Caracas. His situation created the need to explain the theory of criminal law more generally, and the book was a continental success. Lacking in the general literature are studies analyzing the production of Latin American legal teaching materials, or why certain works from within and outside the region were preferred over others.

Apart from the didactic works, production was directed at the general public. Again, these were not works of original research but were of public interest in clarifying contemporary problems. A polemic literature also surfaced, the quality of which varied greatly, including some products of high scholarship that became landmarks in legal literature. For example, Fermín Toro's *Reflecciones [Reflections on the law of April 10, 1834]* became a classic of Venezuelan political philosophy. Frequently this literature was not produced by professors nor ever used in the universities. Later, the code commentaries that predominated in the nineteenth century and beginning of the twentieth were replaced by a more independent erudite literature.

Starting in the mid-1800s and much more in the 1900s, each Latin American country had its own legal magazines where legal works of diverse quality were published along with such items as legislation, judicial decisions, and legal arguments. These works were directed at a national audience. Analysis of the legal magazines and their role appears to have just begun (Leiva, 1997).

Law students and lawyers were very active producers and consumers of more than just legal literature. Legal practitioners and scholars of the era were expected to write literary or historical essays and poetry and to give speeches. Adorno (1988) analyzed the intellectual production of Brazilian legal practitioners and scholars in the nineteenth century. The variety is impressive: side by side with purely legal works were religious, historical, and literary works as well as parliamentary speeches. Adorno ascribes significance to the cultural climate that surrounded law schools in the homogenization of the political elite. He indicates that this was even more stimulating than the ideological or technical legal training provided by the law schools (Adorno, 1988: 142).

THE STUDENTS

The post-independence national constitutions guaranteed equality. Their content would indicate that "pure blood" requirements for university admission had been abolished. The tendency from the outset among Latin American universities and law schools was for education to be paid for by the national budget, free for the student. Thus we might think that anyone from any social level could be admitted if she or he met the academic requirements. In practice, it did not happen in this way, and entrance to law school was reserved predominantly for white men of means.

In some cases, the resistance of universities to admitting new citizens in the first decades of independence has been documented. For example, after great controversy at the Universidad de Córdoba in 1832, a *pardo* was admitted as a philosophy student—but without the right to receive a degree. There were frequent conflicts between university faculty, who wished to maintain the restrictions of the colonial period, and government leaders, who wanted to override the restrictions. Only in 1852 was the "pure blood" requirement eliminated by the Córdoba legislature (Endrek, 1966: 61–68; Bergoglio, 1993). Urzúa (1978: 182), referring to nineteenth-century Chile, indicates that applicants to legal programs were required to attach witnesses' declarations that the applicants "belong to distinguished families and have not committed any crime." The year in which the requirement was revoked is not indicated.

Even when there was no expressed regulation, social norms reserved education for the upper social classes, and university education for the truly elite. Academic prerequisites excluded a sizable portion of the population. To enter law school, one had to have earned a bachelor's degree, which was available only to graduates of high school or other pre-university studies. In the 1800s relatively few people reached such an educational level, and the percentage of illiterates was very high. Economic exclusion operated in the same sense. In low-income families, young people were expected to work at an early age to assist the family materially.

The operation of social norms is even more visible with respect to women. Documentation of their formal exclusion is elusive, but we know that in practice women did not attempt to enroll as university students. It was not considered socially appropriate for women to pursue law studies or university studies in general.

Social selectivity kept the number of students quite low. We will analyze the figures from the end of the nineteenth and early twentieth centuries. In the 1880s in Venezuela there were some 120 law students (6 per 100,000 inhabitants) (Pérez-Perdomo, 1981: 127). For 1887 Colombia we have only the total number of university students. If we suppose that half were law students, this would yield under 300 (9 per 100,000 inhabitants). It is remarkable that the number of university students decreased relative to the immediately preceding decades, and this decline appears to have affected law students in particular—perhaps indicating an overestimation of their number.[23] Chile had 302 law students in 1900 and 564 in 1912 (Chile, 1912), or 16 per 100,000 inhabitants. Brazil had 2,481 law students in 1907 and 2,728 in 1912 distributed among ten schools (Brazil, 1927), or 12 per 100,000 inhabitants.

The law school at the Universidad de Buenos Aires was considered enormous in 1901: 1,098 law students were enrolled in the six-year program, though the student attrition rate was high, with only 90 in the graduating class—a perhaps poor statistic for a city the size of Buenos Aires, population 850,000 (Buenos Aires, 1902: 267).

Only as the twentieth century advanced was there a tendency for an increase in these numbers, in great part due to the region's social changes. The cities began to grow, which meant more people were freed from rural jobs and had easier access to primary and secondary education. Consequently, all of education expanded, not just within the universities. The case of Buenos Aires is a good example: because of its expanding social base, women and people from the lower-middle class began to enter the universities. But the trend may have been halted in some countries with restrictive admission policies, as appears to have been the case in Chile.

The incorporation of women merits special mention. The first women entered universities in the late 1800s. In Mexico the first woman graduated from law school in 1898. In 1924 only two female students were enrolled in the Escuela Nacional de Jurisprudencia (Mendieta y Núñez, 1956: 263). In 1907 Brazil the statistic was just 6 women out of a total of 2,481 law students, and that dropped to 4 out of 2,728 by 1912 (Brazil, 1927: 892, 897). In Venezuela the first woman graduated in law in 1936 (Roche, 2001).

The presence of women continued to be scarce into the mid–twentieth century. In the Escuela Nacional de Jurisprudencia de México, they constituted 8 percent of the 2,396 students in 1946 (Mendieta y Núñez, 1956; Arce Gurza, 1982: 246). In Chile, out of a total of 153 lawyers admitted to practice in 1945, only 11 were women (Merryman et al., 1979: 465). In Brazil, of the 15,566 lawyers in 1950, only 346 (or 2.2 percent) were women (Falcão: 1984: 180).

Despite the slow increase of women students, the growth of registered law students was significant. In 1934 Brazil a total of 8,515 law students were enrolled (Coelho, 1999: 268). In 1918 Chile there were 819 (Mellafe et al., 1993: 148), and 1,558 by 1945 (22 per 100,000 inhabitants) (Merryman et al., 1979). Colombia had 1,456 law students (14 per 100,000 inhabitants) in 1945, Costa Rica had 176 (25 per 100,000 inhabitants), and Peru had 1,033 law students (15 per 100,000 inhabitants) (Merryman et al., 1979). In 1950, Venezuela showed 1,000 law students. (20 per 100,000 inhabitants) (Pérez-Perdomo, 1981: 182). These are considerably higher figures compared to those of fifty years prior. Compared with the hundreds of students per 100,000 inhabitants at the end of the twentieth century, these figures seem low by today's standards.

The increase in the number of law students can be explained as much by the greater demand for education—that is, the higher number of students who had completed secondary education and were prepared to pursue a university degree—as by the perception that the occupation of lawyer offered ample opportunities for income and social position. It is probable that both elements acted concomitantly.

Lawyers and Their Occupations

DEFINITION AND DEMOGRAPHY

Lawyers today are those who have received the formal degree as such. This is not a tautologous observation, because over history, people without a law degree have regularly performed duties that were generally considered the domain of lawyers, such as representing or assisting people in litigation. They were the *tinterillos*, *huizacheros*, and *pica-pleitos* (Lira González, 1984; Aguirre, 2001; Lynch, 1981: 28) and filled a social need for legal representation or advice not met by lawyers.

In general in the period analyzed, legal regulation required that the title of lawyer be awarded by a court (usually the supreme court or appellate court) following studies at a university or similar institution. The length and content of those studies varied considerably and have already been analyzed.

Regulation of the profession also varied over time and among countries (and in some cases, among states and provinces). In Mexico, for example, regulation fluctuated considerably in the years following independence (Staples, 1982: 81ss). Also in Mexico, there were complaints that governors or other officials had awarded the title of lawyer to people who had not met the requirements (Lira González, 1984). The very fact of a complaint underscores the sense of an appropriate process for receiving the title of lawyer. Only in exceptional circumstances was the professional title granted by other than high-level court officials.

The figures in this period are not comparable with those of the colonial period (see Table 3.4). In the latter, access to legal studies and to the title of lawyer was restricted considerably to one social group, and only a limited number of law graduates opted for the title of lawyer. The occupation of lawyer was considerably restricted both in political activity and in legal activity. Formal restrictions on university entrance disappeared after independence, and obtaining a law degree became easier. Restrictions on the right to occupy high political positions also ended. It is thus possible to hypothesize that the number of lawyers rose dramatically following independence; but as we will see below, this was generally not the case.

Estimating the number of lawyers was hindered by the lack of available statistics and by their imprecision. Figures in some cases had to be estimated based on the number of law graduates, when this figure exists. The calculation is possible because every law graduate during the period analyzed generally also received the title of lawyer after fulfilling other formalities. The data on law graduates are generally offered by one-, five-, or ten-year periods. For the calculation we have supposed that all law graduates in a thirty-year period are alive and active, and that none who graduated before that period

TABLE 3.4.

Lawyers in Eight Latin American Countries, 1840–1950

Country and Year	Number of Lawyers	Number per 100,000 Inhabitants
Argentina 1869	439	25
Argentina 1895	1,506	38
Argentina 1914	3,716	47
Brazil 1850	1,383	19
Brazil 1889	4,438	32
Brazil 1950	15,666	30
Chile 1854	282	19
Chile 1875	624	31
Chile 1885	941	36
Chile 1907	1,947	59
Chile 1945	943	17
Colombia 1839	331	20
Colombia 1849	529	24
Colombia 1951	5,813	50
Costa Rica 1945	416	58
Mexico 1869	667	7
Mexico 1900	3,690	27
Mexico 1950	6,258	22
Peru 1945	1,606	23
Venezuela 1840	120	12
Venezuela 1894	246	10
Venezuela 1941	957	25

SOURCES: *Argentina 1869*: Zimmermann, 1999: 111. *Argentina 1895 and 1914*: Bagú, 1961: 131. *Brazil 1850 and 1889*: Barman and Barman, 1976. *Brazil 1950*: Falcão, 1984: 180. *Colombia 1839 and 1849*: Uribe-Uran, 2000: 115. *Colombia 1951*: Estimate from Lynch, 1981: 27. *Costa Rica*: Merryman and Friedman, 1979: 468. *Chile 1854, 1875, and 1885*: Serrano, 1994b: 176. *Chile 1907 and 1945*: Merryman and Friedman, 1979: 465. *Mexico 1869 and 1900*: Bazant, 1982. *Mexico 1950*: Estimate from Lorey, 1992: 91. *Peru*: Merryman and Friedman, 1979: 467. *Venezuela*: Pérez-Perdomo, 1981: 144, 215. For population: Mitchell, 1998.

is either alive or active. Neither supposition is precise, but since they go in opposing directions, they provide us with an approximate idea of the size of the profession. We have used the span of thirty years for all of the countries, although the average life expectancy may have varied across time and by country. It is an admittedly rough method, but the reasons for not attempting to obtain great statistical refinement will become clear.

In other cases, figures with enormous disparities were found. We have not considered clearly incomplete figures and those that do not show any consistency with prior or later data. Analyzing the source of the figures has been important. For example, data derived from population censuses may have overestimated the number of lawyers based on the number of people who say they are lawyers. This may have included *tinterillos* and other legal practitioners who were in fact not lawyers. Data derived from lists of persons registered as lawyers may represent only practicing lawyers and exclude lawyers performing judicial or other public functions. In any case, we know that the statistics here are imperfect, and our purpose is not to attempt exact calculations from them but rather to look at the big picture and important trends.

If we look at the countries as a whole, it is immediately apparent that the absolute figure increases considerably in the period 1840–1950, but relative to the population the increase is rather modest. In sum, the rate around 1840 of 10–20 lawyers per 100,000 inhabitants becomes 20–50 per 100,000 inhabitants just over a hundred years later. Looking at global figures does not have much meaning due to the countries' different methods of counting lawyers. We will therefore discuss the data country by country.

The figures for 1869 Argentina come from the population census of that year (Zimmermann, 1998: 133). Half of the lawyers (222) were located in the province of Buenos Aires, which had close to one-quarter of the population. Córdoba was next with 55 lawyers. By 1895 the number of lawyers in Argentina had increased to 1,506 (38 per 100,000). In 1914 there were 3,716 lawyers (47 per 100,000 inhabitants) (Bagú, 1961: 131). Further, the census figures of 1895 and 1914 distinguish between national and foreign lawyers.

For Brazil in 1850 and 1889 we do not have direct figures but instead have calculated them from the number of law graduates (Barman and Barman, 1976). For the 1850 figure we have added the number of Brazilian graduates in Coimbra between 1821 and 1830 and the number of graduates in the two law schools (Recife and São Paulo) that existed in Brazil between 1831 and 1850. The figure for 1889, the year the Brazilian monarchy ended, represents the number of graduates of Recife and São Paulo between 1850 and 1889. In the figures relative to population, this means an increase from 19 to 30 per 100,000 inhabitants. Over the next sixty years the number of lawyers tripled, reaching 15,566 by 1950. Nonetheless, the relative number remained stable, around 30 per 100,000 inhabitants.

The figures for Chile in the nineteenth century come from the general population censuses, cited in Serrano (1994b: 176), but they coincide rather well with the number of university graduates.[24] According to these figures, lawyers tripled their numbers in the thirty years between 1854 and 1885, while the number of lawyers per 100,000 inhabitants only doubled. Urzúa (1978: 194), citing the census of 1907, indicates a total of 1,947 lawyers that year, but we have discounted that figure because it does not match the total number of law graduates. The figure for 1945 (943 lawyers, or 17 per 100,000 inhabitants) would show a one-half reduction in the relative number of lawyers. The explanation may be the result of the different sources used. The figures for 1854, 1875, and 1885 come from general population censuses. It is probable that some *tinterillos* declared themselves lawyers, given that their social function was very similar.[25] It also is probable that judges and other public officials who could not practice as lawyers were counted as lawyers because they had a law degree. The 1945 figure (943) derives from the Supreme Court's registry of lawyers. It represents only those lawyers authorized to appear as such in the courts and for that reason surely underreports the number of legal professionals, nor does it use the same definition as the census.

With respect to Mexico, Staples's chapter (1982: 81) offers the figure of 414 enrolled in the national *colegio de abogados* de México in 1868. In principle this should include only lawyers in Mexico City, but in fact it extends to those in other jurisdictions where there were law schools, such as Oaxaca, Puebla, and Durango. A more complete figure may result from including lawyers from the principal cities of the country, as offered by Bazant (1982: 208). Her source is the *Almanaque Mexicano y Directorio de la Ciudad de México*, a publication that attempts to provide reliable information about local and national life. In 1869, Mexico had a total of 667 lawyers, 354 of which were in the Federal District, somewhat more than half. Other cities with a fair population of lawyers were Morelia (82), Guadalajara (62), and Toluca (40). The figures refer to the twenty principal cities, seven of which reported having no attorneys.

Thirty years later, in 1900, there is a disproportionate increase, as Mexico's figure rises to 3,690. That is, the number of lawyers multiplied 5.5 times in thirty years. The result is suspiciously high, considering the time and region; the source is the national census and probably includes many *tinterillos*. According to the census data, the Federal District had 22 percent of the country's lawyers, while the remainder appear to have been distributed over the rest of the territory, with significant presence in the states of Jalisco (385), Puebla (267), Michoacán (202), and Guanajuato (195). This heightened distribution of lawyers throughout the nation is rather anomalous and leads one to take this figure with reservation.

No information is available for the end of the period, but statistics regarding law graduates beginning in 1928 do exist (Lorey, 1992). This allows an estimate for 1950, making a projection backward to 1920 by taking an annual average of law graduates from the period 1928–31. The result is a rough figure of 6,258 law graduates between 1920 and 1949. Note that this estimate would mean only a doubling relative to the 1900 figure and a decrease of 5 lawyers per 100,000 inhabitants. It is probable that the estimate is low, but it is more probable that the 1900 census data are quite above the true figure.

The figure for 1850 Colombia is approximate. It is the simple sum of all law graduates for the years from 1820 to 1849. Uribe-Uran (2000: 115) hypothesizes that from independence to midcentury the figure grew very rapidly and the number of lawyers outnumbered job capacity, which was mainly in the official bureaucracy. We have figures for the mid–twentieth century, which we have calculated using the statistics on law school graduates that Lynch (1981: 27) reproduces. Lawyers were outnumbered only by doctors and other medical professionals combined. Unfortunately, neither figures nor a way to estimate them exist for other periods. Based on student enrollment in the latter 1800s and an analysis of higher education policies (Safford, 1976), the hypothesis is that the number of lawyers decreased toward the end of the century and rebounded vigorously in the twentieth century.

The figures for Venezuela are based on lawyer registration lists. Note that the figure is low even though it doubles between 1841 and 1894. Nonetheless, in relative numbers there is a decrease from 12 to 10 per 100,000 inhabitants. Between 1894 and 1941, the absolute figure quadruples and the relative number moves from 10 to 25 per 100,000 inhabitants, a very significant increase.

In summary, and as one would expect, the figures reveal a tendency toward growth in the number of lawyers. However, when those numbers are expressed relative to the population, the increase is less significant and—as in the case of Venezuela in the second half of the nineteenth century and probably in Colombia at the same time—may even show that there was a temporary decrease in lawyers, in relative terms.

THE EMPLOYMENT OF LAWYERS

What were lawyers' occupations? Without a doubt the largest employer of lawyers was the state, and lawyers occupied key political positions during the entire period studied. They tended to spurn low-level bureaucratic positions because of their high social status. Private law practice also was a possibility, perhaps more in accord with the liberal ideology in which lawyers were educated, but apparently it was neither the most desirable nor the most lucrative choice. In practice, during the nineteenth century into the twentieth, employment in the public sector appears to have been most prevalent in most countries. Nevertheless, law was seen as a "liberal profession," due as much to the curriculum reform as to the profession's image. That is, the profession was linked ideally to the market or civil society, and not necessarily to the state. This clearly created a dichotomy between the normative image of the profession and its actual source of employment, between ideals and practice, as Falcão (1979) observes.

This general proposition requires further investigation. The proportion of lawyers employed by the state bureaucracy to those in private practice depended on the quantity of lawyers, on the bureaucracy's capacity to provide jobs for them, and on how attractive private practice was. Public employment capacity depended on the number of such jobs, and there were not many. In the first place, prevalent political and economic theories assign only a limited role to the state. Second, state income was frequently difficult to assess in nearly all the region's countries, in part due to the scant surplus and the limited number of transactions that could be taxed. Last, the status of lawyers and the jobs that were considered acceptable for persons of their social rank limited them to only a small number of public functions.

In our time, the government jobs considered most acceptable to Latin American lawyers are those in the courts and other legal-sector activities such as public registries and the *notarías*. In the analyzed period, especially the nineteenth century, this was not the case. The judges who dealt with the most common issues of the population were not lawyers, because this qualification was not considered necessary for the post (Flory, 1981). The very scarcity of lawyers and their interest in remaining in the capital and principal cities made it difficult to find lawyers to serve on even the higher courts in small cities far from the capital. The *escribanos* and notaries, consistent with colonial tradition, also were not lawyers, although they had some legal training and practical experience. In other words, the state legal system was not an important source of employment for lawyers.

In regard to the positions that lawyers did fill, various studies place them in high state posts. In Argentina in 1908, 53 representatives (out of 120) and 10 senators (out of 30) were lawyers. Landowners and medical doctors made distant seconds (Bagú, 1961: 72). Imaz (1964: 23) analyzed the government teams of 1936, 1941, and 1946 as well as other years outside of the analyzed period in a study that includes presidents, cabinet ministers, and governors. Lawyers were the strongest occupational group and occupied 69 percent of the positions in 1936, 92 percent in 1941, and 30 percent in 1946. Imaz also analyzed political party leadership between 1936 and 1961. His data were not separated by year but rather by party. Lawyers ranged from 100 percent of the conservative party leaders to 48 percent of the *Peronista* leaders, and above half in the remaining parties (Imaz, 1964: 193).

In imperial Brazil, 47–83 percent of the cabinet ministers had law degrees, compared to 5–15 percent of cabinet ministers who were military professionals (Barman and Barman, 1976: 427). For senators, the number ranged from 52 to 81 percent who held law degrees,[26] and military men again came in a distant second.

Chile had twenty democratically elected presidents between 1851 and 1952, nineteen of whom were lawyers (De la Maza, 2001: 89). Of the 782 members of Chile's parliament between 1834 and 1891, at least 226 (29 percent) were lawyers.

In Venezuela between 1830 and 1930, lawyers made up 31 percent of the ministers appointed in each president's first cabinet (Pérez-Perdomo, 1981: 156) and 26 percent of congress members of 1830, 1864, 1890, and 1929 (Pérez-Perdomo 1981: 154). It is worth noting that Venezuelan politics in the nineteenth century and early twentieth century was dominated by military men: of the twenty-four presidents, only three were lawyers, one a medical doctor, and the rest soldiers. One of the three lawyers, Antonio Guzmán Blanco, also was a general. In a turbulent country where civil war was frequent in the latter 1800s and that lived under dictatorship in the twentieth century until 1936, lawyers nonetheless occupied high political positions.

In Mexico, Camp (1996: 137) analyzed the presidential cabinets of presidents Porfirio Díaz in 1884 through Ernesto Zedillo in 1995. The period this chapter studies concluded with Miguel Alemán in 1946. The percentage of lawyers was given relative to other university-trained professions and ranged from 20 percent with President Portes Gil (in 1928) to 81 percent with Porfirio Díaz (in 1905). The most frequent averages were in the 60 and 70 percent range. Moreno, biographer of forty-nine lawyers who were active in or born in the 1800s, has stated that "to write the biographies of the great Mexican legal scholars and practitioners is, in great part, to relate the history of the nation-state, by virtue of the prominent role that they have played in public life" (Moreno, 1979: 5). Smith (1979) analyzed the recruitment of the political elite in the twentieth century, distinguishing three cohorts: the prerevolutionary (1900–1911); the revolutionary (1917–40); and the postrevolutionary (1946–71). Lawyers made up 45 percent of the first group, 31 percent of the second, and 39 percent of the third. These figures refer to the total of 2,551 individuals Smith considered. With respect to the top elite (344 individuals), lawyers represented 44, 39, and 46 percent, respectively. This does not render the Mexican Revolution irrelevant. It brought about important political change that redistributed power among segments of the middle class (Smith, 1979: 102). But Smith observed that lawyers were key figures in those distinct historical moments and that legal studies at the Universidad Nacional Autónoma (formerly the Escuela Nacional de Jurisprudencia) were particularly useful for a young person who wished to pursue a political career.

The significant presence of lawyers in high government positions does not tell us anything about how many lawyers were employed in the state bureaucracy, in private practice, or in other tasks, but scattered data do exist. In Colombia between 1839 and 1849, 30 percent or more of lawyers held bureaucratic positions (Uribe-Uran, 2000: 140ss). In Chile the number of public sector officials reached 2,211 in 1850, and Serrano demonstrated that 277 of the 1,128 law school graduates in the nineteenth century were public servants (Serrano, 1994b: 177). In other words, at least one-fourth of all lawyers became public officials.

In Brazil, Carvalho's analysis (1980) of the selection of government ministers, senators, and representatives in imperial Brazil can be interpreted in two ways. On the one hand, his assertion that several were lawyers and high judges might allow us to presume that these lawyers were in private practice. On the other hand, he counted the lawyers at the time they assumed public office, so we do not know if private practice was a lifelong designation or pursued only briefly before entering public life. This second interpretation is the most plausible for the reasons discussed below. Falcão (1979: 361ss) emphasizes that the majority of law school graduates in Recife between 1870 and 1930 carried out public duties, and only 17 percent pursued private-sector activity. Among the latter, 59 percent did not practice law. A total of only 68 of the 883 lawyers profiled can be considered attorneys completely dedicated to private practice.

Coelho (1999) studied the professional market in imperial Rio de Janeiro. The results could be summarized as follows: a lawyer in the mid-1800s faced grave difficulties making a decent income practicing law. Public employment, especially a judgeship, offered the best alternative. Forty years later, sufficient commercial activity and plentiful litigation meant that some lawyers could become wealthy by practicing law. The situation was more difficult in the provinces. A lawyer in Bahia at the beginning of the 1870s, Rui Barbosa (who later became a great national figure), confessed that "the advocacy in this province is reduced to begging, and day by day, it falls dishearteningly" (Coelho, 1999: 76).

In mid-nineteenth-century Mexico, Rodríguez de San Miguel (1981) complained bitterly about the low income of lawyers and about the complete disproportion between work and income. Certainly, the attractiveness of the legal profession, which he tried to vindicate or praise highly, did not lie in the economic benefits derived from the profession.

In Chile, De la Maza's hypothesis (2001) is that there was not sufficient business to maintain a profession of practicing lawyers, but that the exploitation of nitrates, the presence of foreign firms, and the expansion of economic activity surely changed the scene around 1880. In any case, some lawyers did make large fortunes through the practice of law. Serrano (1994b: 174) described the case of Manuel Antonio Tocornal, son of an admired political leader, who began his legal career without great wealth. He was a lawyer in several important cases, and by the year of his death, 1867, had amassed quite a considerable fortune. Cases such as Tocornal's were not common in Chile, nor were equivalent cases found in the studies of Mexico, Brazil, and Venezuela.

Pérez-Perdomo (1981: 149) indicates that in nineteenth-century Venezuela one could not speak of a legal profession as such because lawyers did not make a living from private practice. Only at the end of the century did the first professional lawyers appear, and they certainly formed an appreciable group by the mid–twentieth century. There are, however, no data that allow us to determine in what sector and in what proportions they were employed. His analysis of the 1936 class of law graduates from the Universidad Central de Venezuela led him to conclude that, at that time, lawyers were still multifunctional, in the sense that they pursued different tasks successively (and sometimes simultaneously). For example, of the 33 graduates of 1936 for whom information was available, all practiced law at some point, 28 carried out important political functions, 17 held positions in the judicial system (such as judges and registrars), 17 published literary works (fiction or literary or historical essays), and 13 held teaching positions at the university or high schools (Pérez-Perdomo, 1981: 337, 338).

In summary, Latin American countries held some clear features in common during the period analyzed: the number of lawyers was rather low, lawyers occupied high political posts, and a high percentage of lawyers was involved in politics. This was a constant throughout the period and for all countries, despite differences among political regimes. Lawyers were influential in imperial and republican Brazil. In Chile under the aristocratic republic of the nineteenth century and in the twentieth-century democracy, lawyers played crucial roles. In "radical" Argentina or under Perón; in the Mexico of Santa Anna or Porfirio Díaz, and during the revolution or the "revolutionary institutionalization"; in the Venezuela of the "conservative oligarchy," the liberal and disjointed country under Guzmán Blanco, the centralized authoritarianism under Gómez, and the post-Gómez liberalization—in all of these different moments and under different political regimes, the importance of lawyers was a constant.

Clearly the practice of law as a profession could support very few at the dawn of the twentieth century, but the situation gradually changed for a growing number of law graduates. As the activity became a true "liberal profession," lawyers represented businesses and individuals without being subordinate to them. They also became judges, registrars, and *notarios* and progressively displaced the numerical and social significance of *tinterillos* by the end of the period under discussion.

Beyond their involvement in politics and their contribution as professionals, the great role of lawyers in this period was to be *public men.* It was up to them to guide public opinion as writers of books and articles, to be public speakers, and to articulate social demands and the state's responses. To be a law student and, later, a lawyer "was to dedicate oneself to journalism, literature, especially poetry, to devote oneself to the theatre, to be a good public speaker, to participate in literary and political associations, in secret societies and Masonic lodges" (Venancio Filho, 1977: 136). It meant being part of the intelligentsia (Adorno, 1988), and it meant being among the best qualified to understand and run government affairs (Bravo Lira, 1998b: 644).

The nineteenth-century lawyer did not monopolize legal knowledge; it was accessible to any educated person interested in politics who read legal works. Moreover, lawyers wrote about (and above all, spoke of) politics, literature, and history. What did it mean to be a lawyer of that era? What was the relationship between legal knowledge and politics? How was it possible that they were so indispensable in such disparate political regimes? Were they servants of the state or of civil society? What is the historical significance of their acts? These are the questions that the conclusion will address.

Lawyers, Law, and the Configuration of the Nation-States

Lawyers were eminent members of the political elite in the different Latin American countries from independence to the end of the analyzed period. Their characteristic of being "public men" was more significant than their positions in the legal system, although those positions became increasingly important as time went on. Their role as builders of nations is worth emphasizing. They were among those in charge of creating and interpreting the rules of the game for national politics and business.

Carvalho (1980) acknowledges lawyers' fundamental contribution in molding nations in his explanation of how Brazil—despite having been two colonial units with limited intercommunication—remained unified as one nation-state, while the Spanish colonies gave way to a plurality of nation-states. Brazilian lawyers had been educated in a single Portuguese university, Coimbra. The majority of them knew one another personally and formed common social circles. In Spanish America, universities had long been established in the principal cities, and political elites of the various *audiencias* were in fact fairly isolated from one another. The configuration of the political map more closely followed the territorial limits of the Spanish American *audiencias* and their respective law schools than those of the *virreinatos*. This observation attests to the central role of universities and law schools in achieving cohesion of the political elite.

Why were lawyers so important in politics? Several explanations have been posed, but most are problematic. Throughout the transition from colonialism to independence, lawyers were formed at the core of the social and economic elite. Thus their social origins offer one explanation to this question. Even when the circles of power expanded to embrace those from the provinces or middle social classes, lawyers remained among the political elite. By this time, of course, they were lawyers representing those sectors. The explanation may thus be reversed: these groups did not reach political power due to their social origins, but rather their groups gained power through those lawyers who developed themselves into political leaders.

Another explanation is that lawyers formed the political elite because they had the best political knowledge of the time. The weakness of this explanation is that legal knowledge was not the exclusive domain of lawyers; learned persons all read and wrote about law. In fact, the authors of important legal works, such as Andrés Bello or Fermín Toro, were neither law graduates nor lawyers. They have been recognized as legal scholars because of the quality of their works on the subject. At the same time, nineteenth-century lawyers did not have extraordinary legal qualifications, and political participation did not require this specialized knowledge. A lawyer or law student was "a type of intellectual, somewhat cosmopolitan, who ventured into other areas of knowledge, not exclusively restricted to the universe of law" (Adorno, 1988: 143). The virtue of law schools was not merely that they taught law, but that they formed generalists who could pursue almost any function of the state or politics, and who could voice expressions of social concern. Because legal knowledge, or general-legal knowledge, was not exclusively a forum by and for lawyers, knowledge as such could not be a good explanation for lawyers' preeminence in politics.

A very suggestive explanation is based on social networks. Law schools were places where professors and students met others who were interested in politics. The professors were frequently important political actors and could serve as recruiting agents for those interested in a political career. In schools and in student meeting places, personal ties were made that could later have incalculable value when a member of the group was endowed with power. The networks operated to recruit the political elite.[27] This is Camp's explanation (1996: 123) for Mexico, and it can be easily extended to the rest of Latin America. In the period analyzed, a law school—or occasionally more than one—in each nation facilitated the formation of such relationships.[28] Dahrendorf (1971) offers a similar explanation to describe the German political elite.

The job, or the historical image of the lawyer's job, provides an explanation similar to that of social networks. The lawyer was defender and representative; that is, he articulated private interests and mediated between private parties and the state. In going about these tasks his use of social networks was essential. He strengthened them and created additional ones. He was definitely the organizer of elites. From this came the complex relationship that needs explanation. A lawyer without adequate social relationships would have enjoyed little success, and in fact they remain crucial today. Law schools and family relationships provided the initial social networks that were indispensable to the lawyer's role, as he needed the right connections in order to resolve his clients' cases. Later, the clients themselves were people with their own social capital that could be useful for lawyers, whether as political support or as contacts with other people.

This explanation makes sense. What it does not explain is how it was possible for lawyers to be at once eminent members of the political elite and participants in a political life that did not run along the channels established by formal law. Revolutions, coups, violations of human rights, and dictatorships were characteristic of political and legal life in the period. What were lawyers doing with regard to these? What was their function?

It is worth distinguishing between periods of great turbulence or very unstable political structures and periods of more controlled conflict. In the former, civil war or military force were means of deciding who was to govern. Soldiers were preeminent. Nonetheless, in order to govern, *caudillos* or military leaders had to come down off of their horses or get out of their combat vehicles and perform as rulers. They needed interpreters and reformers of constitutions and laws, people who could prepare acts and draw up deeds, who spoke the language of law and of the constitution. For them, lawyers were indispensable. If we look at rural *caudillos* in the 1800s, lawyers provided the added service of integrating them with the urban elite. Lawyers became their representatives. Their role was subordinate to the strong will of those dictators and charismatic rulers, though they did enjoy a certain autonomy and did achieve certain specific goals within regimes. For example, the organization of the Venezuelan state under Juan Vicente Gómez was not Gómez's personal work but that of such associates as José Gil Fortoul or Pedro Miguel Arcaya. Latin American novelists tend to depict lawyers in an overly ridiculous way, but in fact they were not necessarily mere pawns. The personality-driven leader did not make all of the decisions. Within a regime, lawyers played some independent roles, even while others in the same regime may be associated with assassination, torture, or corruption. Historical works that have studied regimes such as Juan Vicente Gómez in Venezuela show how this apparently strange collaboration came about (Capriles Méndez, 1991; Segnini, 1987).

In more peaceful times or with more stable structures, these strongmen rulers who considered themselves so providential, were not necessary. Lawyers then did not hesitate to take center stage.

It is important to emphasize that, no matter who led the governments or who exercised power—from police to presidents—Latin American powerholders tended to abuse power and to disrespect citizens' rights. The hypothesis that human rights abuses were more widespread under dictatorial governments, while undoubtedly strong, is impossible to corroborate given the lack of systematic reports of such abuses comparable to those available today. Regimes justified violation of human rights and the resulting legislation with the need to combat subversion, including armed revolts. But the violations probably have a deeper root: the sense that the great mass of people was ignorant and needed a strong hand to keep it disciplined. Subordinate groups were not treated as citizens because they were not seen as such. The difference between democratic and authoritarian governments was that the latter did not distinguish victims of repression by class (Capeller, 1995).

The best example of the need for repression without excessive legal strings attached is criminal procedure law. While France and other European countries reformed criminal procedure that they inherited from absolutism, in Latin America the Spanish inquisitorial procedure that had been developed by the absolute monarchy was codified (Duce and Pérez-Perdomo, 2001). For example, juries—formed of ordinary people—could not be trusted to decide on punishment. The state needed a free hand to maintain order.

Why were lawyers not champions of legality and human rights? Lawyers were perhaps too involved in political activity to have distanced themselves from it. They did not have sufficiently reasonable occupational alternatives to allow their own liberal political knowledge to stop them from taking part in military takeovers or repression. This argument is probably valid as long as those job choices did not exist, but such was not the case in every country or for the entire period under discussion. The argument that we wish to emphasize in this conclusion is that lawyers' own sense of belonging to the elite, and the shared elitist view among legal scholars and practitioners of the danger of social disorder, made these latter selectively legalistic. The notion that a steel hand was required to control subversive or violent groups and populations that tended toward a lack of discipline was one that placed very distinguished legal scholars and practitioners, profoundly knowledgeable about constitutional law, at the side of repressive regimes such as those of Porfirio Díaz and Juan Vicente Gómez. This, more than a lack of formal independence, explains why lawyers, public prosecutors, and criminal law judges looked aside when it was widely known that police interrogations frequently involved torture, even under governments that, from other angles, were shining examples of legalism and democracy.

In conclusion, when we look at Latin American legal life as a whole in this period, we see that constitutions and laws were both important and hollow. We see prominent lawyers taking on the task of writing about law or staunchly defending just and unjust causes. But we also see those groups for which the state system was an instrument of repression, a forgotten group that the principal legal actors did not wish to deal with. Law seen in this way, with all its tradition and classicism, is like a De Chirico landscape painting: formally beautiful architecture, but dreamlike and unreal.

This chapter should not end on this somber note, because the dream of a society truly guided by law and justice, the dream of the rule of law, remains alive. The story of those who had this dream is not a story only about lawyers as a social group, but a story about individual lawyers. Probably the same people have contributed both to maintaining the dream and to despairing of it. Human action has always been complex and many-faceted.

CHAPTER 4

From Development to Globalization

THIS FINAL chapter covers the period closest to the present: the second half of the twentieth century. We can distinguish two subperiods, clearly different in economic and social policies. In the first, from 1950 into the 1970s, Latin American states practiced policies of "national development." These consisted mostly of promotion and protection of national industries and import substitution. In broad outline, these policies were quite successful: from 1950 to 1981, Latin American countries' gross products grew yearly by 5.3 percent, and the per capita incomes by 2.6 percent (French-Davis and Palma, 1998). Simultaneously, the nations tried to promote education and public health, expanding enormously the number of schools and educational institutes of all levels, investing in sanitation, and increasing the number of hospitals and other health-related institutions. Their quick growth was not without inequalities and tensions. Urban populations grew enormously, as did urban poverty and regional inequality. The state took on the functions of investor, regulator, and at times promoter of national development. Thus it is no surprise that public expenditures grew at a vertiginous pace.

Social and economic dysfunctions led to military dictatorships in most Latin American countries. The military governments in Brazil (1964–85), Argentina (1976–82), and Chile (1973–90) became notorious for massive and systematic human rights violations, at a scale not previously known on the continent. Several thousand people were killed or "missing" in each country, and torture attained new heights of systematic cruelty. These acts of institutional crimes were documented by many national and international reports. Only a few countries (Colombia, Costa Rica, Mexico, and Venezuela) avoided military dictators and bloody massive repression.

State-led growth policies generated an enormous public debt. When financial markets changed in 1982, the debt appeared to be beyond control.

This was the "debt crisis" that affected the countries with more aggressive industrialization policies (especially Argentina, Brazil, Chile, Mexico, and Venezuela). Economic growth stopped in the early 1980s, impoverishment especially in urban areas increased, and the gap between Latin America and the most developed countries widened as well. In Latin America, economists and international agencies spoke of the "lost decade."

It was deemed necessary then to rely on the resources of the International Monetary Fund (IMF), the World Bank, and the Inter-American Development Bank (IDB), among other multilateral institutions, and to agree to open up national markets to foreign competition and deregulate the operation of the economy. Many state enterprises were privatized. The market replaced the state as the principal economic regulator, though often more in the imagination of the elites than in everyday practice.

Viewed from some historical distance, the 1980s look far more complex than just an economic slowdown. It was a decade of swift political change. Democracy was restored in most countries: Argentina, Bolivia, Brazil, Chile, Dominican Republic, Ecuador, El Salvador, Guatemala, Honduras, Nicaragua, Panama, Paraguay, and Uruguay. In Mexico the Institutional Revolutionary Party, which had practically dominated Mexican politics until the 1980s, progressively lost its hegemonic character and the political system became more open and democratic. Only Cuba has remained a dictatorship, and only Costa Rica has had a stable democracy for the entire period. For these reasons political scientists prefer to talk of democratization as an incomplete process (Agüero, 1998; O'Donnell, 1986). Argentina, Ecuador, Peru, and Venezuela have continued to be shaken by political crisis at the beginning of the second millennium, thus the consolidation of the rule of law has a long way to go in almost every country.

In the 1990s the Latin American economy resumed its growth, but at an irregular pace, with some national differences and some setbacks. The integration of the world by new telecommunications and Internet systems has brought the world so much closer, permitting the instantaneous transfer of capital or information, that it has been termed *globalization* (Giddens, 2000; García Canclini, 1999).

In this work our interest centers on the aspirations shared by the elites, on ideologies or a certain consensus about goals that were considered valuable to pursue collectively, and on some basic steps for reaching them. Those ideologies have generated public policies and shared behaviors that shape different aspects of social life. The impact of those ideologies on the legal profession is the subject of this analysis.

The policies of national development generated enormous expansion of public administration—in the central state apparatus and state enterprises. This expansion increased emphasis on administrative law at the expense of private law. The resulting labyrinthine and complex regulations have driven a critical segment of the population to an informal economy (De Soto, 1986).

As regulatory legislation increased, traditional codes lost their former importance. Entire branches of law were removed from the codes. Irti (1979) calls this phenomenon the "decodification" of law. The judicial system also lost influence because high political and administrative officials assumed roles in the patronage of business, promotion of investments, and the solving of conflicts among businesspeople.

The social and political transformations of the 1980s and 1990s have been accompanied by changes in the substance of the law, only a few of which will be mentioned here. Almost all of the region's countries have promulgated new constitutions (Argentina, Brazil, Chile, Colombia, El Salvador, Honduras, Nicaragua, Panama, Paraguay, Uruguay, and Venezuela) or have made significant amendments (Mexico). Most older legislation has likewise been replaced in the last two decades. In Mexico, for example, of the 159 federal laws that existed in 1999, 78 were passed in the period 1991–99 and 51 in the previous decade (López-Ayllón and Fix-Fierro, 2003). In Venezuela, 44 percent of the laws in force in December 1999 were passed in the 1990s (Pérez-Perdomo, 2003).

The large substantive codes (civil, penal, commercial) have been less subject to change; the recent trend has been for these codes to regain the ground they lost to regulatory legislation in the 1960s and 1970s. The constitution itself has gained clout as a legal (and not merely political) text. Contractual activity has increased, partially due to the growth of private business. In many countries, changes in procedural legislation have led to an increase in judicial cases presided over by judges.

The international dimension of law also has gained prominence. Governing elites cannot ignore the IMF, the World Trade Organization (WTO), the multilateral banks, the U.S. government, and the European Union (EU). Latin American countries are signatories to regional integration treaties that affect local law and legal culture, namely the North American Free Trade Agreement (NAFTA), Mercosur, and Andean Pact. The Organization of American States, the Inter-American Treaty for Human Rights, and the Inter-American Court of Human Rights have a constant presence in the region. Even the opinions—generally amplified by the mass media—of private-sector international risk evaluators and of nongovernmental organizations (NGOs) such as Amnesty International and Transparency International have an impact on lives in all the countries. As international exchanges have multiplied, foreign laws and legal cultures have become more salient. The national framework is no longer broad enough for the educational needs of lawyers. The tight union between law and the national state has been shaken.

The principal sources for this work are contained in the abundant literature regarding legal education, lawyers, and judges in Latin America. This author has been an active participant in the movements to reform legal education and the administration of justice during the period examined.

This chapter begins by examining the changes in the education of lawyers. It then looks at the legal profession, especially the heightened role of business lawyers. And as judges have become especially important in the latter decades, the last section will be dedicated to them.

Professors and Legal Education

ACADEMIC ACTIVITY

Works in comparative law emphasize the role of scholars—professors and authors of legal works—in the legal system and the politics of countries following the Romanist tradition. Latin America is no exception, but it is noteworthy that an academic career does not constitute a profession in Latin America. The group of people, often situated in the universities, who have dedicated themselves to legal teaching or research do not derive their main source of income from their academic work. University salaries are sufficiently low that the primary compensation is in professional and social prestige. Thus only a few legal scholars can afford to dedicate themselves exclusively to academic activities—because they are independently wealthy or because they are willing to accept an income well below that which they would earn practicing law full-time. Within this group, only a few manage to make a living by developing a secondary (but highly productive) activity, such as specialized consulting. Some professors who participate in public forums are interviewed by the media or publish editorials—activities that give them visibility and influence in public policy. The main advantage of the system is its low cost to both the state and students, while legal education ends up being financed by the sector of lawyers who are hired as professors, as Lynch (1981: 111) observed in Colombia.

Fucito (2000) has studied law professors in the universities of Buenos Aires and La Plata. He found that the pay for university teaching has relatively little importance for most professors, except for those who are dedicated to it exclusively (usually older people and women). Professors tend to devote themselves to their academic duties during weekends and vacations, and to income-producing activities during weekdays. Contrary to what one might expect, interviewees revealed considerable satisfaction with their jobs.

In Chile the number of law professors with a greater commitment to the school beyond just teaching a course varies according to the university, and in some it exceeds half (De la Maza, 2001: 112–13). But in most cases professors limit themselves to teaching, leaving open the possibility that their main income comes from outside the university. The demanding class load for full-time professors rules out any effort at research. Peña (2000: 5) emphasizes the lack of an academic community dedicated to research and teaching.

The situation was not very different forty years ago. In 1966, 95 percent of law professors in Colombia were part-time or paid by the hour. The few who taught full-time were recruited from among the senior professors, who did not need substantial income, or the younger professors, who gained experience and prestige in the process (Lynch, 1981). This was not a general characteristic of Colombian university education, since in other schools or departments the proportion of full-time professors was much greater.

The situation in Brazil was much the same. Rosenn (1969) paid special attention to the method of appointing professors, based on a competition that gave them tenure very quickly. Contrary to the demands placed on tenured positions in other parts of the world, tenure in Latin America frees professors from any obligation to produce academic research or to pay excessive attention to teaching (Rosenn, 1969: 260ss). This explains the low average productivity of university professors, but not the incentives of some professors to become innovators or highly productive.

In Venezuela in the 1960s and 1970s, an effort ensued to professionalize university activity, including law instruction. Later policies of restricted spending affected the incomes of university professors, leaving certain programs such as law unable to compete with offers of lucrative salaries in the marketplace. By the mid- to late-1980s, the recently created law professor–scholar was already an endangered species (Pérez-Perdomo, 1984, 1985). Similar efforts were made in other Latin American countries with much the same results, although probably with less of an investment.

Informal conversations with colleagues reveal that nowadays not many professors are dedicated primarily to academic activity in the Latin American countries. Interestingly, scholarship and the publication of magazine articles and legal works still continue, often carried on in small research centers, NGOs, and consulting firms. Research tends to be very utilitarian. Consultants or researchers who also are university professors conduct their research and teaching concurrently. The model that is spreading in universities and institutes is that of the professor who is offered an office and other research facilities along with a modest salary. In this way, the institution hopes to generate research in its name, and projects and publications can be expected to produce additional income for the professor and for the institution. This is the model expressly adopted by law schools such as Diego Portales University in Chile, Centro de Investigaciones para el Desarollo Económico (CIDE) in Mexico, and Instituto de Estudios Superiores en Administración (IESA) in Caracas, among other institutions. In other cases, it is the implicit model.

Handbooks or textbooks reflecting minimal scholarly work comprise the greatest volume of publications in the legal field. The production of serious work presenting a branch of law as a whole (treatises) has practically disappeared, but some past works are still being reissued, frequently with updated notes.

One innovation is the production of publications that reflect interdisciplinary, applied research, especially in the field of institutional reform. Such an interdisciplinary literature emerged in the 1970s, but not all countries produced it with the same intensity. Brazil, Chile, Colombia, Mexico, Venezuela (see Souto and Souto, 1990; Figueroa, 1978; Correas and Correas Vázquez, 1990; Pérez-Perdomo, 1984; Pérez-Perdomo and Roche, 1990), and to a lesser degree, Argentina (Ves Losada, 1990), Costa Rica, and Peru are the main producers. Recent law and justice reform activities have generated a significant demand for applied interdisciplinary research.[1]

Legal instruction is much more important for its contribution to the establishment of a professional identity than as an occupational activity in itself (Clark, 1999). Since the colonial period, the only feature Latin American lawyers have shared was their university training, reflected in a law degree. In that sense, a university legal education has two crucial roles: to regulate who will form the professional ranks, and to imbue them with a "professional ideology" (Torres Arends, 2001). One should note that the esteem given a university legal education is greater in Latin America than in France, the country generally held up as a model. There, the separate education received by judges and other officials and by the business lawyers weakens the common base of the various legal professions (Boigeol, 2003) The recent trend in Latin America is to promote differentiation among law schools. Some are very selective and academically rigorous. Others have open enrollment and do not make a concerted effort to offer quality education. They graduate lawyers with hugely divergent professional perspectives.

Our analysis will begin with the role that legal education plays in general selection, and later we will see the formation of the professional ideology.

THE STUDENTS

The importance of universities for lawyers' education is a Latin American constant. The professional organizations have practically no educational role. As we will later see, this has important implications for the orientation and structure of legal education.

Most students enter the university at approximately age eighteen, immediately after completing their secondary education. University studies usually last five years. In the predominantly agrarian societies of the past, there were few universities, and a law career was restricted to those who could afford the cost of moving to and living in the capital or a city with a law school as well as the cost of leaving one's agricultural or commercial work. Thus despite the fact that law was one of the most desired university degrees and attracted a high percentage of university students, the number of law students in relation to the national population was relatively low.

The development policies throughout Latin America altered the scene by promoting urbanization, industrialization, and the expansion of primary and secondary education. Table 4.1 shows the number of law students in the latter twentieth century for the nine Latin American countries that, as a whole, represented more than 90 percent of the region's population.

TABLE 4.1.

Law Students in Nine Latin American Countries, 1950–2000

Country and Year	Number of Law Students	Percent of University Students	Number per 100,000 Inhabitants
Argentina 1970	29,045	13.2	124
Argentina 1998	163,881	14.7	443
Brazil 1961	23,519	23.7	25
Brazil 1965, a	33,402	21.5	41
Brazil 1994, a	190,712	11.5	122
Brazil 1998	292,728	14.1	183
Chile 1950, b	2,284	Not available	19
Chile 1965, a	3,431	7.9	39
Chile 1996, a	17,462	6.4	122
Chile 2000	24,478	5.4	163
Colombia 1950, b	1,985	20.5	18
Colombia 1965, a	5,274	11.9	29
Colombia 1996, a	66,778	14	187
Costa Rica 1950, b	205	13.3	24
Costa Rica 1965, a	328	4.5	22
Costa Rica 1994, a	4,262	5.4	125
Ecuador 1965, a	1,706	12.1	34
Ecuador 1991, a	16,903	8.1	170
Mexico 1965, a	16,808	12.6	42
Mexico 1995, a	137,357	11.3	151
Mexico 2000	188,422	11.9	193
Peru 1950, b	1,392	8.7	18
Peru 1965, a	4,624	5.8	40
Peru 1991, a	43,715	9.2	198
Peru 2000	36,986	8.8	142
Venezuela 1950	1,000	13.5	53
Venezuela 1966, a	6,766	12.6	78
Venezuela 2000	44,000	7.4	160

SOURCES: (a) UNESCO, *Statistical Yearbook*, 1973 and 1997; (b) Merryman and Friedman, 1979. *Argentina*: Sistema de Estadísticas Universitaria, Secretaría de Políticas Universitarias, Ministerio de Educación, Buenos Aires; unpublished data collected by M. I. Bergoglio. *Brazil 1961*: Falcão, 1984. *Brazil 1998*: Junqueira, 2003. *Chile 2000*: Persico, 2001: 43. *Mexico 2000*: *Anuario Estadístico de ANUIES*, 2000. *Peru 2000*: Asamblea Nacional de Rectores. *Venezuela 1950*: Pérez-Perdomo, 1981. *Venezuela 1995*: Estimate from Oficina de Planificación del Sector Universitario, unpublished.

Notice that the table indicates fairly low early numbers for each country compared to those at the end of the period, including the figures relative to the total population. The growth in the number of law students can be explained partially by the expansion of primary and secondary education that took place in the mid–twentieth century. By that time, universities felt the pressure of increased enrollment. The response varied by country: restricting entry, increasing the capacity of law schools, or permitting the creation of new law schools. Frequently, more than one policy was tested and changed over time. In any case, university growth paralleled appreciable demographic change in the cities and urban population over the same period.

A few anomalies exist, such as the substantial decrease in the number of law students in Peru between 1991 and 2000, but this may be related to different definitions of "law student," depending on the source. Note that UNESCO, our source for 1991, has no available figures for 2000. The National Assembly of Rectors' figure for 1991 is 30,396.[2]

Attributing the increase in law students to the expansion of higher education is obvious in cases in which the increase in university students outpaced that of law students (as in Brazil, Chile, Ecuador, Venezuela, and to a lesser degree, Mexico). As opportunities for university study diversified, young people could choose from among more majors. Thus the trend is an increase in the number of law students per 100,000 inhabitants, but a decrease of law students as a percentage of university students.

But this is not a general trend. In Argentina, Colombia, and Costa Rica, the increase in law students has been both in absolute numbers and as a percentage of university students. Thus demographic change and more diverse university offerings do not explain everything, since other traditional fields (such as medicine, theology, and philosophy) did not grow in the same proportion as law studies and sometimes decreased in absolute numbers. Other studies—nonexistent until midcentury, such as computer science or business—attract a significant number of students. Without a doubt, the perception of job opportunities after graduation is a powerful incentive in choosing these subjects. Young people are idealist, *ma non troppo.*

The growth in the number of students is a manifestation of a much deeper change: the *democratization of education*—that is, access by groups and social classes previously excluded from university education. Women, for example, began to have greater access to legal education. National figures vary considerably, but women went from a third or fewer of all law students in the 1960s to approximately half around the end of the century. We will provide some examples. In Mexico, women made up 15 percent of law students in 1965 (UNESCO Statistical Yearbook, 1973) and 47 percent in 1997 (López-Ayllón and Fix-Fierro, 2003). In Chile, women constituted 23 percent of the country's 9,308 lawyers in 1992, and 39 percent of the 2,791 graduates between 1995 and 1999 (Santelices Ariztía, 2002; see also Persico, 2001: 33). At the University of Buenos Aires in 1964, 34 percent of law students were female; in 1980, 53 percent (Mackinson de Sorokin, 1984). In 1997, 56 percent of all Argentinean law students were women (Bergoglio, 2003b). At the Universidad Central de Venezuela, women made up 23 percent of law graduates in 1959, and 57 percent in 2000 (Roche, 2001). Women constituted 29 percent of law students in Venezuela in 1960, and 61 percent in 1999 (Pérez-Perdomo, 2003).

Also gaining access to law schools were people from lower-income social strata. For example, in Brazil in the 1970s the majority of law students in Rio de Janeiro and Recife came from high-income groups (Falcão, 1979: 364). The most recent trend everywhere shows the presence of lower-income groups, with higher-income students concentrated in only a few schools. The racial distribution in Latin America is generally not reported, in part because the ideology of equality and integration means that statistics are not categorized by race or ethnic background. The fact that we have located an article that refers to black students and points out their increased presence in Brazilian education institutions reveals not only a trend in the student population but also a disposition to study issues barely looked at until now (Junqueira and Veras, 2001).

In short, in relation to earlier periods not only are there many more students, but due to their diverse origins they also have other social and job expectations. This will have repercussions in the changing social function of law schools. The increased demand for legal studies that occurred in the second half of the last century was by and large met by an increased supply of law schools, as a product of policies of liberalizing education. In other words, supply and demand are not independent of one another. The increase in the number of law schools in recent years could have augmented the demand for legal education. At the same time, the increase in the number of students could lead to the strengthening or consolidation of the supply.

Demographic changes of law students are integral to Latin American political and social systems. The comparison with Cuba is interesting. This is the only Latin American country that has chosen the socialist path. In 1965, when the Cuban Revolution was initiated with great ideological fervor, legal studies almost disappeared: the country's 343 law students represented less than 2 percent of university students, or 5 per 100,000 inhabitants. In 1995 official policy that revalued legal studies bumped the number to 1,848. This did not signify a substantial increase with respect to its weight in the university, but it signified an increase to 17 law students per 100,000 inhabitants, a figure at any rate very low compared to other Latin American countries. In 1995, 70 percent of law students were women, and the proportion appears to have increased since then (data from UNESCO, 1997; see Zatz, 1994; Bermúdez, 2001).[3]

The increase in demand for legal studies partially explains the emergence or strengthening of private legal education. Whether ideological or commercial in origin, only the sustained increase among young people inclined to study law made possible the increase in the number of private law schools and the proportional rise of students in private universities in nearly all of the countries in the region.

CHANGES IN LAW SCHOOLS AND PROGRAMS

A traditional function of law schools was the training of the political elite. In the nineteenth and early twentieth centuries, that was the express function. Legal studies were often called "political science," and parliamentarians, ministers, and high public officials all trained together (Dantas, 1955; Faoro, 1975; Carvalho, 1980; Pérez-Perdomo, 1981; Falcão, 1984; Serrano, 1994b; De la Maza, 2001). Not only did the law curricula include subjects like political economy and sociology, but also students, displaced from their hometowns, tended to gather to discuss politics and literature. Their networks were later reflected in political activity and state administration. The legal training as such was complemented by work in the tribunals or in the offices of lawyers.

By mid–twentieth century, legal studies stressed law more than ever (De la Maza, 2001; Pérez-Perdomo, 1981), but the law schools' function of training the political elite was preserved, in a latent or implicit way. The presence of lawyers in politics and state administration as well as the informal networks that were formed in the law schools explains this latent function, which was concentrated in certain universities such as the Autonomous National University of Mexico (Lomnitz and Salazar, 2002), the University of Chile, and the Central University of Venezuela. Students' political activity, including participation in violent acts, formed part of their political training and establishment of loyalties.

In the last third of the twentieth century, the political function of these large universities came into conflict with their express function of educating lawyers. The intensification of political agitation damaged education at these universities due to a greater frequency of strikes, class suspensions, and acts of violence. Political activity especially affected the large universities of the capitals, where the principal educators of the political elite were concentrated. This contributed to the surge of private universities, as students who wanted a more continuous course of studies and could afford the tuition migrated away from the public schools.

The first private schools, generally around the end of the nineteenth or the first half of the twentieth century, were the Catholic universities.[4] Occasionally, a law school such as the Escuela Libre de Derecho in Mexico

City was developed with purposes of professionalization as an alternative to a politicized official education. In general, private universities in the first half of the twentieth century were few in number, and their education had a largely ideological purpose. In the last thirty years, the number of law schools and programs increased substantially,[5] and anyone hoping to study law in a Latin American country today generally has quite a range of choices.

Two types of private universities can be distinguished: those that consider education a business and aspire to provide education to huge numbers, and those that have decided to maintain a small student body and try to offer a high-quality education. The latter have attracted the offspring of the economic elite and have begun to stress the training of business lawyers. As a consequence, the law schools of the large, traditional universities lost their standing as the educators of the political elite and saw their prestige in the training of business lawyers drop. Likewise, they lost their position as a center of upward social mobility. In the task of training business lawyers, they were quickly replaced by a few private schools.[6]

By the mid–twentieth century there was no longer any difference between private and public education in terms of content and teaching methods; the curricula were fundamentally the same. The trend was to concentrate legal education on the law, increasing the number of classes in civil, criminal, and procedural law, and also including new branches of law to be studied: labor and administrative law, among others. Thus change in the law curriculum was first apparent in the subject offerings, highly concentrated on strict law. As a result, general education courses lost their relative influence and importance. At the same time, universities created departments in economics, sociology, and political science and developed other social science programs. Students began to have a variety of careers and academic disciplines to choose from. Would-be lawyers found themselves confined to basic legal fields and could no longer claim universal knowledge in the political and social fields. Not surprisingly, their preeminence declined (Rosenn, 1969; Steiner, 1971; Urzúa, 1978; De la Maza, 2001).

The overall increase in the number of law students and the weaker social relations of many of the newer students has meant that the parallel informal education that students traditionally obtained by working in established lawyers' offices or in the courts has become more difficult to procure. An increase in the number of subjects for study also has reduced the time that students can dedicate to nonuniversity activities such as internships, which at one time may have been extracurricular but were still prized for their political socialization value. As we have already observed, most law professors only dedicated the minimum necessary class hours to the university, thus limiting themselves to repeating what they had learned, or explaining the content of the most important handbooks in their subject. Thus in the 1960s and 1970s, there was a perception among leading faculty members of the main law schools that legal studies were irrelevant,[7] and they began to try various innovations and to introduce new movements.

Dantas (1955) was one of the first reformist voices. He called for quite radical reform in the law curriculum and for a reexamination of the methods of legal education. He proposed a flexible curriculum, the incorporation of "case teaching," interdisciplinary analysis, and an active or participatory method on the part of the students. This reformist agenda was formulated in a famous discourse and caused an immediate sensation in Brazil (Bastos, 2000: 250ss; Rosenn, 1969: 273; Steiner, 1971). His ideas can be seen in the formation of legal studies at the Federal University of Brasilia.

Four conferences of Latin American law schools occurred between 1959 and 1964, which produced an abundant literature and called for substantial reforms, including the introduction of class discussion, seminars, and an interdisciplinary focus (Wilson, 1989: 393; Brown, 1961). The last one was in 1974 (Riesco, 1976). These conferences were preceded and accompanied by a reaction against the formalism that has been present in Latin American legal studies since the late 1800s (Pérez-Perdomo, 1984).

The Federal University of Brasilia opened in 1961. Its legal studies were planned with a new type of curricular organization and innovations in teaching methodology (Bastos, 2000). The military coup of 1964, however, resulted in the arrest of several professors and the resignation of a sizable part of the others and halted this first experiment (Rosenn, 1969: 258).

In the 1970s a movement known as "law and development" included the efforts of professors from the United States who, conscious of both the important political role of law studies in Latin America and the backwardness of the law schools themselves, traveled to Latin America as missionaries of the case method and the interdisciplinary study of law. A much larger number of young Latin American professors (especially from Brazil, Chile, Colombia, and Peru) earned U.S. master's degrees and doctorates in law, or in some other way familiarized themselves with the teaching of law in the United States (Lynch, 1981: 111ff; Steiner, 1971). A number of professors began to prepare nontraditional instruction materials and made use of new teaching techniques in the "active class," as it was called. A small number were interested in interdisciplinary research. Several of the North American professors who participated in the experiment considered it a failure, as it did not succeed in changing the Latin American legal culture within a few years, after an investment of approximately $5 million (Trubek and Galanter, 1974).

The view from Latin America is somewhat different. The restlessness for change in legal education predated the presence of the visiting professors. A parallel discussion took place of the topics considered relevant at the time,[8] and changes in Latin American legal education continued long after the withdrawal of the North American organizations that financed the projects and the formal declaration of cessation.

The case of Venezuela is significant, as it did not participate in the "law and development" movement yet nevertheless saw considerable reformist activity both at that time and later. In both civil law countries and in common law ones, many Venezuelan law graduates received postgraduate education mostly with national or university funds. An important segment of these graduates are now professors in Venezuela's law schools, and some have been innovators in their pedagogy or in their research (Pérez-Perdomo, 1984, 1985). The Venezuelan case calls attention to the significant number of law graduates in Latin America who have done postgraduate studies in Europe or, increasingly, the United States in the last few decades.

The changes in legal education have been as much in the teaching of law as in legal scholarship. In the 1970s the changes were very controversial and met with open resistance from the part-time lawyer-professors. In Peru the innovators were sarcastically called the "Wisconsin boys," and they experienced more than a few situations of conflict.[9] In Colombia important political conflicts took place within the schools that attempted reform, and some deans and professors lost their jobs in these struggles (Lynch, 1981). In Chile the Pinochet government expelled the reformists from the universities, including the Catholic university. Several professors under suspicion of being part of the political heterodoxy were forced into exile (Fuenzalida, 2003). We have already noted the case of Brasilia.

Later, changes in teaching came about largely because the private schools that focused on training business lawyers needed to diversify. The innovative schools introduced activities such as legal clinics and negotiation, and law courses such as law and economics, law and society, and human rights (Meili, 1999). These schools also placed importance on an education in ethics, which the positivist formalists had banished from law schools. Some professors innovated their teaching methodologies, although the changes were far from general. Which matters were innovated and which stayed the same varied from one school to another. In some schools the "law and economics" mode of analysis has become dominant, generally associated with neoliberal ideas.[10]

In the postgraduate programs, which were not regulated by tradition, the variety of subjects and activities have been much greater, though studies on what happened in this area are scarce or nonexistent.[11] Curiously, the large public universities have created the most developed postgraduate programs, while innovations to law curricula have occurred more frequently in a few private schools.[12] The main characteristic of these reforms is that they have not formed part of a general movement and have tended to remain low profile.

On the other hand, young law graduates have begun to turn to master's programs in North American universities. There, in one year, they familiarize themselves with the language and the problem-solving methods characteristic of legal teaching in the United States. These are abilities that are appreciated among business lawyers today. Some of these students have become law professors in Latin American countries and have incorporated new approaches and teaching methods into the law schools.

One of the characteristics of legal education in Latin America is the scarcity of external evaluations of law schools as guidance to the students. Perhaps Brazil is the leading country in this regard. The Ministry of Education and the *Ordem dos Advogados* evaluated the law schools independently and published their results (Junqueira, 1999, and personal communication). In Colombia an evaluation was conducted by the Ministry of Justice in 1995, and more recently the Ministry of Education has organized a thorough system of accreditation (Silva García and Fuentes-Hernández, personal communications). In Chile the magazine *Qué Pasa* (Dec. 11, 2001) published an evaluation modeled after one from the American magazine *U.S. News and World Report.*

During the entire period, the perception existed among scholars that the law schools had lost step with social change and that legal studies had been left behind. This perception may have come from the perceived speed of social change as opposed to the much slower and more difficult changes in the curricula and teaching methods in the law schools. Latin American societies faced severe problems of poverty, marginality, criminality, and police brutality. At the same time, political transformations took place that were sometimes quite rapid—a communications revolution and greater integration into the global economy, for example—yet these problems and changes did not seem to affect the majority of law schools, which appeared secluded in a culture of codes and old books (Fuentes-Hernández, 2002). Without denying the problems, the argument developed in this chapter does not accept this perception—in the sense that legal education *has* been affected by social change and that the dynamic of reform, driven out through the door, *has* timidly returned through the window. The perception of stasis probably derives from the desire of legal scholars and leading members of the legal profession to have more dynamic law schools, and from resistance to change in only a few schools and a small fraction of the students. Probably, it also derives from the perception that lawyers have lost their role in the social and political leadership. This is a theme that will be analyzed in the next section.

Changes in legal scholarship have in part accompanied changes in education, but they have not always been congruent. One reason is that some educational changes are associated with the transmission of practical skills (negotiation, for example). Another reason is that researchers are not necessarily linked to the law schools and most schools do not support the development of research.

The Lawyers

DEMOGRAPHICS

The definition of lawyer or legal professional within the boundaries of Latin America does not present the difficulties that it has when broader comparisons are made, for example with China and Japan (Clark, 1999; Abel, 1988). In Latin America in the latter 1900s, all lawyers have had a university degree in law. However, the inverse statement is not always true: in some countries, such as Brazil, substantial additional requirements apply, meaning that not all law graduates can practice law as lawyers. This explains why some countries have a high number of law students, but fewer lawyers. In the mid-1990s, Venezuela and Brazil had the same relative number of law students, but Brazil had just over half the number of lawyers, relative to its population. In Peru, Zolezzi's study about the graduates of the Catholic university distinguishes between those who received a bachelor's degree in law and those who are lawyers. Only 72 percent of graduates in the former category also fall into the latter one (Zolezzi Ibárcena, 1982: 35).

The second difficulty is that we depend on national sources to ascertain the number of lawyers. In some countries careful registries are kept in which lawyers' names are removed when they retire from professional service, are designated as judges or public officials, or die.[13] In other countries the lists are kept much less reliably, thus the number of lawyers listed does not always reflect the number of people who actually support themselves as lawyers. Given these qualifications, we present the data in Table 4.2 with the caution that the figures are rough measurements and not to draw hasty conclusions from them.

A good example of difficulties in the figures is the Argentinean case. No national registry exists and each *colegio de abogados* keeps a separate list. The 2000 estimate was made by the Ministry of Justice and reported by Bergoglio (2003a). Given the high number of law students and the lack of bar examinations or any other substantive requisite to register as a lawyer, we prefer this estimate to the 1996 estimate.

Currently we have figures that allow a comparison over time for roughly the past fifty years only in the cases of Brazil, Chile, Costa Rica, Mexico, and Venezuela. Brazil more than tripled its number of lawyers per 100,000 inhabitants between 1950 and 1991. More demanding regulation for admission to the legal profession explains the decrease in the relative number of

TABLE 4.2.

Lawyers in Nine Latin American Countries, 1950–2000

Country and Year	Number of Lawyers	Number per 100,000 Inhabitants
Argentina 1996	66,500	179
Argentina 2000	128,000	345
Brazil 1950	15,666	30
Brazil 1960	30,066	42
Brazil 1970	37,710	41
Brazil 1980	85,716	72
Brazil 1991	148,871	101
Chile 1950, b	1,475	24
Chile 1960, b	2,602	34
Chile 1970, b	4,306	44
Chile 1982	6,546	58
Chile 1992	9,308	70
Chile 2000	11,400	75
Colombia 2000	112,000	254
Costa Rica 1950, b	467	54
Costa Rica 1960, b	682	55
Costa Rica 1970, b	968	57
Costa Rica 1980	1,700	75
Costa Rica 1990	4,400	157
Costa Rica 2000	10,800	309
Ecuador 1991	9,350	85
Mexico 1960	8,426	24
Mexico 1970	14,669	30
Mexico 1990	141,539	174
Mexico 1998	200,000	208
Peru 1950, b	1,970	23
Peru 1960, b	2,960	30
Peru 1970, b	4,080	32
Venezuela 1950	2,087	41
Venezuela 1961	4,256	57
Venezuela 1971	8,102	76
Venezuela 1981	16,045	111
Venezuela 1990	31,350	159
Venezuela 2000	70,000	290

SOURCES: (b) Merryman and Friedman, 1979. *Argentina*: Garavano, 2001. *Brazil 1950, 1960, 1970, 1980*: Falcão, 1984. *Brazil 1991*: Junqueira, 2001. *Chile 1982, 1992, 2000*: De la Maza, 2001. *Colombia*: Fuentes-Hernández, 2002. *Costa Rica 1980, 1990, 2000*: Information from Alfredo Chirinos, Escuela de la Judicatura. *Ecuador*: Chinchilla and Schodt, 1993. *Mexico 1960, 1970*: Estimates from Lorey, 1992. *Mexico 1990*: López-Ayllón and Fix-Fierro, 2003. *Mexico 1998*: Estimate from Lomnitz and Salazar, 2002. *Venezuela*: Pérez-Perdomo, 1981, 1996b, 2003

lawyers in Brazil in the 1960s. Starting in 1970 the growth of the lawyer population sped up again, but the number of law students quintupled between 1960 and 1991. This allows us to calculate that approximately half of the law graduates in Brazil are not lawyers. Chile has a requirement of practice in addition to the university degree, and a similar situation probably prevails in Peru, although we lack data for recent years.

Venezuela and Costa Rica—in complete contrast to the case of Brazil—have not established any limitations on law graduates becoming lawyers. In Venezuela the only requirement to practice professionally, other than a law degree, is formal enrollment in the respective bar association of one's locality and in INPREABOGADOS, an obligatory insurance.[14] The Venezuelan government tried to keep the number of lawyers low between 1960 and 1990 by blocking the creation of new law schools. The public universities and the Catholic university maintained a relatively rigorous selection process that restricted the number of students, but one private university continued the policy of accepting an unlimited number of students. The only restrictions were economic and geographic, as this giant school is situated in Caracas, and tuition plus the cost of living in the capital was prohibitive for many students. Despite this obstacle, the number of lawyers in Venezuela multiplied by a factor of thirty-three between 1950 and 2000, with a sharp acceleration after 1970. After 1990, the ban on new schools was dropped, permitting the creation of law schools in several cities. This has produced an outburst in the number of lawyers in recent years.

The number of lawyers in Mexico grew moderately until 1970. Figures for 1990 and 1998 show a quick acceleration. The takeoff happened in the 1960s, during which 8,100 graduated from law school, compared to only 3,659 in the previous decade. The figures in Table 4.2 for 1960 and 1970 are estimates based on the number of law graduates for the previous thirty years (Lorey, 1992: 91–92). The figure does not include the number of lawyers existent at the beginning of the period nor the deduction of retired or deceased lawyers, assuming that these two figures counteract each other. The 1990 figure comes from the National Institute of Statistics (used by López-Ayllón and Fix-Fierro, 2003). This figure is trustworthy as it comes from a census of professional personnel conducted by this institute. The 1998 figure results from adding the number of lawyers registered in 1990–97 (Lomnitz and Salazar, 2002) and subtracting an estimate of retired or deceased lawyers. As 1990 was probably counted twice, our subtraction took this into account.

The pattern of growth in Costa Rica[15] was similar to that in Venezuela, though its growth was slightly less explosive. The large jump took place in the 1980s and 1990s, and in those two decades the relative number of lawyers doubled.

Between 1950 and 2000, the number of lawyers per 100,000 inhabitants tripled in Chile. The figure is closer to that of Brazil than that of Venezuela. Compared to the number of law students, this figure remained low until 1980 as an express policy not to allow an increase in law schools and to restrict the number of students. The policy changes in this period have produced an explosion in the student population, but the effect on the number of graduates has not yet been felt. It is expected that it will be in the near future (De la Maza, 2001). In any case, it seems clear that the restriction on the number of students admitted into law schools was responsible for Chile's relatively slow growth of the legal profession until approximately 1990.

If we compare countries, we see that the number of lawyers seems to vary substantially. We have figures from the 1990s for eight countries. Argentina, Costa Rica, and Venezuela have the highest number of lawyers relative to population, approximately 300 per 100,000 inhabitants. They are followed by Colombia (254) and Mexico (208). Brazil (101), Ecuador (85), and Chile (75) have the fewest. The gaps among the countries have become greater over the last few decades: they were much smaller in the 1950s and still not very great in 1970. It would be absolutely inappropriate to draw conclusions about the role of lawyers in development. We know too little about what the people who hold the title of lawyer effectively do, and we also would overlook many people who have some legal training and fulfill functions in the legal system. Information about notary and registry activity and about lawsuits could doubtless give us a better overview, but the available studies and data are full of gaps. As a result, this chapter will not attempt to take the quantitative analysis any further. Likewise, the analysis will not support generalizations about the classification of legal cultures based on the control of the number of lawyers or supply of services (which is characteristic of Europe) and expansion of demand (which is characteristic the United States) (Mattei, 1997).[16] This type of theorization would have to include a greater number of national experiences and detailed data in order to be credible. Economic analysis of the formal regulation of the legal profession is not enough.

ACTIVITY AND SOCIAL POSITION

Traditionally, lawyers held a high social position and were conspicuous members of the political elite. The law was considered the preeminent format for obtaining political knowledge, which gave lawyers their political legitimacy. They were members of the elite, because in countries with high illiteracy rates, rural populations, and difficulties in communication only relatively well-off members of the urban sectors had access to a legal education. As we have seen, this situation changed during the 1900s, but at different rates, depending on the country. The situation in the last third of the century is completely different from that of the beginning of the century.

Social change and the change in the organization of education meant that other disciplines came to compete with law as technical forms of knowledge about political action. These disciplines varied according to the time and country. In the 1960s and 1970s, economics, sociology, and planning were considered the preeminent forms of political knowledge. More recently, a new version of economics and public policy has attained preeminence. Lawyers have maintained a presence in politics not only due to the weight of tradition but also because certain sectors are considered reserved for jurists, and because some lawyers individually have concerned themselves with learning the new disciplines. But lawyers no longer seem to have an initial advantage in the field of politics, and their influence has been on the decrease in higher political circles in later years (López-Ayllón and Fix-Fierro, 2003; De la Maza, 2001).

In the 1960s and 1970s, one of the incentives in the effort to transform law schools resulted from the perception of a diminished political role for lawyers in government. Steiner (1971: 59) takes up the complaint that lawyers were rarely consulted in governmental tasks, including legislation, having been replaced by economists, engineers, and other technical professionals. The perception fueled the image of decline of the legal profession, which Steiner (1971) to a large extent blamed on formalist legal education. This diagnosis was probably accurate, but from today's vantage point we would consider other elements as well. For example, the proliferation of military governments (including Brazil from 1964 until 1985) removed lawyers from many key positions.[17] Because of the nature of those regimes, which did not allow any adverse discussion of their decisions, the participation of lawyers no longer made sense. In the countries that maintained a civil government during that period (Colombia, Costa Rica, Mexico, and Venezuela), the participation of lawyers in governmental duties remained high (Arias Sánchez, 1976; Pérez-Perdomo, 1981; Lomnitz and Salazar, 2002).

When the scenario is analyzed in detail, the explanation becomes somewhat more complex. The increase in the number of students and lawyers, and the greater diversity of their social origins, meant that going to law school was no longer equivalent to membership in the political elite. In fact, many lawyers even found entry into the professional market quite difficult. On the other hand, the increase in the number of law schools dispersed the centers of elite education and thus broke its unity. As we have already pointed out, the young people most closely linked to elite groups, especially to those of greater economic power, selected certain private schools that became the educational centers of business lawyers. The large public schools lost their privileged place in the education of the political elite.

The result is a stratified profession. At the top end of income today are the business lawyers who are partners in large law firms, still a novelty in

TABLE 4.3.
Large Law Firms in Six Latin American Countries, 1999

Country	100 or More Lawyers	50–99 Lawyers
Argentina	2	7
Brazil	4	4
Chile	0	1
Mexico	1	4
Peru	0	1
Venezuela	0	2

SOURCE: *Latin Lawyer: A Who's Who of Latin American Law Firms*. London. Law Business Research, 1999.

Latin America. For example, until 1980, the biggest Venezuelan firms did not have even twenty lawyers, and in Peru apparently only one firm exceeded twelve (Pérez-Perdomo, 1981; Zolezzi Ibárcena, 1982).[18] As Table 4.3 shows, even today there are no really large firms, if compared with those in the United States. The situation is just slightly different in continental Europe (Pérez-Perdomo and Friedman, 2003), although a higher number of large firms are found in France and Germany.

A structural explanation for the moderate size of law firms plays upon the predominance of internal business lawyers (in-house counsel). The biggest businesses have veritable law firms within the business itself. For example, the Venezuelan oil company (PDVSA) employed 143 lawyers in 1999, double the figure in the largest Venezuelan law firm (Pérez-Perdomo, 2001). The internal lawyers handle most of the firm's legal matters and decide which matters to send outside. The preference is then to consult individual lawyers or specialized firms. The professional prestige of internal lawyers depends on the importance of the business, with specialists able to demand the highest market value.

This explanation is not valid for all Latin American countries. In Chile, in-house lawyers are not numerous and do not carry high professional prestige. However, another explanation, based on cultural traits, takes the region's high regard for personal relations into account. The extreme trust that develops between businesspeople and their lawyers means that even lawyers from large firms can expect to retain their clients in the event they move or form a new law firm (Ashton, 2002). This explanation is probably valid for most Latin American countries.

The ways of acquiring professional prestige also have changed. Prestige is now determined by one's professional accomplishments. Naturally, recent graduates are by definition less experienced and have had little opportunity to demonstrate their professional qualities. The traditional career path was that of family or mentor relations: the son of a prestigious lawyer, or a young lawyer accepted as an apprentice, had the opportunity to serve important clients or participate in cases that attracted the attention of the media and the public. If one performed well, one earned prestige. This path still exists, but relatively few lawyers profit from it. Many learn "on the street," "asking in the offices," or "crashing and burning," and only some are able to excel given all the difficulties (Fucito, 1997). The firms, the large legal consultants, and certain public organizations have institutionalized the career path: they accept young lawyers, who get the chance to learn and eventually make a name for themselves.

Aside from professional practice, university teaching and publication can garner prestige—though nowadays only the most reputable universities qualify. In a kind of circular argument, these law schools have prestige because, among other reasons, they hire prestigious lawyers for their teaching staff. In practice, social networks exist that allow particular people to join prestigious firms or businesses or obtain university teaching positions. Of course, personal ability acts as a regulating mechanism in obtaining as well as keeping these privileged positions.

Of course, the biggest employer of lawyers will continue to be the state. But the meaning of government employment can differ greatly depending on the state agency in question. The most specialized or important legal duties, such as those of the lawyers who advise or represent high governmental offices, are generally professionally prestigious positions that carry with them considerable political power (although not necessarily a high salary). Legal positions in the agencies that regulate private economic activity usually supply the necessary credentials to enter the private sphere at a very advantageous position. The state also takes in a large number of graduates in low-level jobs in the judicial system (such as the police force or document registry), or in jobs unrelated to the law. These jobs tend to lack professional prestige.

The lowest professional stratum is made up of law graduates with no ready access to the job market. These lawyers have trouble surviving financially and may resort to very mundane types of activity—such as those associated with the *gestorías* in Venezuela, or *coyotes* in Mexico. Their duties center on low bureaucratic activities such as making useful but illegal payments to accelerate procedures or avoid the lines in front of public offices. Others visit jails to offer their services or sell their wares close to public offices where legal procedures are carried out. The difficulty in entering the job market has been called the "proletarianization" of the profession; it is a phenomenon that appeared in the latter 1900s at different times, depending on the country.

SOCIAL CHANGES, CULTURAL CHANGES, AND LAWYERS

Many questions arise along with this description of the profession. What social and economic changes explain the increase in the number of lawyers? Why, despite the enormous expansion of the market for lawyers and the high incomes of successful lawyers, does there exist a perception of crisis? What effects have the policies of national development and later of globalization had on the legal occupations?

The policies of national development involved the expansion of the state and required a vast army of officials to operate the machinery as well as a good number who could help citizens navigate it. Citizens needed licenses and permits in order to obtain privileges and favors. A maze of regulations applied to all these acts. For many officials and brokers, a university education was necessary or at least useful. Lawyers, as traditional university graduates, were prepared to occupy many of the positions in the expanded bureaucracy or at a minimum to serve as brokers with them. The informal networks among lawyers were an advantage in getting the machinery to operate for the benefit of clients and, obviously, for the lawyers themselves (Lomnitz and Salazar, 2002). A well-connected lawyer was able to find the proper person to navigate the bureaucratic labyrinths or to help avoid them. This explains why the study of law maintained its appeal, as it provided work and social respectability to a significant number of people—including many who came from the modest social strata of the population and might be the first in their families to earn a university degree.

Among elite lawyers, the situation was seen differently. This younger group was not intellectually well equipped to occupy the important posts of the interventionist state. Economists, planners, and sociologists seemed better equipped for those tasks and better suited to occupy the high state positions, which had been lawyers' traditional turf. Hence, lawyers sensed the necessity to change legal education and to educate themselves to the ideals of the social engineer—as the North American lawyers trained under the policies of the New Deal had preached. It is not surprising that the reform attempts of 1970 found vigorous champions in the elite but not among the majority of lawyers at that time; the problems of social reform did not concern them (Lynch, 1981).

The reduction in the size of the state, brought about in the wake of new policies of privatization and decentralization, has been more programmatic than real. In practice, the central state has generally diminished in size, but decentralization has heightened the roles of the municipal and regional governments and in the process generated problems of competing powers. Under the policies of privatization, many state enterprises are now private. This has affected very important spheres—such as the production and distribution of energy, telecommunications, and public services. In those sprawling and high-profile areas, new regulations and regulatory bodies were required, especially since political hierarchies and networks had lost part of their power.

Although no studies support this, the perception is that governments continue to be large and that complexity in legal relations has only increased. This in turn has probably boosted the need for lawyers who can maneuver amid the decentralized powers and the new private enterprises that provide public services. In any case, the state continues to be a substantial employer of lawyers, and the private business sector requires a growing number. At the same time, more lawyers require knowledge and skills that many law schools have been unable to provide.

Under the regulatory state, some brokers (and "fixers") were not necessarily lawyers, and in each country they were referred to by different names. In Mexico they were *coyotes*; in Venezuela, *gestores*. They were (and still are) used as brokers or fixers only for the most everyday tasks. Yet their activities have completely lost legitimacy and today are classified as corrupt.[19] Under the de-bureaucratization and the anticorruption fight going on in almost every country, these intermediaries still remain, but their ranks have thinned. Lawyers tend to assume the social function formerly served by intermediaries, but in a way considered more legitimate.

Cultural change is undeniably another agent resulting in a greater need for lawyers, and it is pertinent to mention it here. The central idea is that the mass media, especially television, have spread a modern, individualist vision throughout society and that this has caused a greater tendency in the population to pursue claims through legal channels. If one adds to this the growing exchanges taking place among people who do not form multiconnected groups such as families or the inhabitants of a small city, then the need for contracts and the probability of conflicts also increase (Friedman, 1985, 2001). The cultural changes that we label globalization involve an increased use of lawyers. Many of the claims against the state that are generally pursued with the help of lawyers eventually involve *amparos*[20] and administrative actions, two areas of litigation that have clearly increased. In short, our analysis suggests that the new policies have increased rather than reduced the need for lawyers.

The second large theme is whether Latin American lawyers are "globalized," whether they are active in that process, and whether their profession has sacrificed either its local or national character. In that sense, the answer has to be mixed. Legal education has tended to preserve a strongly national character despite the enormous changes in law and society that have accompanied globalization (Faria, 2000). Law studies center on the large national codes, along with the principles of law that are believed to be universal. The result could not be more lamentable. As a hypothetical example, a recent graduate of a Venezuelan law school (most likely female) believes she knows Venezuelan law and the universal principles of law, but if presented with a case involving the law of Colombia or of the state of Florida, she would feel absolutely lost. Belief in the universality of law does not help in the slightest when trying to understand and utilize foreign law. It is likely that the young Venezuelan lawyer has never studied comparative law and does not even suspect the existence of the multitudes of legal systems. One can hypothesize that this is true for the majority of law graduates and lawyers throughout Latin America. The exceptions are the young graduates who decide to get their postgraduate degree abroad—with growing frequency in the United States—and the few law schools that place importance on comparative law or international training.

Naturally, the lawyers who work in business firms or for companies in frequent contact with foreign providers or clients soon feel the need to learn a foreign language, the fundamentals of other legal cultures, and other bodies of law that permit them to interact with foreign clients and lawyers. An apprenticeship with a mentor can serve this purpose, or better, a postgraduate degree from a foreign country. Only a small percentage of all Latin American lawyers work in an international environment, but they are at the top in terms of professional prestige: they have the most income, and they belong to the most reputable firms or work for the most important businesses. They are at the top of the ladder in terms of professional knowledge and stratification. As such, they are significantly more influential than their numbers would suggest, and they are valuable role models for ambitious young people.

The effects of stratification can be seen even among lawyers who work for the same company. For instance, the internal lawyers for the Venezuelan oil company (Pérez-Perdomo, 2001) fall into two groups: those who deal with lawsuits or matters in the oil fields, who must know national law and Spanish; and those who work in the corporate sector of the company and participate in negotiations with foreign companies, who must know other legal cultures and languages, especially English. It is not surprising that the latter tend to have higher salaries and more recognition within the company. Globalization can be reflected in one's pocketbook.

Foreign training—whether in universities, law firms, or international or multilateral organizations—is valued highly. Lawyers with such training encounter better job opportunities not only in firms and businesses but also in the most important state agencies. Interest in working in the official sector, as well as the sector's willingness to receive transnationalized lawyers, can vary from country to country (see Dezalay and Garth, 2002) depending on the culture and political structures of the state. Unlike in the past, lawyers with foreign experience today generally serve as technocrats, rather than in traditional political roles. They do have a role in legitimizing the political system in the international arenas, and on the other hand, they have new capacities and titles to compete in the national political arena. In other words, globalization has not eliminated the political role of lawyers; it has transformed it. It also has given preeminence to a postgraduate education in the United States, instead of Europe (Dezalay and Garth, 2002). These themes will be discussed more thoroughly when we analyze the profession as a whole, not only the occupation of lawyer. Thus we should first examine what has happened in the realm of judges.

The Judges

The occupation of judge in Latin America did not traditionally carry great professional prestige. Lawyers who were uncertain about building a career in private practice or with a specialized state agency usually sought a judgeship as an alternative choice. Naturally, a lot depended on the available judicial post: municipal judgeships in small provincial towns were the least desired, while a seat on the Supreme Court or in an appellate court in the capital carried far greater prestige.

Working as a judge was not so different from working as a lawyer. In fact, a lawyer became a judge simply by being designated as such, but without special training to fulfill those functions. In most Latin American countries, a judge occupied his position for only a short period, often with no way of knowing how long, because a political retaliation could cost him his post at any juncture. However, the position of judge could be useful training and a way of gaining access to the informal networks that could help in the practice of law or in politics. As a result, after spending a couple of years as a judge, it was normal for him to return to practicing law or to move on to a position as a state official. After 1970, however, in countries like Brazil, Chile, Costa Rica, and Venezuela, judges could expect to be retained and to gain regular promotions. Most of the countries now have a judicial career path, even if political upheavals affect the system from time to time.

Globalization has affected judges differently than lawyers. With few exceptions, Latin American judges tend not to have had training abroad or have command of a foreign language. Nor have they felt the pressure to understand other legal cultures. Nonetheless, there have been changes. The political and social importance of judges has increased. In most countries in the region, judges can aspire to stay in their posts until retirement. Also, judicial schools or academies have been formed, which provide specific technical training. Thus technically, judgeships have been professionalized in the style of what occurred earlier in European countries. In this section of our study we analyze this change, starting with some demographic information.

THE DIFFICULTIES OF QUANTIFICATION

Curiously, less data exist concerning the number of judges than lawyers, probably because judges were considered less crucial. What we have been able to compile is presented in Table 4.4.

TABLE 4.4.

Judges in Eight Latin American Countries, 1970–2001

Country and Year	Number of Judges	Number per 100,000 Inhabitants
Argentina (Córdoba) 1971	167	8
Argentina (Córdoba) 1998	447	11.9
Argentina 1996	4,030	10.9
Bolivia 1988	424	6.6
Brazil 1970	3,624	3.9
Brazil 1991	8,050	5.5
Chile 1970	604	6.2
Chile 1995	483	3.4
Colombia 1970	2,724	12.8
Colombia 1990	4,800	16
Colombia 1999	3,272	8.9
Costa Rica 1970	148	8.6
Costa Rica 1990	299	10.7
Costa Rica 2000	567	16.2
Mexico (federal) 1970	77	0.2
Mexico (federal) 1999	366	0.4
Mexico (states) 2000	3,677	3.7
Venezuela 1971	783	7.3
Venezuela 1997	1,165	5
Venezuela 2001	1,772	7.5

SOURCES: *Argentina*: Bergoglio, 2003b. *Bolivia*: Gamarra, 1991. *Brazil*: Junqueira, 2003. *Colombia 1970*: Merryman and Friedman, 1979; *Colombia 1990*: Giraldo Angel, 1993 (includes instructor judges who later became officials of the Public Ministry). *Colombia 1999*: Fuentes-Hernández and Amaya-Osorio, 2001. *Costa Rica 1970*: Merryman and Friedman, 1979. *Costa Rica 2000*: A. Chirinos, Director of Escuela Judicial. *Chile 1970*: Merryman and Friedman, 1979. *Chile 1995*: Vargas, Peña, and Correa, 2001. *Mexico* (Federal Justice Dept.): López-Ayllón and Fix-Fierro, 2002. *Mexico* (State Justicia): Concha-Cantú and Caballero-Juárez, 2001. *Venezuela 1971, 1997*: Consejo de la Judicatura (the figure does not include the Supreme Court, military courts, or justices of the peace). *Venezuela 2001*: Tribunal Supremo de Justicia (Aug. 15, 2001, Universal, pp. 1–4; the figure probably excludes military courts and justices of the peace).

The figures can be deceptive, since the definition of *judge* is not always straightforward. Military judges, for example, are active members of the military who work under the ministry of defense and generally are not tallied as judges. Yet their jurisdictional functions can be quite broad (Mera Figueroa, 1998). Crimes committed by the military police in Brazil, for example, are tried in military courts. These courts deal with numerous cases, including homicides, which frequently go unpunished (Holston and Caldeira, 1998). Aguirre (1998) has quantified the use of military tribunals in post-Pinochet Chile and has found the numbers to be significant.

The term *judge* is defined differently by different sources. In the case of Chile, the 1970 figure in Table 4.4 includes auxiliary judges, while the 1995 figure apparently does not. Thus it becomes not a matter of a change in the number of judges, but one of changing parameters in defining who should be counted. In the case of Venezuela, the number of judges between 1997 and 2000 appears to have jumped. Although the increase might reflect the creation of more judicial posts as part of a progressive judicial reform, more likely it reflects a new way of counting judges.

Another example involves administrative officials with jurisdictional duties. In Venezuela the greatest number of cases heard in labor courts today concerns the classification of a job dismissal as either justified or unjustified. The labor reform of 1990 eliminated the tripartite commissions that previously decided these cases and passed them on to labor judges (Pérez-Perdomo, 2003). In Colombia, however, the number of judges declined substantially between 1990 and 1999 because of the constitutional reform of 1991 and the subsequent change in criminal justice that gave quasi-jurisdictional powers to the prosecutors of the public ministry and eliminated the role of the instructing judge (Rodriguez et al., 2003).

In short, it is difficult to make generalizations concerning either judges' duties or their designation as judges, as they may be defined as judges or as officials more or less at random. The most obvious observations to be made are regarding the disparity among countries, or the disparity over time within the same country. These disparities generally are linked to the duties that judges perform in society, which vary from country to country and over time. Argentina has triple the number of judges per capita than Chile, and Costa Rica has quadruple. The central hypothesis that explains the relatively greater number of judges in Argentina, Colombia, and Costa Rica (in comparison with Brazil, Chile, Mexico, and Venezuela) is that in the first set of countries judges cover more routine duties than in countries where there are fewer judges. This is certainly true in Costa Rica, the Latin American country with the highest number of judges and judicial cases. However, that enormous number does not necessarily signify more social conflict or a greater judicialization of conflicts, but perhaps merely that traffic violations are handled by judges in that country and not in others (Mora, 2001, and personal communication). It would be erroneous to draw the conclusion that there is greater control of legality or a greater respect for individual rights in Argentina or Colombia than in Chile based on the greater number of judges in those countries.

CHANGES IN THE JUDICIAL FUNCTION

In countries with a tradition of civil law, judges played a relatively less important role in the legal system (legislators and professors were more highly valued) and in the political system than in countries with a tradition of common law (Merryman, 1985). It was often held by the nineteenth century that judicial duties were less creative than mechanical: they consisted of applying the law to the facts proven in the proceeding. This relegated judges to a secondary position in the legal system. The concept of judges as officials linked to the government likewise made them less important and less independent. This perception was still dominant in the 1970s. In that decade legislative changes were proposed regarding the credentialing of jurists (including lawyers and judges) to make them more sensitive to the needs of development. Thus a principal task became the modification of legal education, not the transformation of judges. This, too, has changed in the period analyzed in this chapter; judges have become more involved in the definition of public policies, the resolution of conflicts among private individuals, and the regulation of political conflicts (Pérez-Perdomo and Friedman, 2003). This trend is worldwide (Toharia, 2003; Tate and Vallinder, 1995; Pérez-Perdomo, 2000) and, as we will later show, can be considered part of the transformation associated with globalization. Certainly, Latin America participates in this trend.

In the tradition of most Latin American countries, political conflicts tended to be resolved either by violence or with the mediation of powerful men. The *caudillos* and dictators were very influential (typifying *personalismo politico*, or political personalism, to use Soriano de García Pelayo's term, 1996). Military men tended to fill strategic government positions during times of domestic repression. In the periods of military government, and in more than a few periods of civil government with a strong military presence, massive violations of human rights were frequent. Judges had a very limited and often shameful role. They made a concerted effort to look the other way and continued to put themselves at the service of the government—even when gross human rights violations were committed (Galín, 1984; Frühling, 1984; Pásara, 1982, 1984; González, 2001; Rodriguez et al., 2003).

Between World War II and the 1970s, most of the governments in Latin America were committed to development, at least verbally. Ideologically, this meant that certain aspects of law, especially the role of judges, were relegated to a lesser position. Issues like the defense of individual rights and concern with legality appeared almost petty in contrast with national security and national development (or the "revolution"). The Latin American political systems side-stepped the legality of governmental acts and protection of human rights, which theoretically were the domain of judges. With some very honorable exceptions, the typical judge in almost all of the countries in the region did not dare take firm action in these matters. The few that did met with serious difficulties or ceased to be judges. Pásara (1982) has defined the role of the judge as that of accomplice and victim.

Rosenn (1987) has cataloged various forms of interference into the judicial systems of Latin America. In some cases, especially as a result of a coup, as in Uruguay in 1977, judicial independence was formally eliminated. This path has been rather exceptional. A more frequent measure was to grant jurisdiction to military tribunals in politically important cases. This means was used in almost every country in Latin America, especially when there was a subversive or guerilla movement. Military dictatorships had a strong inclination to use military courts for as many crimes as possible Another frequently used tactic was massive dismissal of high court magistrates, as occurred in Argentina under Perón and the later military governments; in El Salvador in 1979; and in Peru in 1969 and 1973 under military rule, and more recently under Fujimori. A similar procedure was used in Venezuela in 1999.[21] Another method was the increase or reduction in the number of magistrates, as occurred successively under the Brazilian military governments and in Venezuela in 2004. Rico and Salas (1990) identify similar conduct in the Central American countries.

The most common way to control judges politically was to make the system a vertical hierarchy, with great power at the top, whether in the Supreme Court or a judicial council (Zaffaroni, 1995: 119ss). Control had to be secure at the top, which was not especially difficult, given the political instability and frequent purging of the high ranks of the judiciary. In the case of Venezuela, administration of the system was in the hands of the Judicial Council, a body that was completely controlled by the main political parties and used for shameless clientist purposes (Pérez-Perdomo, 2003). From 1999 onward this control has passed to the Supreme Court. Thus the frequent call in all of Latin America has been for judicial independence—that is, the liberation of judges from improper pressure from the executive branch or the political parties, and even from the Supreme Court judges themselves.

Beyond the lack of independence, the main characteristic of the judicial system was its marginality. Thus in business matters, the policies of intervention and state protection reduced the number of competing enterprises and tied them to the government. This meant that in any case of conflict with the state, or between businesses, resolution of the conflict was in the hands of figures with political power (Pérez-Perdomo, 1991). And as the government could decisively influence any legal decision, recourse to the judicial system was relatively useless. It is interesting that the discussion about law and development in the 1970s did not turn its attention to judges.

Rosenn (1987) sees the lack of independence and the marginality of Latin American judges as a feature rooted in Latin American legal culture, going back to Iberian colonization and associated with the civil law tradition. On the contrary, this work maintains that such features are associated with political and economic structures that are by no means permanent. Changes in economic policy and democratization not only have given rise to new actors but also have diminished the power of the government and political parties in most countries. In countries where this has occurred, businesspeople have liberated themselves from government protection and judges have become more independent. This is a general tendency, with some exceptions (Hammergren, 1998, 1999). In some countries democratization produced a greater concentration of power in a person or group, as was true of Peru under Alberto Fujimori,[22] Argentina under Carlos Menem (Garrido, 1993), or Venezuela first under the parties and later under Hugo Chávez (Quintero, 1983, 1988; Pérez-Perdomo, 2004). In these cases, control over judges was an explicit job that these populist governments assumed. Not to be overlooked is the praiseworthy performance of the Constitutional Court of Colombia or the Supreme Court of Justice of Venezuela in the 1990s. The federal judiciaries of Mexico and Brazil also have acted with independence and have decided cases of enormous political and economic importance (Rodríguez et al., 2003; Pérez-Perdomo, 2003; Junqueira, 2003; López-Ayllón and Fix-Fierro, 2003). That affirmation of the principles of law often took place in situations of great political and social turbulence. To invoke the civil law tradition or the Hispanic character is a weak argument, as the cases of Spain and Italy themselves make clear (Clark, 2003; Cassesse, 2003; Toharia, 2003).

The abandonment of the policies of economic intervention has limited the power of political leaders and has caused new economic actors to emerge, including foreign investors. Naturally, this increases the possibility of conflict among the new players and simultaneously diminishes the ability of politicians to act as regulators of conflicts. This creates a heightened role for judges, although in practice there has been no explosion of business litigation or anything like it (Pérez-Perdomo, 1996b).

The massive human rights violations in the past, and democratization during the period that we analyze, have given rise to a felt need for more independent judges to protect the human rights of the population and to effectively control the legality of governmental acts (Correa Sutil, 1993). There is also the problem of "transitional justice"—that is, what to do with massive violators of human rights when democracy is reestablished. The fact that many countries have decided to use judges to punish the leaders of those sinister regimes has increased the prestige and importance of judges and legal proceedings. This has been especially true in Chile and Argentina, where the worst abuses by military governments took place (Correa Sutil, 1997; Acuña and Smulovitz, 1997; Nino, 1996).

Democratization, accompanied by a more active press and greater political conflict, has meant that more cases of corruption come to light and that corruption is used as a powerful political argument. Corruption scandals have facilitated the use of judges to decide the fate of high-ranking political figures—leading presidents, ministers, and other high officials in Brazil, Colombia, Ecuador, Mexico, Peru, and Venezuela to be implicated in legal cases (Pérez-Perdomo, 1996a). Several have lost their posts as a result, and some have spent time in prison. The most severe punishment is the scandal itself and the ruin of more than a few political careers.

These political and economic changes have produced a true juridification and judicialization of Latin American societies.[23] The trend is for political and economic conflicts to lead to lawsuits and disputes over legality. This does not necessarily mean that the judicial decisions really solve the conflicts, but that they are important elements in negotiation strategies (Fix-Fierro and López-Ayllón, 2001; Pérez-Perdomo, 2003).

Legal professionals now have attained the social and political importance that the jurists of the 1960s and 1970s feared they were losing. Very significant changes are in progress. That law should serve as an instrument of development is no longer a central necessity; what is desired now is that law should provide legal certainty for businesses and investors, and better protection of human rights. Naturally, the protection of property rights and respect for contracts is what interests businesspeople and investors most, while other social actors give more weight to other rights. Reform projects are no longer called "law and development" but are instead referred to as modernization projects or efforts to strengthen the rule of law. These especially concentrate on judges and the judicial system. Critics of the projects generally complain that not enough importance is given to the emancipating elements of reform (Santos, 1999). There is greater awareness that respect for human rights and access to justice must be taken into consideration in the process of reform. Thus the "law and development" programs and the "rule of law" programs—certainly not totally congruent, have become topics of debate. However, there are those who do affirm the congruence and continuity of these two movements (Rodríguez, 2001).[24]

In this age of globalization there is a dominant perception of the importance of judges, that judges are indispensable umpires in a functioning market economy and a democratic society. Simultaneously, the perception exists that mortal judges cannot live up to the high performance expected of them. These figures, forgotten for so long, are perceived as largely unqualified, too obedient to the government, with a tendency toward corruption, with little ability to do justice efficiently as a public servant (Zaffaroni, 1995; Garrido, 1993; Soberanes Fernández, 1993; Zolezzi Ibárcena, 1993; Pérez-Perdomo, 1996b). Hence, there is great pressure to reform the judiciary, to establish good programs to train judges, to sensitize judges to the problems of human rights and the needs of the population, to turn the courts into efficient organizations, and to make judges more independent and impartial. Evaluation of judges and of judicial activity is another central theme of reform. In short, the topic of judicial reform has moved onto the political agendas of every Latin American country. Multilateral organizations such as the World Bank, the Inter-American Development Bank, the U.N. Development Program, and several foundations have understood the importance of the judiciary and have financed reform projects.[25] The judicial reform movement has reached the point where judges have created their own international organizations, such as the Iberoamerican Association of Supreme Courts, which have institutionalized annual meetings and common projects. There is also an international association of democratic judges.

The task of reforming the judicial systems has turned out to be overwhelming. No country in the region is considered to have found a suitable formula, much less to have a completely desirable judicial system. Even in Costa Rica, the country that has most consistently invested abundant resources in the system for the longest time (Rivera-Cira, 1993), the matter of judicial reform is still seen as a continuous process that has barely begun (Mora, 2001).

In practice, judges have become more valuable politically. European judges from countries culturally very close to Latin America have contributed to this change. The actions of the Italian judges and prosecutors who started the operation *mani pulite* (or the "robed revolution," as it was called), or the Spanish judges who caused the downfall of the socialist government and the crisis of that party, have been followed very closely by Latin American judges. Antonio Di Pietro and Baltazar Garzón, among others, frequently have been invited to speak in Latin American countries about their experiences.

This stage of globalization marks a new era of reform enthusiasm and of attention to the law. The subject raised is not how to make the law an instrument of development, as in the "law and development" stage. The modernization that is spoken of today focuses on how to strengthen the power of judges and at the same time make them more responsible for the operation of a true rule of law; how to make them protectors of human rights and at the same time protectors of property and business security; how to make justice more accessible and more efficient.

For purposes of this work, the important thing is to emphasize that the judiciary is in the process of consolidating itself as a separate career, following the European model. Training is one instrument of professionalization—specific training that will qualify judges to exercise their functions. The investment made by the state makes sense only if it is anticipated that the judge will stay in the judiciary for a long time. The schools for judges can have many social functions (Binder, 2001), but especially in establishing the judgeship as a distinct career or profession. At about the same time that judges had acquired more political power and more independence, the occupation of judge began to earn the prestige never previously enjoyed. Efforts to consolidate it as a career include giving judges the training, the job stability, and the certainty of promotion that will make the occupation attractive to good lawyers. Naturally, this is merely a trend. Not all of the judicial schools in the region are fulfilling the function that is expected of them, nor are the judicial careers and judgeships as a profession consolidated in all of the countries of Latin America.[26]

Awareness of the political importance of judges explains why more attention is being paid to their education than to legal education in general. There has been a definite neglect of the latter, probably out of confidence in market forces to differentiate among good law schools that will train business lawyers, judges, and academics; and other schools that will train the rest of the lawyers, including the taxi driver–lawyers or the lawyers who are minor officials.

The Professions and Globalization

Social change does not affect all people and institutions equally. Some people become agents of change, and others are affected in a more or less passive way. For example, modernization at the beginning of the twentieth century turned some small industrialists into large enterprises, while in the case of muleteers, they were replaced by other methods of transportation altogether.

In the beginning of the period that we examined, elite lawyers worried that other professionals—economists, planners, and engineers—were replacing them in their traditional positions of political power. There was also a perception that businesses employed few lawyers and that business lawyers were subordinate to the businessmen and professionals more directly involved in the planning and operation of corporations. Litigious activity, which was considered the preeminent field of lawyers, lacked the capacity to absorb the great number of graduates. What conclusions can we reach, after our analysis of the occupation of lawyers and judges? This is the topic of this final section.

First, we look at the globalized or globalizing portion of the legal profession. The most obvious examples are the large international firms of business lawyers. Most firms originate in the United States, with branches or partner firms in many countries. "In the early 1990s, U.S. firms had more that 18,000 'affiliates overseas'; German firms had even more" (Friedman, 2001: 354). These firms are true legal transnationals (Armitage, 1990; Trubek et al., 1994; Dezalay, 1992; Flood, 1996). The lawyers of these firms have a common language and individually often speak one or more foreign languages. Even more to the point, they have common professional and legal cultures. Their communication is not hindered by legal or national cultural differences, and the common culture is not restricted to lawyers in international firms; lawyers for the multinational corporations also share the same fundamental traits (Pérez-Perdomo, 2001).

This is more than a trend toward the worldwide Americanization of legal culture. Internationalization also created challenges for U.S. lawyers and established a clear distinction between international and purely domestic lawyers. Some U.S. publications address the interests of these American international lawyers as well as practical aspects of negotiation in different cultures, the use and significance of time in different countries, and the rules of courtesy that should be followed (Sunwolf, 1997). Lawyers in the United States and Canada are worried by the growth of multidisciplinary firms, mostly controlled by business consultants, that have extended their reach very quickly in Europe (Paton, 2002).

The globalized culture sometimes resembles a club, as is true of international arbitration (Dezalay and Garth, 1996). It can undergo changes and its actors can change, but global culture itself continues to thrive. In Latin America there are other clublike manifestations of globalization, such as the panels formed as a result of the free trade agreement (NAFTA) between the United States, Canada, and Mexico (López-Ayllón and Fix-Fierro, 1999). The purpose of the panels composed of jurists from different legal cultures is the resolution of commercial disputes. Since their inception, these panels became institutions that transformed legal cultures, especially the Mexican one.

Among international organizations, such as the World Trade Organization, the strong presence of lawyers has displaced the diplomatic culture in favor of a more law-oriented one (Weiler, 2001). At the World Bank the Legal Vice-Presidency has grown in size and in stature.

The international courts are another example of the creation of globalized spaces. In Latin America the Inter-American Court of Human Rights has become a supranational instance for cases involving human rights and is central to the transformation in legal culture that emphasizes human rights.

Several legal occupations have been internationalized. Apart from business lawyers, an influential group of law scholars can be included; they generally know several legal cultures and languages and have frequent contacts among themselves. Human rights lawyers also have frequent international meetings and communicate often with each other. Thus globalization involves many different groups, with very different predominant ideologies, and with relatively little contact among the groups. Their common characteristic is that they possess high professional prestige and the ability to influence public policies by means of their professional tools.

Our analysis is not equated to an assertion that all conflict resolution and regulatory institutions in the international or global sphere are necessarily related to the law. Gessner (1998) and Appelbaum et al. (2001) identify various cases in which globalized institutions have chosen to avoid the use of law and lawyers. The opposition between the option of juridification and what is generally called relational capitalism should not be exaggerated (Dezalay and Garth, 1997), but as we will later see, globalization seems to be tuned more to juridification.

Related to globalization is the multiplication of legal relations that cross national boundaries. Not only is this a matter of contracts involving parties of different nationalities, but it also includes transactions that can produce effects in countries different from those of the parties' nationalities. In personal relations as well, national borders seem to mean less in this age. For example, it is not unusual for a Mexican to marry a Brazilian and for the couple to settle in the United States, where they have children. Matrimonial conflict can arise in one country and involve investments in a fourth or fifth country. Private international law, which is the formal way of resolving this type of conflict, may turn out to be completely inappropriate: the parties could be completely surprised by the application of an unexpected legal rule; judges and lawyers, who would find themselves compelled to work with foreign laws, would not feel comfortable either. Hence, when the situation is foreseeable, lawyers seek to define in advance the applicable law and the way in which conflicts will be resolved. In the same way, electronic commerce can involve parties located in distant countries, with the property subject to negotiation located in a third place and delivered in a fourth country. It is not easy to determine who should pay taxes to whom or, if a conflict arises, what the appropriate court and laws might be.

The study of how the parties or courts handle these types of conflict, or how those who do business look for legal certainty in a context like the ones described, is a challenge for researchers who study transnational legal activity. Gessner (1996, 1998) has found that legal institutions and most lawyers are poorly equipped to handle these matters and that the tendency everywhere is to apply national law. National laws and states have thus shown themselves to be much more resistant to the onslaught of globalization than is generally supposed. This fact can be read two ways: descriptively, it testifies to the lasting importance of states and national legal systems; normatively, it suggests the necessity of a stronger international order that can provide legal certainty in times of globalization. Likewise, a greater sensitivity seems necessary on the part of legal professionals to relations that cross national borders. Globalized institutions and personnel will surely only intensify.

Pérez-Perdomo (2001) found that even in the case of international businesses, the weight of *lex mercatoria* (supranational law) is small; rather, in contracts, a national law is selected—not necessarily that of either one of the parties; lawyers choose a mutually convenient law, whether it be English maritime law, Delaware corporation rules, or the financial law of New York. International arbitration bodies also may be selected to decide future cases. This produces a division between the lawyers who know only one law and legal culture, and those who have a broader knowledge. In short, perhaps globalization will not bring about a transnational culture but rather a greater interaction of national laws and cultures.

The burgeoning of relations among people with greater geographic mobility and of different nationalities and cultures has another dimension as well. People who do not belong to the same community constantly enter into business relations. Less and less common are the ethnically homogeneous communities, connected to the same small towns (Landa, 1994), which can provide the mechanisms for social control and predictable behavior. Communities that share the same religious culture, like the diamond merchants (according to Bernstein, 1992), also become less able to function in a more globalized world on an informal basis. This means that law—and above all, lawyers and contracts—become first-string players (Pérez-Perdomo, 1993). Without a doubt, the visible increase in the market for legal services is a function of modern times.

This assertion is not a prediction that the law will permeate every sphere of business and life. In minor transactions, especially since the rise of electronic commerce, confidence has to be reestablished, giving new roles to existing institutions: the "charge back" mechanism used by credit card companies is an example.[27] This avoids juridification that would be excessively complicated and too costly for that type of case (Pichler, 2000).

Friedman (1985, 1999) has emphasized the importance of globalization's impact on the law. He has examined how our age of intense communication has spread values and attitudes that have caused the vertical mechanisms of social control to lose force. The family and other authorities that used to be perceived as natural socialization checks and balances already lack their former strength. We think of ourselves more than ever as individuals who have rights and the liberty to make choices. The legitimacy of authority, including that of professionals and experts, is questioned. Hence, there is an increase in legal actions against various state agencies and in lawsuits over professional malpractice. This more horizontal society is one that aspires to total justice (Friedman, 1999, 1985). We have, therefore, a culture of the complaint (see also García de la Cruz Herrero, 1999) and thus a greater use of lawyers and courts. The enormous increase in lawyers that we have seen in Latin America derives not only from the spread of higher education but also from a societal transformation that requires more lawyers, more efficient courts, and more willingness to seek remedies for various wrongs.

In this way, globalization affects not only those who enter into international interactions but also people whose relations are entirely domestic and confined to a single national space, yet who are exposed to new values through the media. The increase in the number of lawyers cannot be explained solely by a rise in the number of people who receive a higher education; it also reflects the social desirability of a profession that helps us demand our rights and to arrange social relations in accordance with the law.

After a few decades of "national development" efforts—that is, of state interventionism—the project was abandoned during the 1980s or early 1990s. Economic liberalization and the opening up of markets (an important aspect of globalization) have erased many of the perceptions of the 1970s. One effect of liberalization is the greater ease of creating new universities. The creation of programs in legal studies was an irresistible temptation, as traditional teaching methods made them very cheap. In fact, a classroom, a blackboard, and a few lawyers ready to lecture a few times a week were enough to establish a law school. As a result, university promoters could make a quick profit off such courses. The negative aspect of the expansion does not require further analysis: the exponential increase in lawyers and the deterioration of the quality of education in many universities are quite evident. On the positive side, it is important to note that competition between schools causes those universities interested in attracting the best students to make an effort to diversify their offerings. The substantial effort to modernize legal education—which occurred mainly in private universities—and the growth in postgraduate studies also should be noted on the positive side of this balance.

In the present climate of the legal profession, the main preoccupations of the past (including the recent past) have lost much of their force. The demand for legal services has expanded in such a way that now a huge number of lawyers have sufficient work. Perhaps lawyers no longer run the state, as they used to. However, the dividing up of knowledge means that many different kinds of professionals can aspire to run those areas of state operation that best match their training. But the growing importance of the judicial sphere as a forum for debate about the most pressing political and economic problems means that lawyers and judges have a great task ahead of them in carrying out their specific functions. People with far-reaching responsibilities should be able to rely on a lawyer's good advice to ensure that their actions will be able to withstand the challenge of lawsuits and media scandals.

Nevertheless, globalization has not been without problems for the legal profession. In the first place, the image of the lawyer as a liberal professional offering services to a wide array of clients no longer reflects reality. Most lawyers work in organizations—that is, they work for other lawyers or are employees of businesses or public organizations. In an age of technological advances and the accumulation of financial power, these organizations can do enormous damage to the community or can find themselves implicated in scandals that destroy them. The role of lawyers in these organizations is a subject that should be given the most serious consideration. Legal professionals, today more than ever, must stand up and notice issues of ethics and professional responsibility.

Another matter of concern is the stratification of law schools. As Lomnitz and Salazar (2002) have observed, in this new age the role that social mobility had in the recent past has weakened. Young people from separate social groups now go to different law schools, and likewise the graduates have different job opportunities. The coveted market for business lawyers is reserved for the children of the elite (who also control the businesses) and talented young people from the middle class. Mobility now takes place within a much more reduced space. Everyone else has a lower-quality legal education and a much less desirable job market. For them, law schools really turn out to be "dream factories," to use Junqueira's (1999) metaphor. The quality of legal education has an impact that extends beyond the professionals themselves. A system of legal education with a bottom layer of poor schools especially affects people with fewer resources, who will receive the worst-quality legal services, and as a result, access to justice will be most difficult for them. The systems could exploit the most destitute. The deepening poverty of one sector of the population, which we see associated with globalization, is not merely an economic problem.

For those who work with the education of professionals, the scene is changing—as it is for the judges and lawyers themselves. Without a doubt, legal education is more demanding with respect to the social and professional responsibility of lawyers, judges, and scholars. At least, this is the case if we think that legal professionals have something to do with justice and with the fairer functioning of society.

REFERENCE MATTER

Notes

CHAPTER 1

1. These dates are not entirely fixed. Schulz (1946) distinguishes the following periods: Archaic, Hellenistic, classical, and bureaucratic. In this work we include the Hellenistic in the classical period, but within it we distinguish the republican and the imperial eras.

2. Publius Mucius Scaevola (died around 115 B.C.) is considered one of the first jurisconsults. He himself was a *pontifex maximus* in 130 B.C. Pontifices traditionally formulated opinions but only communicated them upon request (D'Ippolito, 1986). Later jurisconsults were not necessarily pontifices and began to publish their opinions.

3. Today we use the word *rhetoric* predominantly as an adjective, and it carries pejorative connotations referring to empty and embellished discourse. Its meaning in ancient thinking could not be more different; it signified the art of reasoning with rigor in the matters up for discussion (Aristotle, *Rhetoric*, sec. 1354; Perelman, 1953).

4. Quintus Mucius Scaevola (son of Publius Mucius Scaevola and also *pontifex maximus* like his father, and later consul in 95 B.C.) was the first jurist to order the law according to genre (*Digest*, 1.2.2.41); that is, he clearly applied the Greek model to the elaboration of law (Stein, 1966: 36).

CHAPTER 2

1. An *escribano* is "the official or public secretary assigned to record the trial and to authorize the writings of the acts and contracts that are executed between individuals" (Escriche, 1837: 211). Clerks obtained their positions through appointment by the king or through provisional appointment by viceroy, governor, or local council. The fact that the post was able to be purchased explains the king's interest in controlling the appointments, as it was a source of royal income. Two types of clerks prevailed: those *of the chamber*, civil servants for a governmental body who certified the acts that came out of that agency; and *public*, equivalent to today's notaries.

The number of escribanos was considerable, but there are no comprehensive studies quantifying their presence in the colonies. Luján Muñoz (1982: 213–20) lists two hundred clerks for the colonial period in Guatemala City alone.

2. The book was a best seller in the sixteenth century, first published in 1563 and reissued in 1566 and 1587 (Madrid, National Library, Catalog of pre-1830 works).

3. *Procuradores* had elementary legal training and were officially recognized by a court. *Tinterillos* practiced law without any formal training or official recognition.

4. It is fitting to cite the words of the *Ordenamiento de Alcalá* (28, 1) (1348): "Et porque al Rey pertenesce, è ha poder de facer fueros, è leys, è de la interpretar, è declarar . . . tenemos por bien que si . . . fuere menester interpretacion, ò declaracion, ò enmmendar, ò annadir, ò tirar, ò mudar, que Nos lo fagamos. Et si alguna contrariedad apesciere en la leys sobredichas entre si mesmas . . . que nos que seamos requeridos sobrello." However, the same text orders that the ancient scholars be read in general studies: "porque en ellos hay mucha sabiduria, è queremos dar logar que nuestros naturales sean sabidores, è sean por ende mas onrrados."

5. A search in the Collective Catalog of the Spanish Patrimonial Bibliography; National Library of Madrid; Library of Congress–Washington, D.C.; and British Library–London revealed editions from 1681, 1754–56, 1774, and 1791. The lack of editions for certain years was not accidental. In 1748, for example, the compilation was commonly considered to have many unapplied or inapplicable rules and was therefore not reedited that year (Tau Anzoátegui, 1992: 189). However, it was reissued, without changes, six years later. It is noteworthy that the work seems to have raised interest only in the latter 1700s, when royal legislation was reevaluated as a consequence of the Enlightenment. Some private collections were printed prior to 1681 (Manzano, 1950–56), and some later compilations of the legislation appeared—such as that of the erudite Antonio Pérez y López (1791–98).

6. Polanco Alcántara bases this on the distinguished careers and intellectual production of a number of ministers from the American *audiencias*, but he does not consider the bibliography that examines a visit to some *audiencias* or one that shows the abusive conduct of several ministers (see Albornoz de López, 1987; Puente Brunke, 1997).

7. *Alcalde* comes from the Arabic *al cadí*, or judge. The terminology in the provinces presents some difficulties, but it is not necessary to examine them here (García-Gallo, 1972: 695ss).

8. The University of Mexico began operations in 1553, the University of Santo Domingo probably in 1558, and the University of San Marcos in 1576 (Lanning, 1940: 14–21).

9. In contrast, abandoned sons were acceptable. This was because it was thought that only honorable parents abandoned their children for reasons of honor. Such was the case of the abandoned José Felix Blanco, to whom the staff of the University of Caracas refused to grant the degrees of bachelor of philosophy and doctor of law, canonical law, and theology in 1809. A royal order was necessary, reminding the staff of the rule that the abandoned should be allowed degrees as long as they are not certain of their true parents (Pérez-Perdomo, 1981: 97).

10. The text is not clear about whether the opposition was to *pardos'* obtaining university degrees in law, or to their becoming lawyers (granted by the *audiencia*), or both.

11. Uribe-Uran (2000: 115) has different figures for New Granada (Colombia). In a chart of law graduates in 1790–1850, he noted 61 graduates from 1790 to 1806—approximately a quarter of Silva's (1992) figure, already cited. My impression is that he confused the number of law graduates with the number of lawyers, which were two very different things in the colonial period.

12. Vinnius (1586–1657) was a representative of what is called humanist jurisprudence. His edition of *Institutes* was originally published in 1618, and numerous editions appeared in the seventeenth and eighteenth centuries. Arnaud (1969: 319) notes that Vinnius "represents a first stage in the process of the transformation of law . . . it was frequently through the reading of his works that the French jurists were introduced to the modern natural law." Since 1726 "el Vinnio," as it was called, generally contained a preface and commentaries by Heineccius, an integral member of the school of natural law and of peoples. The work was required reading in courses on Roman law in all universities under the Spanish crown from 1771 on. Tau Anzoátegui (1992) considers this book to be key in the transition between traditional casuist teaching and modern, systematic teaching in Spain and Latin America.

13. "La Constitución no impone sino la obligación de explicar en esta cátedra los cuatro libros de la Instituta de Justiniano desde las tres hasta las cuatro de la tarde; pero como aquí no hay otra jurisprudencia civil, es necesario ampliar las lecciones sobre todas aquellas materias propias de las catedráticos de Prima y Vísperas para enseñanza del derecho de los romanos, con las luces que prestan los comentarios de Arnoldo Vinnius y Antonio Pérez. Esta fue la conducta que observaba en la regencia de la expresada cátedra mi maestro y antecesor el difunto doctor Juan Francisco Zárate, haciendo por sí solo lo que hacen tres en otras universidades bien surtidas y dotadas: y no contento con la exposición de las Pandectas, Instituto y Código, sin faltar al estatuto y asignación de la cátedra, dictaba y explicaba el derecho real de España e Indias, añadiendo las leyes patrias pertenecientes al título, materia o parágrafo de la lectura diaria, tanto las concordantes como las contrarias, modificativas o derogatorias. Por consecuencia de esto, en los actos literarios o disputas públicas proponía siempre entre los puntos de Instituta un título de las Partidas: y de este modo, con la única investidura de Catedrático de Instituta lo era también, verdaderamente hablando, de Prima, Víspera y Derecho Práctico, enseñando con frecuencia por vía de ilustración necesaria para unos vasallos que no debían ser gobernados ni juzgados por otras leyes que las españolas, casi todas aquellas de que no se halla noticia alguna de los Digestos y Códigos del Imperio Romano. Yo he seguido constantemente las huellas de mi preceptor desde el día 9 de febrero de 1798 en que, por fallecimiento suyo, el Venerable Claustro me hizo el honor de confiarme en propiedad esta Cátedra de Instituta; cuyas relaciones con otras artes y ciencias exigen muchas veces su tratado y doctrina en cuanto a conducentes al mejor conocimiento y auxilio de las cuestiones civiles."

14. *Siete Partidas*, part III, heading 6, law 3, explains the reasons: First, because it is not honest nor appropriate ("*guisado*") that a woman take a man's position, mixing herself up with men in order to reason for others. The second is a historical explanation, citing a "wise" and "shameless" woman named Calfurnia in the days of antiquity and contending that when women lose their shame "it is a hard thing to listen to them, and to contend with them." Thus historically, women have been punished by being prohibited from practicing law.

15. This image of lawyers in this first stage of the colonial period can be appreciated in the pointed epitaph that appeared on the tomb of Antonio de las Peñas, who died in 1569 while dining at the home of a judge (cited in González Echenique, 1954: 322): "Aquí yace un famoso licenciado, primero que hubo en Chile, y por más

señas/ a honra tuvo el ser desnarigado y llamarse Antonio de las Peñas./ Aunque nunca sirvió como letrado, en cambio, desque algún embrollo vido, dejando los escrúpulos de lado/ trató con maña de sacar partido. Murió como es ya guisa de abogados/ y como mueren otros con frecuencia/ con la bolsa y el vientre bien hartados/ y a la vez muy gravada la conciencia."

16. The number of lawyers and law graduates seems to have declined in Spain during the 1600s and early 1700s. The available data are indirect and derive from the law schools themselves: Salamanca experienced a continuous decline in enrollment from 1640 on. In Valladolid the number of law students decreased by 70 percent over the course of the century (Navas, 1996: 17).

17. In 1819 the Lima bar had 120 members, of which 40 were originally from Arequipa and 40 resided in Arequipa (Ramos Núñez, 1993: 30).

18. Note that this figure is out of proportion with the rest of the colonies. The source is a report by the governor of Cuba, not from the *audiencia*; thus we question its exactness.

19. Montevideo had four lawyers in 1791 (Ferrés, 1944: 291), who surely are included in the figure cited by Levene.

20. According to the report of the councilmen, there were four lawyers in San Juan in addition to the lieutenant governor. More than fourteen graduates were also still doing their apprenticeships (Delgado Cintrón, 1970: 8).

21. In 1789 the Spanish king prohibited (with some exceptions) the admission to law school of natives or neighbors of the island of Cuba as lawyers, but he ordered to "be admitted . . . those who studied in the universities of Spain and practiced in their reputable superior tribunals . . . having practiced for six years" (cited in Del Arenal Fenochio, 1980: 541). Note that the prohibition was not absolute and that there was a clear discrimination against the American universities.

22. The concern did not exist solely with respect to the colonies. In eighteenth-century Spain various works were published criticizing the "crowd" ("*muchedumbre*") of lawyers and their poor preparation, considered one of the most ruinous and destructive plagues of any republic (see Del Arenal Fenochio, 1980). In 1794 a royal order set the number of lawyers who could practice in Madrid at two hundred (Del Arenal Fenochio, 1980: 535; Levene, 1959: 10). The basic complaint was that lawyers caused the number of lawsuits to multiply and it was thus preferable to direct youth toward more useful occupations.

23. This explanation derives from personal experience: in an informal conversation, a Stanford hospital traumatologist insisted that riding a bicycle on campus was very dangerous because the hospital had received numerous badly injured cyclists. I found it difficult to accept his assertion not only because of my own experience as a cyclist but also because I knew very few cases of people who had been injured.

24. Carlos Aguirre comments on the frequently negative portrait of the *tinterillos* as depicted by lawyers and other elites. In this portrait, the *tinterillo* "is always a man, racially or culturally mestizo, literate, knowledgeable (or at least pretending to be so) in legal affairs although without formal legal training. He is totally unscrupulous, a real master of legal trickeries who almost always responds to his own personal greed" (2001: 3). Aguirre indicates that the real figure must have been less negative and must have responded to a real social need because the profession persisted into the

twentieth century. The perception that *tinterillos* exploited the poor may have resulted from the fact that they in fact charged their clients, contrary to the prevailing moral obligation of lawyers to represent the poor for free. It was incongruous that a poor person or a person of relatively low social status would have to pay a lawyer, someone of high social status, for his services. On the other hand, it was socially acceptable for the *tinterillo* to charge for his services.

25. We take as an example Tomás Hernández de Sanabria (1752–1838), the son of a captain who arrived in Venezuela in 1720. Sanabria graduated from the University of Caracas with a bachelor's degree in canons (1776), master's degree in arts, doctorate in philosophy and one in civil law (1778). He was received as a lawyer in Santo Domingo in 1781. "Without desire for profit he served the powerful and also humble and simple people, among them many small farmers" of the Tuy region, where he had two pieces of land (Parra Márquez, 1973: 7). He was a professor at the university in Latin, arts, and eloquence; head of the bar association in 1793–94; and Rector of the university in 1794–95 and 1809–11. He was prosecutor of the Ecclesiastical Tribunal, defender of the Capuchin Missions, consultant of the Santo Oficio of the Inquisition, and prosecutor of the Corps of Artillery and Engineers. Juan Lovera, renowned painter of the period, painted a portrait in which Hernández de Sanabria, dressed very richly and exuding satisfaction, appears with his son, also a lawyer. Without doubt, the multiple positions to which he was named provided him with income and honor. Hernández de Sanabria aspired to being granted a title of nobility by the king (Parra Márquez, 1973).

26. The title of "lawyer before the Royal Councils" also was granted. This title permitted a lawyer to exercise the profession in other jurisdictions, but it required membership in the local bar association if one existed.

27. Roscio presented long writings before the bar and the *audiencia* of Caracas in which he argued that the legislation and traditional politics of Spain had been to accept the equality of indigenous people, and criticized those who supported the idea of inequality through birth. His thesis, clearly influenced by Enlightenment philosophy and the exhibition of an erudite knowledge of Spanish and *Indiano* law, deeply irritated the authorities of the bar, and the dispute took on a sour personal dimension.

28. Gil also explains the circumstances of how the dishonorable conduct came to pass. He indicates that he had preferential treatment along with the other whites invited to the wedding, and he explains that he began to play cards with the whites, but little by little mulattos took their places. He also alleges his previous faultless conduct. This defense reveals that Gil shared the social norm or considered it counterproductive to attack it.

29. Although lawyers were obligated to defend Indians and the poor for free, in practice they did not desire such clients. Thus the bar association of Caracas designated a defense attorney for these clients, who would be released from the other duties of lawyers (Parra Márquez, 1952). One hundred pesos covered approximately the basic, annual, per capita costs of a person in the province of Cumaná or in Caracas (McKinley, 1993: 40ss). Note that law graduates and lawyers often served in positions without remuneration or as pro bono advisors to town councils or other organizations, in the interest of "making merits" for a remunerated position later.

30. In 1809 the criollo lawyer Ignacio Herrera y Vergara (Sindico Procurador General of the city council of Bogotá and later member of the *Junta Suprema*) complained that many young recent graduates of Salamanca and Alcalá, who had no knowledge of *Indiano* law, were appointed as judges in the colonies, despite the fact that the legislation required at least ten years of practical experience. In contrast, the lawyers born in Spanish America, despite their experience and merits, were rarely appointed (quoted in Uribe-Uran, 2000: 52–53). Navas (1996: 152) points out that it was not easy to find lawyers with merit to fill positions in the Indies. With respect to the reproachable conduct of the judges in Caracas, see Albornoz de López (1987). With respect to the lack of preparation and experience among judges in Quito (although in a period far from independence), see Herzog (1995: 40ss).

31. The original reads: "Sereis vosotros mismos menos victoriosos en vuestras defensas que lo han sido los inmortales abogados de Buenos Ayres, Santa Fé, Quito, Chile, Caracas y Cartagena, que ya ganaron el reñido pleyto de la libertad de aquellos países?" (*Diario Secreto de Lima* [periodical manuscript] no. 3, Feb. 6, 1811, cited in Chassin, 1998: 255).

32. "Dos fueron señaladamente las clases que comunicaron a la infeliz América esos tenebrosos rayos de luz . . . La primera fue la de los doctores en leyes, o abogados, quienes en retribución a los mayores beneficios de que eran deudores a la paternal solicitud del Monarca español por haberles proporcionado universidades y maestros para seguir la noble carrera de la toga, fueron los primeros en sellar su negra ingratitud maquinando los planes de subversión, creando juntas populares, redactando constituciones, manejando los actos legislativos y judiciales, y convirtiendo en daño de su propio país las luces y conocimientos que se les habían comunicado para afianzar la justicia, conducir al pueblo por el camino de la obediencia y subordinación, consolidar el orden, y fomentar la prosperidad pública." The other class referred to by Torrente was the youth.

33. The maps of García-Gallo (1997: 243) are particularly useful as schemes.

34. The ecclesiastics voted 18–6, the military 49–11, and the businessmen 25–22 (Levene, 1959, note 8).

35. Domínguez's (1980: 192) description of the typical rebel leader is a sort of spoken portrait of lawyers: "The typical Mexican rebel leader was a white, middle-aged male, born in America, with fairly substantial education. He was likely to have access to junior appointments in the civil, military, or ecclesiastical bureaucracies."

36. For a general look at the independence process in Chile that has been especially useful for our analysis of the independence process, see Jocelyn-Holt Letelier (1999).

37. I am grateful to José Antonio Caballero for his guidance in understanding Mexican independence. A work that has followed in the matter is Rodríguez (1989).

CHAPTER 3

1. Botana (1994) attempts an evolutionary typology of nineteenth-century constitutions. His work is very suggestive, but the diversity of constitutions and the pitfalls in his typology suggest a more cautious approach.

2. For the constitutional texts and principal political documents of these periods, see Tena Ramírez (1999).

3. For the economic and social history, see Liévano Aguirre (1972). The constitutional texts are found in Restrepo Piedrahita (1995). On the legal history of Colombia, see Aguilera (1965).

4. For the constitutional texts with a preliminary study, see Brewer Carías (1985).

5. Soriano de García Pelayo (1996, 2000) and her disciples have analyzed in detail the relationship between personalist leaders and constitutions and codes (for example, Serrada, 2000; Guardia, 2000).

6. Toro's (1845) comments on Venezuela's Freedom of Contract Law of 1834 is one of the classics of legal-political-economic thought from the first half of the nineteenth century.

7. The restrictions on property are the *retroventa* (sell back), the *retracto* (repurchase option), and the *rescisión por lesión* (nullification due to insurmountable differences regarding just price). Our analysis is based on the text of the 1836 Civil Code of the North Peruvian State, due to the impossibility of obtaining the original 1831 Bolivian text. A detailed commentary may be found in Ramos Núñez (2001).

8. Andrés Bello (Caracas 1781–Santiago 1865) is known as a great literary man and grammarian. His Spanish grammar branded an age in the history of this discipline. In addition to the celebrated civil code, he wrote didactic books on Roman and international law (Hanisch Espíndola, 1982; Pérez-Perdomo, 1982).

9. The law that abolished the entailment was very controversial, and Bello, who participated in the special commissions that drafted the special legislation, had many doubts. The law was approved in 1857 (Mobarec Asfura, 1982).

10. The doctrinal books did not mention slavery either (González, 1981: 47), although Justinian's *Institutes* from which the expository plan was taken did speak of slaves when dealing with the same material. In practice, the theme of slavery was controversial and each country had its own, particular regulation for the matter.

11. Teixeira de Freitas's *Consolidação* has the structure and style of a modern code, with short articles and length similar to that of other civil codes. We doubt that it is in fact a consolidation, in the sense that the legal rules of colonial Brazil were just as complex as those of Spanish America. In such a situation, the consolidator has to decide which rule to select and, under the pretext of consolidation, can innovate. For an analysis of the *Consolidação* and the criticism it received in its day, see Pontes de Miranda (1984).

12. Martínez Marina (1966[1820]: 380) offers testimony from that time about this difficulty: "Who is today capable, even after many years of study and continued investigations, to understand all the parts of the Spanish law? The most expert judge . . . the most studious lawyer cannot help but ignore a large part of the Spanish legislation."

13. Juan de Sala y Bañuls (1731–1806) was a professor at the University of Valencia who was famous for his erudition. In 1779 he published *Vinnius castigatus ad usum tironum hispanorum accomodatus*, an edition of Vinnius's *Institutiones de Justiniano* adapted for the Catholic orthodoxy. He also edited the *Digest* in 1794. *Ilustraciones* was his most famous work, and several shortened versions later appeared in 1827 and 1833. (Information based on the catalogs of the National Library of Madrid.)

14. Legal scholars before the codification were less legalist. Tau Anzoátegui (1987: 92) sums up his analysis of the Argentinean legal scholars' mentality: "Our 19th century legal scholars—especially in the era before 1870—ostensibly held a critical attitude toward the inherited legal order, but they needed to serve the system. At the same time, they admitted the existence of natural law above the positive laws and appreciated the value of justice. For these reasons, said legal scholars present themselves in practice—in relation to posterior generations—less attached to the letter of the law and to the impositions of the legal order, and more predisposed to take advantage of the diverse elements within their reach in a wide legal horizon. It was a way of reasoning that aimed more at Law than at laws."

15. María del Refugio González (1984: 405), analyzing speeches of lawyers who speak of their profession, detects the passing from an oral tradition to a written one over the course of the nineteenth century. In the early speeches, good oratory and speaking skills were put forth as important virtues for lawyers. In later speeches, the importance of writing was highlighted.

16. The *colegios* were houses for the students usually run by a religious order. Frequently they offered teachings that were sometimes recognized by the university.

17. Jean Baptiste Say (1767–1832) is generally known as a spreader of Adam Smith's ideas. His *Traité d' economie politique* (1803) was subtitled *Simple exposition de la manière dont se forment, se distribuent et se consommnent les richesses*. Prohibited by Napoleon, it later became a true best-seller in France, in the United States (28 printings between 1821 and 1880), and in Spanish-speaking countries (Palmer, 1997). Its success was due to the author's articulate expression and simple style, quite superior to that of the great economists who were his contemporaries (A. Baptista, personal communication, April 2002).

18. Bentham considered traveling to Venezuela to write the country's laws: "If I go hither it will be to do a little business in the way of my trade, to draw up a body of laws for the people there . . . The good which I could do for mankind if I were in the House of Commons or even if I were minister is inconsiderable in comparison with that which I may hope to do if I go there: for having, by the ignorant and domineering Spaniards, been purposely kept in ignorance, they have the merit of being sensible of it, and disposed to receive instruction from England in general, and from your humble servant in particular. Whatever I give them for laws they will be prepared to receive as oracles . . . " (Letter to Mr. Mulford, cited in McKennan, 1978). Bentham was lucky not to receive or to accept the invitation. His most probable destiny would have been death by firing squad as soon as the conservatives came to power.

19. For an analysis of the controversy over Catholic universities in Chile, see Serrano (1994a: 450).

20. Heinrich Ahrens was professor in Brussels, Graz, and Leipzig, successively, in the mid–nineteenth century. Trazegnies Granda (1979) analyzes his thought and finds that he is a student of Krause and a second-string eclectic thinker. His fame in Latin America was probably due to his grave reservations about the equality principle and his emphasis on the place of history and the national spirit. Ahrens maintained that the role of the state could not be limited to the protection of its citizens' liberty, but rather that it should strive for what is good. In other words, the state

should take care that liberty not affect loyalty to the traditional structure of society, which is a product of history worth preserving (Trazegnies Granda, 1979: 86). Conservatives and liberals adopted him, but the conservatives had reservations and included the explanation that creating a legal foundation without reference to God and religion was dangerous.

21. Bravo Lira (1998a: 98) appears to have a different idea when he affirms that "Chile became one of the focal points of the lawyer culture that predominated in Hispanic America until at least the middle of the twentieth century." The issue could be resolved by empirically analyzing the number of students from other Latin American countries who studied at the Universidad de Chile law school or another school thought to have continental importance. My hypothesis is that the majority of lawyers were trained nationally. Biographic works of lawyers (for example: Moreno, 1979; Azpúrua, 1877; Garrido Mezquita, 1953) mention professional formation in the same country as their citizenship. It is worth comparing with the United States, where elite law schools do not attempt to educate students on the law of the state in which the school is located. Thus universities such as Harvard, Yale, and Stanford receive students from all states and, more recently, a good number of international students.

22. For example, *Principios de Derecho de Gentes* (*Law of Peoples*, later called *Principles of International Law*) by Andrés Bello was published in Santiago (1832), Valparaíso (1844), Caracas (1847), and Madrid (1883).

23. The decrease in the number of university students, especially law students, appears to have resulted from a well-thought-out conservative policy based on the perception that political damage resulted from an abundance of people with university degrees and a shortage of technical personnel (Safford, 1976). In a given university, for example, engineering slots might be encouraged and law spaces limited. Thus in 1874, Colombia's Universidad Nacional had 30 law students versus 65 in engineering, 59 in medicine, and 30 in natural sciences (Safford, 1976: 194). If we extrapolate these figures for 1887 and for all of Colombia, the number falls by at least half; that is, to some 4 law students per 100,000 inhabitants.

24. The Universidad de Chile awarded 1,014 basic law degrees between 1844 and 1879 (Serrano, 1994b: 166). This degree was a prerequisite for later receiving the title of lawyer. The 1885 census shows 944 lawyers. The approximate sum of the law degrees in the 1850s, 1860s, and 1870s is 922.

25. This is the probable explanation for the completely anomalous figure for 1907, suggested by E. Fuenzalida (personal communication, March 2002).

26. Carvalho (1980: 79–81) offers more disaggregated data, in which he distinguishes judges, lawyers, and professors. He therefore looks at the occupation, not the training. The judges come out on top, with a total of 30 percent of government ministers, followed by military members (22 percent) and lawyers (21 percent). Judges made up 36 percent of the senators, followed by lawyers (14 percent).

27. Silva García (2001: 43) describes the case of Gabriel Giraldo, S.J., dean of law for a long period at the Universidad Javeriana, who cultivated relationships with graduates and helped them to attain positions of power, "placing himself thus at the head of a powerful interest group, run in patriarchal form."

28. Colombia may be the special case in which a principal university very early lost the ability to form the political elite. There, private universities, created with different ideological tendencies, assumed this role and shaped very ideological and intensely rival separate social networks. This may be an element to consider in explaining the extremely conflictive nature of Colombian politics.

CHAPTER 4

1. The meeting *Nuevos Enfoques para Atender la Demanda de Justicia* (Regional Conference of the World Bank for Latin American and the Caribbean, CIDE, Mexico, May 2001) was the occasion for the presentation of works of applied research, generally at the request of the judiciaries, ministries of justice, the World Bank, and the IDB.

2. For example, in some countries law students begin with a basic cycle of courses and also can draw from a cycle of professional courses in their chosen field. Different sources may include, or exclude, these students. The same thing can occur with postgraduate students. The definition of *university student* also varies, as one of the important changes in the latter 1900s was the growth of university-level institutes of technology, university colleges, and institutes of higher education that technically are not universities.

3. The very low number of law students and lawyers was a characteristic of the socialist countries (see Clark, 1999).

4. For example, the Universidad Católica de Chile was created in 1889; the Pontificia Universidad Católica del Perú (Lima) in 1917; the Universidad Católica Andrés Bello, of Caracas, in the 1950s. In almost all Latin American capitals is found a Catholic university with a law school.

5. For example, of Chile's 40 law schools, 6 were created before 1979, 13 between 1980 and 1990, and 21 between 1991 and 2000 (De la Maza, 2001). Venezuela had 7 law schools until 1980, and 16 in 2001, of which 12 are private (Information from the Oficina de Planificación del Sector Universitario).

6. Among these schools are the Catholic universities in Caracas, Lima, Quito, Rio de Janeiro, and Santiago; Universidad de los Andes y la Javeriana in Bogotá; Libre, ITAM, and Iberoamericana in Mexico City; Diego Portales in Santiago; Belgrano, Torcuato di Tella, and Palermo in Buenos Aires; Monte Avila and Metropolitana in Caracas. The characteristic feature of these schools is that they are private, they recruit the majority of their students from the social elite, and they have made diverse reform efforts in the teaching of law. A new school (CIDE) in Mexico City was founded in 2001 with the intent of innovating legal education and educating the elite, but it has two distinguishing characteristics: it is financed by the federal government, and it strives to recruit its students (who must pass very rigorous tests) among people of modest income who live in less populated regions of the country.

7. At the time, the perception was not necessarily shared by the majority of legal professionals. A study among Colombian lawyers showed that 64 percent were "very satisfied" with their legal education, 24 percent were "satisfied," and only 9 percent were "unsatisfied" (Lynch, 1981: 113).

8. For a look at subjects in legal education that interested Latin American academics, see Witker (1978). It is important to point out that the type of teaching that uses the class or the professor's lecture as the main instrument of instruction has been consistently criticized from different perspectives. Pérez-Perdomo (1974), for example, places it at the root of skepticism and lack of compromise with the rule of law among lawyers. More recently, Torres Arends (1997, 2001) has emphasized that teaching trains abstract reasoning but does not develop the capacity to tackle problems, and that it produces an inconsistent construction of the concept of law.

9. The innovation in teaching and approach generated rivalries at the law school. This aspect mixed with a more liberal behavior and ideas of young professors who had studied law at the University of Wisconsin.

10. An example is the law school of Universidad de Ciencias Aplicadas, Lima. The new tendency was mostly the work of professors with U.S. law degrees, some of whom had important roles in the Fujimori regime. The law graduates are called "generation X" and are associated with very pragmatic attitudes (Gorki González, personal communication, March 2002).

11. Some examples: In Venezuela the first graduate programs were created in the 1960s. In 2002, 9 universities offered a total of 15 "specialization" programs, 13 master's programs, and 2 doctoral programs. Several programs and courses are interdisciplinary (H. Njaim, personal communication, July 2002). Colombia has several master's programs and a doctoral program at Universidad del Externado (G. Silva García, personal communication, August 2002). The postgraduate programs in both Colombia and Venezuela have a strict system of evaluation. In recent years the Legal Research Institute of Universidad Nacional Autónoma de México (UNAM) and the National University of Chile in Santiago have created doctorates in law with an interdisciplinary focus.

12. Mexico seems to be a somewhat different case. The law school with the greatest weight in the training of business lawyers (Escuela Libre) is private and considerably traditional. ITAM and Iberoamericana, two private universities, also are devoted to the training of business lawyers and have made innovations with different degrees of success. The most radical innovation is being made in a public school (CIDE) that has barely gotten under way. One of its characteristics is its attention to admitting very promising students with limited resources and providing them with scholarships (A. L. Magaloni, personal communication).

13. The differences can be substantial. Spain, for instance, keeps records of practicing and nonpracticing lawyers: in 1999 there were 97,826 practicing lawyers (249 per 100,000 inhabitants), and 34,661 nonpracticing. The sum of both would raise the number of lawyers in the population to 337 per 100,000, a misleading figure. The way in which the registry is set up and maintained is clearly helpful.

14. The number of lawyers in Venezuela in 1961 and 1981 is derived from the national population census for those years. The figure probably does not include *tinterillos* or *procuradores* because their numbers were negligible. The 1971 figure comes from the INPREABOGADO registry. It was a new institution in 1971, and the figure probably reflects the total number of active legal professionals. The figures for 1990 and 2000 also are based on the registry, but as retired or deceased lawyers are

not excluded, we have estimated the figure using the registry as a base. The most recent registry figure is 87,190 in 2001. Our estimate is rough and is at best a measure only of potentially active lawyers.

15. The source of this figure is the *colegio de abogados* de Costa Rica. The 1980, 1990, and 2000 figures are unpublished, and we thank Alfredo Chirinos, Director of Escuela de la Judicature, for providing them.

16. The generalization ignores the case of Spain, which does not control law school entry nor does it have policies of expansion of demand. Venezuela and, since 1980, Chile belong to this heterodox model, apparently without economic rationality, if we accept the premises of Mattei (1997).

17. Military governments go through stages. Usually there is a very harsh stage, followed by an opening in which discussion and later the election of a civil government is permitted. The harsh stage of the Brazilian dictatorship ended in 1974 (Alcántara, 1999: 91ss).

18. Zolezzi's work is a social and occupational study of lawyers who graduated from the Catholic university in Lima, and in the group interviewed only one firm reports more than twelve lawyers.

19. The coyotes' intermediary activity is the typical transactional bribe (or *jeito*, in Brazil), as described by Reissman (1979) and Rosenn (1971). Today these are considered unacceptable, and the trend is for the simplification of everyday procedures. Lawyers act as intermediaries only when the procedure is more complicated. For that reason, their work is considered to have a technical element, and their fees are not merely disguised bribes. In fact, much of lawyers' procedural work involves using informal connections that do not technically qualify as bribes.

20. *Amparo* is an injunction addressed to stop the violation of a constitutional right, or to prevent the imminent violation. It is much used in most Latin American countries.

21. Starting in 1992 the Supreme Court of Justice of Venezuela showed signs of considerable independence in its decisions, some of which were politically sensitive. Among these was one that permitted the convocation of a constituent assembly in order to prepare a new constitution—a procedure that was not provided for in the constitution of 1961. Subsequently, the supreme court modified the terms of the summons prepared by President Chávez. The 1999 Constituent Assembly substantially transformed the court and renamed it the Tribunal Supremo de Justicia (Supreme Tribunal). Upon elimination of the Judicial Council, the Supreme Tribunal was given the power to manage the judiciary. Once the new tribunal was established, justices were "provisionally" appointed. One year later, the national assembly, which had an overwhelming majority of Chávez supporters, appointed permanent justices, some of them better known as political activists. All of this can be understood as an attempt to control the Supreme Tribunal politically. Some later decisions indicated that this political control was not firm, and in 2004 a new change in legislation put the justices and judges in complete control of the National Assembly.

22. The case of Peru is paradigmatic. Fujimori, through his "security advisor" Montesinos, was able to control the judges and falsify the system of checks and balances established in the constitution. Among the many abuses was the dismemberment of the constitutional court when it made a decision that might have impeded

Fujimori's third attempt at reelection. For a general analysis, see Zolezzi Ibárcena (1993) and González (2001).

23. *Juridification* refers to a greater importance of the law; *judicialization*, to the greater importance and use of courts. Both phenomena do not necessarily occur simultaneously.

24. It is a question of degree. Articles like those by Rosenn (1969) and Steiner (1971) gave surprisingly little notice to the fact that Brazil was under a dictatorship that committed massive human rights violations. From later works of these authors, one can assume that their treatment of the same topic today would be very different.

25. The literature generated on judicial reform in Latin America, and the role of the multilateral banks in the 1990s, is enormous. Some examples: Inter-American Development Bank (1993); Dakolias (1996); Rowat et al. (1995); Hammergren (1998); Varela (1999); Van Puymbroeck (2001); Rodríguez (2001).

26. A panorama of the situation of judicial training appears in the journal *Sistemas Judiciales* (no. 1, 2001). For a thorough study of training in Chile, see Correa Sutil (1998). For Mexico: Instituto de la Judicatura Federal (2001). For a general overview of the problems of consolidation of the judicial career, see Hammergren (1999).

27. When "charge back" is allowed, the credit card company serves as an arbitrator. If a customer refutes a charge and the credit card company finds the complaint justified, it will "charge back" the customer and the merchant. This mechanism generates trust, especially for e-commerce transactions.

References

Abel, Richard L. 1988. "Lawyers in the civil law world." In R. Abel and P. Lewis (eds.), *Lawyers in society: The civil law world*. Berkeley: University of California.

Acuña, Carlos, and C. Smulovitz. 1997. "Guarding the guardians in Argentina: Some lessons about the risks and benefits of empowering the courts." In A. J. McAdams (ed.), *Transitional justice and the rule of law in new democracies*. Notre Dame, Ind.: University of Notre Dame Press.

Adorno, Sergio. 1988. *Os aprendizes do poder: O bacharelismo liberal na política brasileira*. São Paulo: Paz e Terra.

Agüero, Felipe. 1998. "Conflicting assessment of democratization: Exploring the fault lines." In F. Agüero and J. Stark (eds.), *Fault lines of democracy in post-transition Latin America*. Miami: North-South Center Press.

Aguilera, Miguel. 1965. *La legislación y el derecho en Colombia*. Bogotá: Lerner.

Aguirre, Carlos. 2001. "'Litigantes de mala fé': Towards a history of legal intermediaries in modern Peru." Term paper. Department of History, University of Oregon, Portland.

Aguirre, Luppy. 1998. "Justicia militar: Una mirada en cifras." In J. Mera Figueroa (ed.), *Justicia militar y estado de derecho*. Santiago: Universidad Diego Portales.

Albornoz de López, Teresa. 1987. *La visita de Joaquín Mosquera y Figueroa a la Real Audiencia de Caracas (1804–1809): Conflictos internos y corrupción en la administración de justicia*. Caracas: Academia Nacional de la Historia.

Alcántara, Manuel. 1999. *Sistemas políticos de América Latina*. Vol. 1: *América del Sur*. Madrid: Tecnos.

Aljovín de Losada, Cristóbal. 2000. *Caudillos y constituciones: Perú 1821–1845*. Lima: Pontificia Universidad Católica del Perú; and Mexico City: Fondo de Cultura Económica.

Appelbaum, Richard, W. Felstiner, and V. Gessner. 2001. "Introduction." In R. Appelbaum, W. Felstiner, and V. Gessner (eds.), *The legal culture of global business transactions*. Oxford: Hart.

Arce Gurza, Francisco. 1982. "El inicio de una nueva era, 1910–1945." In F. Arce Gurza et al. (eds.), *Historia de las profesiones en México*. Mexico City: Colegio de México.

Archi, Gian Gualberto. 1979. "Giustiniano e l'insegnamento del diritto." In A. Giuliani and N. Picardi (eds.), *L'educazione giuridica: Profili storici*. Perugia: Librería Editrice Universitaria.

Archivo General de la Nación. 1958. *Los abogados de la colonia.* Caracas: Archivo General de la Nación.

Arias Sánchez, Oscar. 1976. *¿Quién gobierna en Costa Rica?* San José: Educa.

Armitage, W. 1990. "From club to global firm: Forging international links." *International Financial Law Review*, May.

Arnaud, André-Jean. 1969. *Les origines doctrinales du Code Civil.* Paris: Librairie Général de Droit et Jurisprudence.

Arnold, Linda. 1988. *Bureaucracy and bureaucrats in Mexico City, 1742–1835.* Tucson: University of Arizona Press.

Ashton, Scott. 2002. "El torneo de abogados: Law firms in Chile." Term paper for seminar, Law in Latin America, Stanford University Law School.

Azpúrua, Ramón. 1877. *Biografías de hombres notables de Hispano América.* Caracas: Imprenta Nacional.

Bagú, Sergio. 1961. *Evolución histórica de la estratificación social en la Argentina.* Buenos Aires: Instituto de Sociología, Universidad de Buenos Aires.

Barman, Roderick, and J. Barman. 1976. "The role of the law graduates in the political elite of imperial Brazil." *Journal of Interamerican Studies and World Affairs* 18.

Barrientos Grandón, Javier. 1993. *La cultura jurídica en la Nueva España.* Mexico City: Universidad Nacional Autónoma de México.

Bastos, Aurélio Wander (ed.). 1977. *Criação dos cursos jurídicos no Brasil.* Brasilia: Câmara dos Deputados; and Rio de Janeiro: Fundação Rui Barbosa.

Bastos, Aurélio Wander. 1978. "O estado e a formação dos currículos jurídicos no Brasil." In A. W. Bastos (ed.), *Os cursos jurídicos e as elites políticas brasileiras.* Brasilia: Câmara dos Deputados.

Bastos, Aurélio Wander. 2000. *O ensino jurídico no Brasil* (2nd ed.). Rio de Janeiro: Lumen Juris.

Bauer, Arnold J. 1995. "Iglesia, economía y estado en la historia de América Latina." In M. P. Martínez López-Cano (ed.), *Iglesia, estado y economía: Siglos XVI al XIX.* Mexico City: Universidad Nacional Autónoma de México.

Bauman, Richard A. 1983. *Lawyers in Roman Republican politics.* Munich: C.H. Beck.

Bauman, Richard A. 1985. *Lawyers in Roman transitional politics.* Munich: C.H. Beck.

Bauman, Richard A. 1989. *Lawyers and politics in the early Roman Empire.* Munich: C.H. Beck.

Bazant, Mílada. 1982. "La República restaurada y el Porfiriato." In F. Arce Gurza et al. (eds.), *Historia de las profesiones en México.* Mexico City: Colegio de México.

Bergoglio, Maria Inés. 1993. "Castas y estamentos en Córdoba." *Revista de la Universidad Blas Pascal* (Córdoba) 3.

Bergoglio, Maria Inés. 2003a. "Argentina: The effects of democratic institutionalization." In L. Friedman and R. Pérez-Perdomo (eds.), *Legal cultures in the age of globalization: Latin America and Latin Europe.* Stanford, Calif.: Stanford University Press.

Bergoglio, Maria Inés. 2003b. "Las facultades de derecho en Argentina: Entre las tradiciones y los esfuerzos de cambio." Paper presented at seminar, Educación Jurídica. Instituto de Direito e Sociedade, Itaipava, Brazil, February.

Bermúdez, Carlos M. 2001. "Studying law in Cuba: A law student's perspective." Term paper for seminar, Law in Latin America, Stanford University Law School.

Bernstein, Lisa. 1992. "Opting out of the legal system: Extralegal contractual relations in the diamond trade." *Journal of Legal Studies* 21.

Binder, Alberto. 2001. "Los oficios del jurista: La fragmentación de la profesión jurídica y la uniformidad de la carrera judicial." *Sistemas Judiciales* 1.

Boigeol, Anne. 2003. "The rise of lawyers in France." In L. Friedman and R. Pérez-Perdomo (eds.), *Legal cultures in the age of globalization: Latin America and Latin Europe*. Stanford, Calif.: Stanford University Press.

Bolívar, Simón. 1970. "Carta de Jamaica." In S. Bolívar, *Escritos selectos*. Caracas: Presidencia de la República. (Originally published 1815.)

Borah, Woodrow. 1970. "Juzgado general de indios en el Perú, o juzgado particular de indios en el cercado de Lima." *Revista chilena de historia del derecho* (Santiago) 6.

Borah, Woodrow. 1983. *Justice by insurance: The General Indian Court of colonial Mexico and legal aid of half a real*. Berkeley: University of California.

Botana, Natalio. 1994. "Las transformaciones del credo constitucional." In A. Annino, L. Castro Leiva, and F. X. Guerra (eds.), *De los imperios a las naciones: Iberoamérica*. Zaragoza: IberCaja.

Bravo Lira, Bernardino. 1998a. "Estudios de derecho y cultura de abogados en Chile 1758–1998: Tras la huella del ius commune, la codificación y la descodificación en el Nuevo Mundo." *Revista de estudios históricos-jurídicos* (Valparaíso) 20.

Bravo Lira, Bernardino. 1998b. "Estudios jurídicos y estado modernizador: La cultura de abogados en Chile 1758–1998." *Revista chilena de derecho* (Santiago) 25.

Brazil (Ministerio da Agricultura, Industria e Comercio). 1927. *Anuario estatístico do Brasil*. Vol. 3. Rio de Janeiro: Typografia da Estatistica.

Brewer Carías, Allan Randolph (ed.). 1985. *Las constituciones de Venezuela*. Madrid: Centro de Estudios Constitucionales; and San Cristóbal: Universidad Católica Andrés Bello.

Brown, Brenda. 1961. "Recent significant trends in legal education in the Americas." *Inter-American Law Review* 3.

Buenos Aires (Municipalidad de la Capital, República Argentina). 1902. *Anuario estadístico de la Ciudad de Buenos Aires*. Buenos Aires: Compañía Sud Americana de Billetes de Banco.

Bulmer-Thomas, Víctor. 1994. *The economic history of Latin America since independence*. Cambridge: Cambridge University Press.

Burkholder, Mark. 1980. *Politics of a colonial career: José Baquijano Carrillo and the Audiencia de Lima*. Albuquerque: University of New Mexico.

Burkholder, Mark, and D. S. Chandler. 1977. *From impotence to authority: The Spanish Crown and the American audiencias, 1687–1808*. Columbia: University of Missouri Press.

Calasso, Francesco. 1954. *Medio evo del diritto*. Milan: Giuffrè.

Camp, Roderic. 1996. *El reclutamiento político en México*. Mexico City: Siglo XXI.

Capeller, Wanda de Lemos. 1995. *L'engrenage de la repression: Stratégies sécuritaires et politiques criminelles*. Paris: Librairie Général de Droit et Jurisprudence.

Capriles Méndez, Ruth. 1991. *Los negocios de Román Delgado Chalbaud*. Caracas: Academia Nacional de la Historia.

Carrera Damas, Germán. 1980. *Una nación llamada Venezuela*. Caracas: Universidad Central de Venezuela.

Carvalho, José Murilo de. 1980. *A construção da ordem: A elite política imperial.* Rio de Janeiro: Editora Campus.

Carvalho, José Murilo de. 1995. *Desenvolvimiento de la ciudadanía en Brasil.* Mexico City: Colegio de México; and Fondo de Cultura Económica.

Cassesse, Sabino. 2003. "The Italian legal system, 1945–1999." In L. Friedman and R. Pérez-Perdomo (eds.), *Legal cultures in the age of globalization: Latin America and Latin Europe.* Stanford, Calif.: Stanford University Press.

Castro Leiva, Luis. 1994. *Insinuaciones deshonestas: Ensayos de historia intelectual.* Caracas: Monte Ávila.

Catalano, Pierangelo. 1983. "Consolato e dittadura: L'esperimento romano della Reppublica del Paraguay (1813–1844)." In G. Meloni (ed.), *Dittadura degli antichi e dittadura dei moderni.* Rome: Editori Riuniti.

Catalano, Pierangelo. 1986. *Modelo institucional romano e independencia: República del Paraguay 1813–1870.* Asunción: Comuneros.

Cavanna, Adriano. 1979. *Storia del diritto moderno in Europa.* Milan: Giuffrè.

Chassin, Joelle. 1998. "Lima, sus élites y la opinión durante los últimos tiempos de la colonia." In F. Guerra and A. Lempérière et al. (eds.), *Los espacios públicos en Iberoamérica.* Mexico City: Fondo de Cultura Económica.

Chile, República de. 1912. *Anuario estadístico: Año 1912.* Santiago: Sociedad Impresora y Litográfica Universo.

Chocano Mena, Magdalena. 1999. *La fortaleza docta: Elite letrada y dominación social en México colonial (siglos XVI y XVII).* Barcelona: Bellatierra.

Chocano Mena, Magdalena. 2000. *La América colonial (1492–1763): Cultura y vida cotidana.* Madrid: Síntesis.

Clark, David S. 1999. "Comparing the work and organization of lawyers worldwide: The persistence of legal traditions." In J. Barceló III and R. Cramton (eds.), *Lawyers' practice and ideals: A comparative view.* The Hague: Kluwer.

Clark, David S. 2003. "Italian styles: Criminal justice and the rise of an active magistracy." In L. Friedman and R. Pérez-Perdomo (eds.), *Legal cultures in the age of globalization: Latin America and Latin Europe.* Stanford, Calif.: Stanford University Press.

Coelho, Edmundo Campos. 1999. *As profissões imperiais: Medicina, engenharia e advocacia no Rio de Janeiro, 1822–1930.* Rio de Janeiro: Record.

Collier, Simon, and W. Sater. 1996. *A history of Chile, 1808–1994.* Cambridge: Cambridge University Press.

Concha-Cantú, Hugo, and A. Caballero-Juárez. 2001. *Diagnóstico sobre la administración de justicia en las entidades federativas: Un estudio institucional sobre justicia local en México.* Mexico City: Instituto de Investigaciones Jurídicas, Universidad Nacional Autónoma de México.

Correa Sutil, Jorge. 1993. "The judiciary and the political system in Chile: The dilemmas of judicial independence during the transition to democracy." In I. P. Stoltzky (ed.), *Transition to democracy in Latin America: The role of the judiciary.* Boulder, Colo.: Westview.

Correa Sutil, Jorge. 1997. "No victorious army has ever been prosecuted: The unsettled story of transitional justice in Chile." In A. J. McAdams (ed.), *Transitional justice and the rule of law in new democracies.* Notre Dame, Ind.: University of Notre Dame Press.

Correa Sutil, Jorge (ed.). 1998. *Necesidades de capacitación de los funcionarios del poder judicial: Informe a la Academia Judicial de Chile.* Santiago: Universidad Diego Portales.

Correas, Oscar, and F. Correas Vázquez. 1990. "La sociología jurídica en México." In V. Ferrari (ed.), *Developing sociology of law.* Milan: Giuffrè.

Cutolo, Vicente Osvaldo. 1964. "El primer abogado criollo que actuó en Buenos Aires." *Revista Chilena de historia del derecho* (Santiago) 3.

Cutolo, Vicente Osvaldo. 1968–85. *Nuevo diccionario biográfico argentino, 1730–1930.* Buenos Aires: Elche.

Dahrendorf, Ralf. 1971. "Las facultades de derecho y la clase alta alemana." In V. Aubert (ed.), *Sociología del derecho.* Caracas: Tiempo Nuevo.

Dakolias, Maria. 1996. "The judicial sector in Latin America and the Caribbean: Elements of reform." Working paper. World Bank, Washington, D.C.

Dantas, San Tiago. 1955. "A educação jurídica e a crise brasileira." *Revista Forense* 159.

David, René. 1988. *Les grands systèmes de droit contemporains* (9th ed.). Paris: Dalloz.

De la Maza, Iñigo. 2001. "Lawyers: From the state to the market." SPILS Master's thesis, Stanford University Law School.

Del Arenal Fenochio, Jaime. 1980. "Los abogados en México y una polémica centenaria, 1784–1847." *Revista de investigaciones juridicas,* Escuela Libre de Derecho (Mexico).

Delgado Cintrón, Carmelo. 1970. *Libro de matrículas del Ilustre Colegio de Abogados de Puerto Rico 1840 a 1910 (Abogados puertorriqueños de 1840 a 1910).* San Juan: Colegio de Abogados de Puerto Rico.

De Soto, Hernando. 1986. *El otro sendero.* Lima: El Barranco.

Dezalay, Yves. 1992. *Marchands de droit: La restructuration de l'ordre juridique international par le multinationales de droit.* Paris: Fayard.

Dezalay, Yves, and B. Garth. 1996. *Dealing in virtue: International commercial arbitration and the construction of a transnational legal order.* Chicago: Chicago University Press.

Dezalay, Yves, and B. Garth. 1997. "Law, lawyers and social capital: 'Rule of law' versus relational capitalism." *Social and Legal Studies* 6.

Dezalay, Yves, and B. Garth. 2002. *The internationalization of palace wars: Lawyers, economists, and the contest to transform Latin American states.* Chicago: University of Chicago Press.

D'Ippolito, Federico. 1986. *Giuristi e sapienti in Roma arcaica.* Rome: Laterza.

Domínguez, Jorge I. 1980. *Insurrection or loyalty: The breakdown of the Spanish American empire.* Cambridge, Mass.: Harvard University Press.

Duce, Mauricio, and R. Pérez-Perdomo. 2001. "Seguridad ciudadana y reforma de la justicia penal en América Latina." *Boletín Mexicano de Derecho Comparado* 102.

Edwards Vives, Alberto. 1936. *La fronda aristocrática.* Santiago: Ediciones Ercilla.

Endrek, Emiliano. 1966. *El mestizaje en Córdoba: Siglo XVIII y principios del XIX.* Córdoba: Universidad Nacional de Córdoba.

Escriche, Joaquín. 1837. *Diccionario razonado de legislación civil, penal, comercial y forense.* Mexico City: Galván.

Escriche, Joaquín. 1840. *Diccionario razonado de legislación civil, penal, comercial y forense.* Caracas: Valentín Espinal.

Eyzaguirre, Jaime. 1957. *Ideario y ruta de la emancipación chilena.* Santiago: Editorial Universitaria.

Eyzaguirre, Jaime. 1966. *Historia constitucional de Chile*. Santiago: Editorial Universitaria.

Falcão, Joaquim. 1978. "Os cursos jurídicos e a formação do estado nacional." In A. W. Bastos (ed.), *Os cursos jurídicos e as elites políticas brasileiras*. Brasilia: Cámara dos Deputados.

Falcão, Joaquim. 1979. "Lawyers in Brazil: Ideals and praxis." *International Journal of the Sociology of Law* 7.

Falcão, Joaquim. 1984. *Os advogados: Ensino jurídico e mercado de trabalho*. Recife: Fundação Joaquim Nabuco, and Editora Massangana.

Faoro, Raymundo. 1975. *Os donos do poder: Formação do patronato político brasileiro* (2nd ed.). Porto Alegre: Editora Globo.

Faria, Jose Eduardo. 2000. "Globalização, direito e ensino jurídico." *Revista da Faculdade de Direito da UFF* (Rio de Janeiro) 4.

Ferrés, Carlos. 1944. *Epoca colonial: La administración de justicia en Montevideo*. Montevideo: Casa A. Barreiro y Ramos.

Figueroa, Gonzalo. 1978. "Investigaciones socio-jurídicas emprendidas en Chile." In G. Figueroa (ed.), *Derecho y sociedad*. Santiago: Corporación de Promoción Universitaria.

Fix-Fierro, Héctor, and S. López-Ayllón. 2001. "Legitimidad contra legalidad: Los dilemas de la transición jurídica y el estado de derecho en México." *Política y Gobierno* 7.

Flood, John. 1996. "Megalawyering in the global order: The cultural, social and economic transformation of global legal practice." *International Journal of the Legal Profession* 3.

Flory, Thomas. 1981. *Judge and jury in imperial Brazil, 1808–1871*. Austin: University of Texas Press.

French-Davis, Ricardo, and J. G. Palma. 1998. "The Latin American economies, 1950–1990." In L. Bethell (ed.), *Latin America: Economy and society since 1930*. Cambridge: Cambridge University Press.

Friedländer, Ludwig. 1947. *La sociedad romana*. Madrid: Fondo de Cultura Económica.

Friedman, Lawrence. 1985. *Total justice*. New York: Russell Sage Foundation.

Friedman, Lawrence. 1999. *The horizontal society*. New Haven, Conn.: Yale University Press.

Friedman, Lawrence. 2001. "Erewhon: The coming global legal order." *Stanford Journal of International Law* 37.

Frühling, Hugo. 1984. "Poder Judicial y política en Chile." In J. de Belaúnde (ed.), *La administración de justicia en América Latina*. Lima: Consejo Latinoamericano de Derecho y Desarrollo.

Fucito, Felipe. 1997. "La profesión jurídica: Un estudio cualitativo." *Revista de Sociología del Derecho* (Buenos Aires) 12.

Fucito, Felipe. 2000. "El profesor de derecho en Argentina." *Revista da faculdade de direito da UFF* (Rio de Janeiro) 4.

Fuentes-Hernández, Alfredo. 2002. "Globalization and legal education in Latin America: Issues for law and development in the 21st Century." American Association of Law Schools, New Orleans.

Fuentes-Hernández, Alfredo, and C. Amaya-Osorio. 2001. "Demanda y oferta judicial: Dificultades de ajuste." Paper presented at meeting, Nuevos Enfoques para

Atender la Demanda de Justicia. World Bank Regional Conference for Latin America and the Caribbean, CIDE, Mexico City, May.

Fuenzalida, Edmundo. 2003. "Law and legal culture in Chile, 1974–1999." In L. Friedman and R. Pérez-Perdomo (eds.), *Legal cultures in the age of globalization: Latin America and Latin Europe*. Stanford, Calif.: Stanford University Press.

Gaitán Bohorquez, Julio. 2002. *Huestes de estado: La formación universitaria de los juristas en los comienzos del estado colombiano*. Bogotá: Centro Editorial de la Universidad del Rosario.

Galín, Pedro. 1984. "La independencia del Poder Judicial argentino en la dictadura 1976–1980." In J. de Belaúnde (ed.), *La administración de justicia en América Latina*. Lima: Consejo Latinoamericano de Derecho y Desarrollo.

Gálvez Montero, José Francisco. 1990. "La Real Audiencia y su configuración en el virreinato." *Boletín del Instituto Riva Agüero* (Lima) 17.

Gamarra, Eduardo. 1991. *The system of justice in Bolivia: An institutional analysis*. Monograph series, no. 4. San José, Costa Rica: Centro para la Administración de Justicia; and Miami: Florida International University.

García Belaúnde, Domingo (ed.). 1993. *Las constituciones del Perú: Textos institucionales, cuadros comparativos*. Lima: Ministerio de Justicia.

García Canclini, Néstor. 1999. *La globalización imaginada*. Mexico City: Paidós.

García Chuecos, Héctor. 1937. *Estudios de historia colonial de Venezuela*. Caracas: Tipografía Americana.

García de La Cruz Herrero, Juan José. 1999. "La cultura de la reclamación como indicador de desarrollo democrático: Tres perspectivas de análisis." *Politeia* (Caracas) 22.

García-Gallo, Alfonso. 1972. *Estudios de historia del derecho indiano*. Madrid: Instituto Nacional de Estudios Jurídicos.

García-Gallo, Alfonso. 1977. "La ciencia jurídica en la formación del derecho hispanoamericano de los siglos XVI al XVIII." *La formazione storica del diritto moderno in Europa: Atti del terzo congresso internationale della societá italiana de storia del diritto*. Florence: Leo Olschki.

Garcia-Gallo, Alfonso. 1997. *Atlas histórico-jurídico*. Mexico City: Universidad Nacional Autónoma de México; and Porrúa.

Garrido, Carlos Manuel. 1993. "Informe sobre Argentina." In J. Correa Sutil (ed.), *Situación y políticas judiciales en América Latina*. Santiago: Universidad Diego Portales.

Garrido Mezquita et al. (eds.). 1953. *Diccionario biográfico de Venezuela*. Madrid: Blass.

Gessner, Volkmar. 1996. "The institutional framework of cross-border interactions." In V. Gessner (ed.), *Foreign courts: Civil litigation in foreign cultures*. Aldershot: Dartmouth.

Gessner, Volkmar. 1998. "Globalization and legal certainty." In V. Gessner and A. C. Budak (eds.), *Emerging legal certainty: Empirical studies on the globalization of law*. Aldershot: Dartmouth.

Giddens, Anthony. 2000. *Runaway world: How globalization is reshaping our lives*. New York: Routledge.

Gilmore, Myron. 1963. *Humanists and jurists: Six studies on the Renaissance*. Cambridge, Mass.: Harvard University Press.

Giraldo Angel, Jaime. 1993. "Informe sobre Colombia." In J. Correa Sutil (ed.), *Situación y políticas judiciales en América Latina*. Santiago: Escuela de Derecho, Universidad Diego Portales.

González, Gorki. 2001. "La carrera judicial: Estudio analítico y comparativo." *Pensamiento constitucional* (Lima) 8.

González, María del Refugio. 1981. *Estudios sobre la historia del derecho civil en México en el siglo XIX.* Mexico City: Universidad Nacional Autónoma de México.

González, María del Refugio. 1984. "El derecho y la función del abogado. (Discursos en la Academia de Jurisprudencia Teórico-Práctica en México, 1831–1862)." In *Estudios jurídicos en memoria de Roberto L. Mantilla Molina.* Mexico City: Porrúa.

González, María del Refugio. 1988. *El derecho civil en México 1821–1871.* Mexico City: Universidad Nacional Autónoma de México.

González, María del Refugio. 1998. *Historia del derecho mexicano.* Mexico City: Universidad Nacional Autónoma de México; and McGraw-Hill.

González, María del Refugio. 2000. "Las transiciones jurídicas en México del siglo XIX a la Revolución." In M. R. González and S. López-Ayllón (eds.), *Transiciones y diseños institucionales.* Mexico City: Universidad Nacional Autónoma de México.

González Echenique, Javier. 1954. *Los estudios jurídicos y la abogacía en el Reino de Chile.* Santiago: Imprenta Universitaria.

Grases, Pedro. 1978. *La conspiración de Gual y España y el ideario de la independencia.* Caracas: Ministerio de Educación.

Grotius, Hugo. 1724. *Le droit de la guerre et de la paix.* Amsterdam: P. de Coup.

Guardia, Amelia. 2000. "Estado de derecho y desarrollo discrónico: Problemas de la codificación hispanoamericana." *Politeia* (Caracas) 24.

Guerra, François-Xavier. 1992. *Modernidad e independencias: Ensayos sobre las revoluciones hispánicas.* Madrid: Editorial MAPFRE.

Gutiérrez, Carlos José. 1969. "Santa Cruz y Carrillo: Opinión sobre una vieja polémica." *Revista de Ciencias Jurídicas* (San José, Costa Rica) 69.

Guzmán Brito, Alejandro. 2000. *La codificación civil en Iberoamérica: Siglos XIX y XX.* Santiago: Editorial Jurídica de Chile.

Halliday, Terence, and L. Karpik. 1997. "Politics matter: A comparative theory of lawyers in the making of political liberalism." T. Halliday and L. Karpik (eds.), *Lawyers and the rise of western political liberalism.* Oxford: Clarendon Press.

Halperin Donghi, Tulio. 1985. *Reforma y disolución de los imperios ibéricos.* Madrid: Alianza.

Halperin Donghi, Tulio. 1993. *Historia contemporánea de América Latina* (14th ed.). Madrid: Alianza.

Halperin Donghi, Tulio. 1994. "The colonial *letrado* as a revolutionary intellectual: Deán Funes as seen through his 'Apuntamientos para una biografía.'" In M. Szuchman and J. C. Brown (eds.), *Revolution and restoration: The rearrangement of power in Argentina, 1776–1860.* Lincoln: University of Nebraska Press.

Hammergren, Linn. 1998. *The politics of justice and justice reform in Latin America: The Peruvian case in comparative perspective.* Boulder, Colo.: Westview Press.

Hammergren, Linn. 1999. "The judicial career in Latin America: An overview of theory and experience." Working paper. World Bank, Washington, D.C.

Hanisch Espíndola, Hugo. 1982. "Los ochenta años de influencia de Andrés Bello en la enseñanza del derecho romano en Chile." In Departamento de Ciencias del Derecho, Facultad de Derecho, Universidad de Chile, *Congreso internacional Andrés Bello y el derecho.* Santiago: Editorial Jurídica de Chile.

Hanke, Lewis. 1949. *The Spanish struggle for justice in the conquest of America.* Philadelphia: University of Pennsylvania Press.

Haslip-Viera, Gabriel. 1999. *Crime and punishment in late colonial Mexico City, 1692–1810*. Albuquerque: University of New Mexico Press.

Herzog, Tamar. 1995. *La administración como un fenómeno social: La justicia penal de la ciudad de Quito (1650–1750)*. Madrid: Centro de Estudios Constitucionales.

Holston, James, and T. Caldeira. 1998. "Democracy, law and violence: Disjunctions of Brazilian citizenship." In F. Agüero and J. Stark (eds.), *Fault lines of democracy in post-transition Latin America*. Miami: North-South Center Press at the University of Miami.

Honores González, Renzo. 1993. "Litigando en la Audiencia: El devenir de un 'pleito.'" *Historia y Cultura* (Lima) 22.

Imaz, José Luis de. 1964. *Los que mandan*. Buenos Aires: Editorial Universitaria.

Instituto de la Judicatura Federal. 2001. "La formación de los jueces federales en México: Notas para un análisis de la situación actual y perspectivas." Paper presented at meeting, Empowerment, Security and Opportunity Through Law and Justice, World Bank, St. Petersburg, July 2001.

Inter-American Development Bank (ed.). 1993. *Justicia y desarrollo en América Latina y el Caribe*. Washington, D.C. Inter-American Development Bank.

Jiménez de Asúa, Luis. 1945. *La ley y el delito*. Buenos Aires: Sudamericana.

Jocelyn-Holt Letelier, Alfredo. 1999. *La independencia de Chile: Tradición, modernización y mito* (2nd ed.). Santiago: Planeta-Ariel.

Junqueira, Eliane. 1999. *Faculdades de direito ou fábrica de ilusões?* Rio de Janeiro: IDES; and Letra Capital Editora.

Junqueira, Eliane. 2003. "Brazil: The road of conflict bound for total justice." L. Friedman and R. Pérez-Perdomo (eds.), *Legal cultures in the age of globalization: Latin America and Latin Europe*. Stanford, Calif.: Stanford University Press.

Junqueira, Eliane, and C. V. Veras. 2001. "Estudantes e profissionais negros de direito: Perspectivas para o novo milênio?" Working paper. Rio de Janeiro: Instituto de Direito e Sociedade.

Kagan, Richard L. 1974. *Students and society in early modern Spain*. Baltimore, Md.: Johns Hopkins University Press.

Kagan, Richard L. 1981. *Lawsuits and litigants in Castile. 1500–1700*. Chapel Hill: University of North Carolina Press.

Kicza, John. 1984. "The legal community of late colonial Mexico: Social composition and career patterns." In R. Spores and R. Hassig (eds.), *Five centuries of law and politics in central Mexico*. Nashville, Tenn.: Vanderbilt University.

Koschaker, Pablo. 1955. *Europa y el derecho romano*. Madrid: Editorial Revista de Occidente.

Landa, Janet Tai. 1994. *Trust, ethnicity and identity: Beyond the new institutional economics of ethnic trading networks, contract law, and gift exchange*. Ann Arbor: University of Michigan Press.

Lanning, John Tate. 1940. *Academic culture in the Spanish colonies*. Folcroft, Penn.: Folcroft Press.

Leal, Ildefonso. 1963. *Historia de la Universidad de Caracas*. Caracas: Universidad Central de Venezuela.

Leiva, Alberto David. 1997. "Del periodismo forense a las revistas jurídicas: Un aspecto de la evolución de la literatura jurídica argentina." In V. Tau Anzoátegui (ed.), *La revista jurídica en la cultura contemporánea*. Buenos Aires: Ediciones Ciudad Argentina.

Leonard, Irving A. 1992. *Books of the brave: An account of books and of men in the Spanish conquest and settlement of the sixteenth-century New World.* Berkeley: University of California Press.

Levaggi, Abelardo. 1992. "Alberdi-Vélez Sarsfield: Una polémica transcendental sobre la codificación argentina." In A. Levaggi (ed.), *Fuentes ideológicas y normativas de la codificación latinoamericana.* Buenos Aires: Universidad del Museo Social Argentino.

Levaggi, Abelardo. 1994. "La réception du système espagnol par les systèmes indigènes en Amerique." In M. Doucet and J. Vanderlinden (eds.), *La réception des systémes juridiques: Implantation et destin.* Brussels: Bruylant.

Levene, Ricardo. 1941. *La Academia de Jurisprudencia y la vida de su fundador Manuel Antonio de Castro.* Buenos Aires: Facultad de Derecho y Ciencias Sociales.

Levene, Ricardo. 1957. *Manual de historia del derecho argentino* (2nd ed.). Buenos Aires: Kraft.

Levene, Ricardo. 1959. "Nota para la historia de los abogados en Indias." *Revista Chilena de historia del derecho* (Santiago) 1.

Liévano Aguirre, Indalecio. 1972. *Los grandes conflictos sociales y económicos de nuestra historia* (4th ed.). Bogotá: Tercer Mundo.

Lira González, Andrés. 1984. "Abogados, tinterillos y huizacheros en el México del siglo XIX." In J. L. Soberanes Fernández (ed.), *Memoria del III Congreso de Historia del Derecho Mexicano (1983).* Mexico City: Universidad Nacional Autónoma de México.

Lockhart, James, and S. Schwartz. 1983. *Early Latin America: A history of colonial Spanish America and Brazil.* Cambridge: Cambridge University Press.

Lohmann Villena, Guillermo. 1974. *Los ministros de la audiencia de Lima en el reinado de los Borbones (1700–1821).* Seville: Escuela de Estudios Hispano-Americanos.

Lomnitz, Larissa, and R. Salazar. 2002. "Cultural elements in the practice of law in Mexico. Informal networks in formal systems." In Y. Dezalay and B. Garth (eds.), *Global prescriptions: The production, exportation, and importation of a new legal orthodoxy.* Ann Arbor: University of Michigan Press.

López-Ayllón, Sergio, and H. Fix-Fierro. 1999. "Communications between legal cultures: The case of NAFTA's Chapter 19 binational panels." In L. Perret (ed.), *Evolution of free trade in the Americas.* Montreal: Wilson & Lafleur.

López-Ayllón, Sergio, and H. Fix-Fierro. 2003. "'Faraway, so close!': The rule of law and legal change in Mexico, 1970–1999." In L. Friedman and R. Pérez-Perdomo (eds.), *Legal cultures in the age of globalization: Latin America and Latin Europe.* Stanford, Calif.: Stanford University Press.

López Bohórquez, Alí E. 1984. *Los ministros de la audiencia de Caracas, 1786–1810.* Caracas: Academia Nacional de la Historia.

Lorey, David. 1992. *The rise of the professions in twentieth-century Mexico: University graduates and occupational change since 1929.* Los Angeles: University of California.

Loveman, Brian. 1993. *The constitution or tyranny: Regimes of exception in Spanish America.* Pittsburgh, Penn.: University of Pittsburgh Press.

Lowenstein, Steven. 1970. *Lawyers, legal education, and development: An examination of the process of reform in Chile.* New York: International Legal Center.

Luján Muñoz, Jorge. 1982. *Los escribanos de las Indias Occidentales.* Mexico City: Universidad Nacional Autónoma de México.

Lynch, Dennis O. 1981. *Legal roles in Colombia.* Uppsala: Scandinavian Institute for African Studies; and New York: International Center for Law in Development.

Lynch, John. 1973. *The Spanish American revolutions 1808–1826.* New York: Norton.

Mackinson de Sorokin, Gladys. 1984. "La mujer y el derecho: Estudio sobre las variaciones de la matrícula femenina en la Facultad de Derecho y Ciencias Sociales de la Universidad de Buenos Aires." *Revista de sociología del derecho* 2.

MacLachlan, Colin. 1974. *Criminal justice in 18th century Mexico: A study of the Tribunal of the Acordada.* Berkeley: University of California Press.

Malagón Barceló, Javier. 1966. *Estudios de historia y derecho.* Xalapa: Universidad Veracruzana.

Manzano, Juan. 1948. *La incorporación de las Indias a la Corona de Castilla.* Madrid: Cultura Hispánica.

Manzano, Juan. 1950–56. *Historia de las recopilaciones de Indias.* Madrid: Ediciones Cultura Hispánica.

Maravall, José Antonio. 1972. *Estado moderno y mentalidad social (siglos XV al XVII).* Madrid: Revista de Occidente.

Maravall, José Antonio. 1977. *Poder, honor y élites en el siglo XVII.* Madrid: Siglo XXI.

Mariluz Urquijo, José María. 1988. "Maziel, jurista del setecientos." *Revista de historia del derecho* (Buenos Aires) 16.

Martínez Marina, Francisco. 1966. *Juicio crítico de la Novíssima Recopilación.* Madrid: Biblioteca de Autores Españoles. (Originally published 1820.)

Martínez Peñaranda, Yanick. 1981. "Los estudios de derecho en la práctica." Thesis. Universidad de los Andes Escuela de Derecho, Bogotá.

Mattei, Ugo. 1997. *Comparative law and economics.* Ann Arbor: University of Michigan Press.

McKennan, Theodora. 1978. "Jeremy Bentham and the Colombian Liberators." *The Americas* 34.

McKinley, P. Michael. 1993. *Caracas antes de la independencia.* Caracas: Monte Ávila.

Meili, Stephan. 1999. "Legal education in Argentina and Chile." In L. Trubek and J. Cooper (eds.), *Educating for justice around the world: Legal education, legal practice and the community.* Aldershot: Dartmouth.

Mellafe, R., A. Rebolledo, and M. Cárdenas. 1993. *Historia de la Universidad de Chile.* Santiago: Universidad de Chile.

Méndez Calzada, Luis. 1944. *La función judicial en las primeras épocas de la independencia.* Buenos Aires: Losada.

Mendieta y Núñez, Lucio. 1956. *Historia de la Facultad de Derecho.* Mexico City: Universidad Nacional Autónoma de México.

Mera Figueroa, Jorge (ed.). 1998. *Justicia militar y estado de derecho.* Santiago: Universidad Diego Portales.

Merryman, John Henry. 1981. "On the convergence (and divergence) of the civil law and the common law." *Stanford Journal of International Law* 17.

Merryman, John Henry. 1985. *The civil law tradition* (2nd ed.). Stanford, Calif.: Stanford University Press.

Merryman, John, D. Clark, and L. Friedman. 1979. *Law and social change in Mediterranean Europe and Latin America: A handbook of legal and social indicators.* Stanford, Calif.: Stanford University Law School.

Mitchell, Brian R. 1998. *International historical statistics: The Americas 1750–1993*. London: Macmillan; and New York: Stockton Press.

Mobarec Asfura, Norma. 1982. "Bello y las leyes de exvinculación." In Departamento de Ciencias del Derecho, Facultad de Derecho, Universidad de Chile, *Congreso internacional Andrés Bello y el derecho*. Santiago: Editorial Jurídica de Chile.

Moccia, Luigi. 1988. "Il legislatore del 'diritto comune' continentale (secc XVI–XVIII) nell'opera di Gino Gorla." In A. Giuliani and N. Picardi (eds.), *Modelli di legislatore e scienza della legislazione*. Perugia: Edizione Scientifiche Italiane.

Molina Martínez, Miguel. 1986. *El Real Tribunal de Minería de Lima (1785–1821)*. Seville: Diputación Provincial de Sevilla.

Mora, Luis Paulino. 2001. "Presentación del caso de Costa Rica." Paper presented at meeting, Nuevos Enfoques para Atender la Demanda de Justicia. World Bank Regional Conference for Latin America and the Caribbean, CIDE, Mexico City, May.

Moreno, Daniel. 1979. *Grandes juristas mexicanos*. Mexico City: Pax.

Navas, José Manuel. 1996. *La abogacía en el siglo de oro*. Madrid: Ilustre Colegio de Abogados de Madrid.

Nino, Carlos S. 1996. *Radical evil on trial*. New Haven, Conn.: Yale University Press.

O'Donnell, Guillermo. 1986. "Introduction to Latin American cases." In G. O'Donnell, P. Schmitter, and L. Whitehead (eds.), *Transitions from authoritarian rule: Latin America*. Baltimore, Md.: Johns Hopkins University Press.

Palmer, R. R. 1997. *J. B. Say, an economist in troubled times*. Princeton, N.J.: Princeton University Press.

Pareja Paz-Soldan, José. 1954. Las constituciones del Peru. Madrid: Ediciones de Cultura Hispanica.

Parra Aranguren, Gonzalo. 1966. "Los antecedentes de la codificación civil y del derecho internacional privado venezolano (1810–1862). *Revista de la Facultad de Derecho de la Universidad Católica Andrés Bello* 2.

Parra Aranguren, Gonzalo. 1974. "Nuevos antecedentes sobre la codificación civil venezolana (1810–1862)." In Academia Nacional de Historia, *La codificación de Páez*. Caracas: Academia Nacional de Historia.

Parra Márquez, Héctor. 1952. *Historia del colegio de abogados de Caracas*. Vol. 1. Caracas: Imprenta Nacional.

Parra Márquez, Héctor. 1973. *Historia del colegio de abogados de Caracas*. Vol. 2. Caracas: Colegio de Abogados del Distrito Federal.

Pásara, Luis. 1982. *Jueces, justicia y poder en el Perú*. Lima: CEDYS.

Pásara, Luis. 1984. "Perú: administración de ¿justicia?" In J. de Belaúnde (ed.), *La administración de justicia en América Latina*. Lima: Consejo Latinoamericano de Derecho y Desarrollo.

Paton, Paul D. 2002. "Process, policy and politics: Regulatory responses and the multidisciplinary practice debate in Canada." SPILS JSM thesis, Stanford University Law School.

Pelorson, Jean-Marc. 1980. *Les letrados juristes castillans sous Philippe III*. Poitiers: Université de Poitiers.

Peña, Carlos. 1994. "Hacia una caracterización del ethos legal: De nuevo sobre la cultura jurídica." In A. Squella (ed.), *Evolución de la cultura jurídica chilena*. Santiago: Corporación de Promoción Universitaria.

Peña, Carlos. 2000. "Características y desafíos de la enseñanza legal." Unpublished paper.

Perelman, Chaim, and L. Olbrechts-Tyteca. 1953. *Rhetorique et philosophie.* Paris: Presses Universitaires de France.

Perelman, Chaim, and L. Olbrechts-Tyteca. 1958. *Traité de l'argumentation.* Paris: Presses Universitaires de France.

Pérez-Perdomo, Rogelio. 1968. "Modernismo y tradicionalismo en la filosofía del derecho del siglo XVIII español." *Derecho* (Pontificia Universidad Católica del Perú, Lima) 26.

Pérez-Perdomo, Rogelio. 1974. *Tres ensayos sobre los métodos de la educación jurídica.* Caracas: Universidad Central de Venezuela.

Pérez-Perdomo, Rogelio. 1981. *Los abogados en Venezuela.* Caracas: Monte Ávila.

Pérez-Perdomo, Rogelio. 1982. "Bello y la literatura didáctica en derecho." *Revista nacional de cultura* (Caracas) 249.

Pérez-Perdomo, Rogelio. 1983. "Ensayo de periodización de la historia social del derecho en Venezuela." In *Libro Homenaje a José Melich Orsini.* Caracas: Universidad Central de Venezuela.

Pérez-Perdomo, Rogelio. 1984. "La investigación jurídica en Venezuela contemporánea." In H. Vessuri (ed.), *Ciencia académica en la Venezuela moderna: Historia reciente y perspectivas de las disciplinas científicas.* Caracas: Fondo Editorial Acta Científica Venezolana.

Pérez-Perdomo, Rogelio. 1985. "La producción de los investigadores de la Facultad de Ciencias Jurídicas y Políticas de la Universidad Central de Venezuela." *Archivos Latinoamericanos de metodología y filosofía del derecho (1981–85)* 2.

Pérez-Perdomo, Rogelio. 1987. "Teoría y práctica de la legislación en la temprana República (Venezuela 1821–1870)." In A. Giuliani and N. Piccardi (eds.), *Modelli di legislatori e scienza della legislazione.* Perugia: Edizioni Scientifiche Italiane.

Pérez-Perdomo, Rogelio. 1990. "La organización del estado en el siglo XIX (1830–1899)." *Politeia* (Caracas) 14.

Pérez-Perdomo, Rogelio. 1991. "Liberalismo y derecho en el siglo XIX de América Latina." *Sociologia del Diritto* (Milan) 19.

Pérez-Perdomo, Rogelio. 1993. "La justicia en tiempos de globalización: Demandas y perspectivas de cambio de la administración de justicia en América Latina." In Inter-American Development Bank, *Justicia y desarrollo en América Latina y el Caribe.* Washington, D.C.: Inter-American Development Bank.

Pérez-Perdomo, Rogelio. 1996a. "Corrupción: La difícil relación entre política y derecho." *Politeia* (Caracas) 19.

Pérez-Perdomo, Rogelio. 1996b. "De la justicia y otros demonios." In M. E. Boza and R. Pérez-Perdomo (eds.), *Seguridad juridical y competitividad.* Caracas: Ediciones IESA.

Pérez-Perdomo, Rogelio. 2000. "Jueces y estado hoy." In Fundación Manuel García-Pelayo (ed.), *Constitución y constitucionalismo hoy.* Caracas: Fundación Manuel García-Pelayo.

Pérez-Perdomo, Rogelio. 2001. "Oil lawyers and the globalization of Venezuelan oil business." In R. Appelbaum, W. Felstiner, and V. Gessner (eds.), *Rules and networks: The legal culture of global business transactions.* Oxford: Hart.

Pérez-Perdomo, Rogelio. 2003. "Venezuela 1958–1999: The legal system in an impaired democracy." In L. Friedman and R. Pérez-Perdomo (eds.), *Legal cultures in the age of globalization: Latin America and Latin Europe.* Stanford, Calif.: Stanford University Press.

Pérez-Perdomo, Rogelio. 2004. "Reforma judicial, estado de derecho y revolución en Venezuela." In L. Pásara (ed.), *En búsqueda de una justicia distinta: Experiencias de reforma en América Latina.* Lima: Consorcio Justicia Viva.

Pérez-Perdomo, Rogelio, and L. Friedman. 2003. "Latin legal cultures in the age of globalization." In L. Friedman and R. Pérez-Perdomo (eds.), *Legal cultures in the age of globalization: Latin America and Latin Europe.* Stanford, Calif.: Stanford University Press.

Pérez-Perdomo, Rogelio, and C. L. Roche. 1990. "Balance de la sociología del derecho en la Venezuela actual." In V. Ferrari (ed.), *Developing sociology of law.* Milan: Giuffrè.

Pérez Vila, Manuel. 1997. "Miguel José Sanz." *Diccionario de historia de Venezuela* (2nd ed.). Caracas: Fundación Polar.

Pérez y López, Antonio Xavier. 1791–98. *Teatro de la legislación universal de España é Indias, por orden cronológico de sus cuerpos y decisiones no recopiladas y alfabético de sus títulos y principales materias.* Madrid: Imprenta de Antonio Espinosa.

Persico, Pablo. 2001. *Informe sobre la educación superior en Chile: Análisis de tendencias de la última década.* Santiago: Corporación de Promoción Universitaria.

Piano Mortari, Vincenzo. 1980. *Gli inizi del diritto moderno in Europa.* Naples: Liguori Editore.

Pichler, Rufus. 2000. "Trust and reliance. Enforcement and compliance: Enhancing consumer confidence in the electronic marketplace." SPILS JSM thesis, Stanford University Law School.

Polanco Alcántara, Tomás. 1992. *Las reales audiencias en las provincias americanas de España.* Madrid: Mapfre.

Pontes de Miranda, Francisco Calvacanti. 1984. *Fontes e evolução do direito privado no Brasil.* Rio de Janeiro: Forense.

Puente Brunke, José de la. 1997. "Justicia e intereses particulares: El caso de un oidor del siglo XVII." *Boletín del Instituto Riva Agüero* (Lima) 24.

Quaglioni, Diego. 1988. "Legislazione statutaria e dottrina della legislazione nel pensiero giuridico del trecento italiano: Le 'questiones statutorum' di Alberico da Rosate (c1290–1360)." In A. Giuliani and N. Picardi (eds.), *Modelli di legislatore e scienza della legislazione.* Perugia: Edizione Scientifiche Italiane.

Quevedo y Villegas, Francisco. 1951. *Los sueños.* Buenos Aires: Losada. (Originally published 1622.)

Quintero, Maria Olga. 1983. "Independencia del poder judicial." In *Libro homenaje a José Melich Orsini.* Vol. 2. Caracas: Universidad Central de Venezuela.

Quintero, Maria Olga. 1988. *Justicia y realidad.* Caracas: Universidad Central de Venezuela.

Ramos Núñez, Carlos A. 1993. *Toribio Pacheco, jurista peruano del siglo XIX.* Lima: Pontificia Universidad Católica del Perú.

Ramos Núñez, Carlos A. 2001. *Historia del derecho civil peruano.* Lima: Pontificia Universidad Católica del Perú.

Rasi, Piero. 1957. "Avvocati e procuratori: Diritto romano." In *Novissimo Digesto Italiano*. Torino: Unione Tipografico Editrice.

Restrepo Piedrahita, Carlos (ed.). 1995. *Constituciones nacionales de Colombia*. Bogotá: Universidad del Externado.

Rey, Juan Carlos. 1989. *El futuro de la democracia en Venezuela*. Caracas: IDEA.

Rico, José María, and Luis Salas. 1990. "Independencia judicial en América Latina: Replanteo de un tema tradicional." Paper. San José, Costa Rica: Centro para la Administración de Justicia.

Riesco, José Antonio. 1978. "Conclusiones de la V conferencia de facultades y escuelas de derecho de América Latina. Informe del Relator General." In J. Witker (ed.), *Antología de estudios sobre la enseñanza del derecho*. Mexico City: Universidad Nacional Autónoma de México.

Rivera-Cira, Tirza. 1993. "Informe sobre Costa Rica." In J. Correa (ed.), *Situación y políticas judiciales en América Latina*. Santiago: Universidad Diego Portales.

Roche, Carmen Luisa. 2001. "The feminization of the legal profession in Venezuela: Its meaning for the profession and for women lawyers." Paper presented at the Joint Meeting of the Law and Society Association and ISA Research Committee on Sociology of Law, Budapest, May 2001.

Rodríguez, César. 2001. "Globalization, judicial reform and the rule of law in Latin America: The return of law and development." *Beyond Law* 23.

Rodríguez, Cesar, M. García-Villegas, and R. Uprimny. 2003. "Justice and society in Colombia: A sociological analysis of Colombian courts." In L. Friedman and R. Pérez-Perdomo (eds.), *Legal cultures in the age of globalization: Latin America and Latin Europe*. Stanford, Calif.: Stanford University Press.

Rodríguez Cruz, Agueda. 1973. *Historia de las universidades hispanoamericanas: Período hispano*. Bogotá: Instituto Caro y Cuervo.

Rodríguez de San Miguel. 1981. "Vindicación de los que se dedican a la abogacía." *Revista de investigaciones jurídicas* (Mexico) 5.

Rodríguez O, Jaime. 1989. "From royal subject to republican citizen: The role of autonomists in the independence of Mexico." In J. Rodríguez (ed.), *The independence of Mexico and the creation of the new nation*. Los Angeles: University of California.

Rodríguez O, Jaime. 1996. *La independencia de la América española*. Mexico City: Fondo de Cultura Económica.

Romero, José Luis. 1978. *Breve historia de Argentina*. Buenos Aires: Huemul.

Rosenn, Keith S. 1969. "The reform of legal education in Brazil." *Journal of Legal Education* 21.

Rosenn, Keith S. 1971. "The jeito: Brazil's institutional bypass of the formal legal system and its development implications." *American Journal of Comparative Law* 19.

Rosenn, Keith S. 1987. "The protection of judicial independence in Latin America." *University of Miami Inter-American Law Review* 19.

Rouquié, Alain. 1986. "Dictadores, militares y legitimidad en América Latina." In J. Labastida Martín del Campo (ed.), *Dictaduras y dictadores*. Mexico City: Siglo XXI.

Rowat, M., W. Malik, and M. Dakolias (eds.). 1995. *Judicial reform in Latin America and the Caribbean*. Washington, D.C.: World Bank.

Ruiz Guiñazú, Enrique. 1916. *La magistratura indiana*. Buenos Aires: Facultad de Derecho y Ciencias Sociales.

Safford, Frank. 1976. *The ideal of the practical: Colombia's struggle to form a technical elite.* Austin: University of Texas Press.

Santelices Ariztía, Fernando. 2002. "Informe sobre la enseñanza legal en Chile." Paper. Centro de Estudios de Justicia de las Américas, Santiago.

Santos, Boaventura de Sousa. 1999. "The GATT of law and democracy." In J. Feest (ed.), *Globalization and legal cultures.* Oñati, Spain: Instituto Internacional de Sociología Jurídica.

Sarfatti, Magali. 1966. *Spanish bureaucratic patrimonialism in America.* Berkeley: University of California.

Schipani, Sandro. 1992. "Los códigos latinoamericanos de la 'transfusión' del derecho romano y de la independencia hacia los códigos de la 'mezcla' y 'códigos tipo.'" In A. Levaggi (ed.), *Fuentes ideológicas de la codificación latinoamericana.* Buenos Aires: Universidad del Museo Social Argentino.

Schulz, Fritz. 1946. *History of Roman legal science.* Oxford: Clarendon Press.

Segnini, Yolanda. 1987. *Las luces del gomecismo.* Caracas: Alfadil.

Sepúlveda, Juan Ginés de. 1951. *Demócrates Segundo; o de las justas causas de la guerra con los indios.* Madrid: Consejo Superior de Investigaciones Científicas.

Serrada, Tibisay. 2000. "El mito de la constitución en Hispanoamérica: La Gran Colombia." *Politeia* (Caracas) 24.

Serrano, Sol. 1994a. "La ciudadanía examinada: El control estatal de la educación en Chile, 1810–1870." In A. Annino, L. Castro, and F. X. Guerra (eds.), *De los imperios a las naciones: Iberoamérica.* Zaragoza: IberCaja.

Serrano, Sol. 1994b. *Universidad y nación: Chile en el siglo XIX.* Santiago: Editorial Universitaria.

Silva, Renán. 1992. *Universidad y sociedad en el Nuevo Reino de Granada.* Bogotá: Banco de la República.

Silva García, Germán. 2001. *El mundo real de los abogados y de la justicia.* Vol. 4: *Las ideologías profesionales.* Bogotá: Universidad Externado de Colombia; and Instituto Latinoamericano de Servicios Legales Alternativos.

Smith, Peter H. 1979. *Labyrinths of power: Political recruitment in twentieth-century Mexico.* Princeton, N.J.: Princeton University Press.

Soberanes Fernández, José Luis. 1980. *Los tribunales de la Nueva España.* Mexico City: Universidad Nacional Autónoma de México.

Soberanes Fernández, José Luis. 1993. "Informe sobre México." In J. Correa (ed.), *Situación y políticas judiciales en América Latina.* Santiago: Universidad Diego Portales.

Socolow, Susan M. 1987. *The bureaucrats of Buenos Aires, 1769–1818: Amor al real servicio.* Durham, N.C.: Duke University Press.

Soriano de García Pelayo, Graciela. 1996. *El personalismo político hispanoamericano del siglo XIX: Criterios y proposiciones metodológicas para su estudio.* Caracas: Monte Ávila.

Soriano de García Pelayo, Graciela. 2000. "La teoría del desarrollo discrónico y su manifestación en el derecho: Para entender la historia política de Hispanoamérica." *Politeia* (Caracas) 24.

Souto, Claudio, and S. Souto. 1990. "Sociology of law in Brazil: The recent years." In V. Ferrari (ed.), *Developing sociology of law.* Milan: Giuffrè.

Squella, Agustín. 1988. "La cultura jurídica chilena." In A. Squella (ed.), *La cultura jurídica chilena.* Santiago: Corporación de Promoción Universitaria.

Staples, Ana. 1982. "La construcción del estado nacional." In F. Arce Gurza et al. (eds.), *Historia de las profesiones en México*. Mexico City: Colegio de México.

Stelling-Michaud, Sven. 1955. *L'Université de Bologne et la pénétration des droits romain et canonique en Suisse au XIIIe et XIVe siècle*. Geneva: Droz.

Stein, Peter. 1966. *Regulae iuris: From luristic rules to legal maxims*. Edinburgh: Edinburgh University Press.

Stein, Peter. 1988. "Legislation in English law." In A. Giuliani and N. Picardi (eds.), *Modelli di legislatore e scienza della legislazione*. Perugia: Edizione Scientifiche Italiane.

Steiner, Henry. 1971. "Legal education and socio-economic change: Brazilian perspectives." *American Journal of Comparative Law* 19.

Sunwolf. 1997. "Communication between legal cultures: Strategies, perceptions and beliefs of American lawyers who practice international litigation." Paper presented at the Workshop on Changing Legal Cultures, Oñati, Spain.

Tanck de Estrada, Dorothy. 1982. "La colonia." In F. Arce Gurza et al. (eds.), *Historia de las profesiones en México*. Mexico City: Colegio de México.

Tate, C. Neal, and T. Vallinder (eds.). 1995. *The global expansion of judicial power*. New York: New York University Press.

Tau Anzoátegui, Víctor. 1977. *La codificación en Argentina, 1810–1870: Mentalidad social e ideas jurídicas*. Buenos Aires: Imprenta de la Universidad.

Tau Anzoátegui, Víctor. 1987. *Las ideas juridicas en la Argentina (siglos XIX y XX)*. 2nd ed. Buenos Aires: Perrot.

Tau Anzoátegui, Víctor. 1992a. *Casuismo y sistema*. Buenos Aires: Instituto de Investigaciones de Historia del Derecho.

Tau Anzoátegui, Víctor. 1992b. *La ley en la América Hispana. Del descubrimiento a la emancipación*. Buenos Aires: Academia Nacional de la Historia.

Tau Anzoátegui, Víctor. 1997. *Nuevos horizontes en el estudio histórico del derecho indiano*. Buenos Aires: Instituto de Investigaciones de Historia del Derecho.

Tau Anzoátegui, Víctor, and E. Martiré. 1967. *Manual de historia de las instituciones argentinas*. Buenos Aires: La Ley.

Taylor, William. 1979. *Drinking, homicide, and rebellion in colonial Mexican villages*. Stanford, Calif.: Stanford University Press.

Tena Ramírez, Felipe (ed.). 1999. *Leyes fundamentales de México, 1808–1999*. Mexico City: Porrúa.

Thieme, Hans. 1967. "Le rôle des doctores legum dans la societé de l'Allemagne du XVIe siècle." In *Recueil des memoires et travaux, publiés par la Societé d'Histoire du Drot de des Institutions des Ancien Pays de Droit Ecrit*. Montpellier: Université de Montpellier.

Toharia, José Juan. 2003. "The organization, functioning, and evaluation of the Spanish judicial system, 1975–2000." In L. Friedman and R. Pérez-Perdomo (eds.), *Legal cultures in the age of globalization: Latin America and Latin Europe*. Stanford, Calif.: Stanford University Press.

Toro, Fermín. 1845. *Reflexiones sobre la ley del 10 de abril de 1834*. Caracas: Valentín Espinal.

Torrente, Mariano. 1829. *Historia de la revolución hispano-americana*. Madrid: Imprenta de D. Leon Amarita.

Torres Arends, Irene. 1997. *Educación jurídica y razonamiento*. Caracas: Universidad Central de Venezuela.

Torres Arends, Irene. 2001. "Cultura jurídica y estudiantes de derecho: Una medición de cultura jurídica en Venezuela." Unpublished paper. Facultad de Ciencias Jurídicas y Políticas, Universidad Central de Venezuela, Caracas.

Torrubiano Ripoll, Jaime. 1917. "Notas biográficas y razones bibliográficas." In F. de Vitoria (ed.), *Relecciones teológicas*. Madrid: Librería Religiosa Hernández.

Trazegnies Granda, Fernando de. 1979. *La idea del derecho en el Perú republicano del siglo XIX*. Lima: Pontificia Universidad Católica del Perú.

David Trubek, Yves Dezalay, Buchanan, and Davis. 1994. "Global restructuring and the law: The internationalization of legal fields and the creation of transnational arenas." *Case Western Reserve Law Review* 44.

Trubek, David, and M. Galanter. 1974. "Scholars in self-estrangement: Some reflections on the crisis in law and development studies in the United States." *Wisconsin Law Review*, p. 1,062.

Urbaneja, Diego. 1975. "Caudillismo y pluralismo en el siglo XIX venezolano." *Politeia* (Caracas) 4.

Uribe, Victor M. 1995. "Educación legal y formación del Estado colombiano durante la transición de la colonia a la República, 1780–1850." In J. Guerrero Baron (ed.), *Etnias, educación y archivos en la historia de Colombia*. Tunja: Universidad Pedagógica y Tecnológica de Colombia.

Uribe-Uran, Victor M. 2000. *Honorable lives: Lawyers, family, and politics in Colombia, 1780–1850*. Pittsburgh, Penn.: University of Pittsburgh Press.

Urzúa, Raúl. 1978. "La profesión de abogado y el desarrollo: Antecedentes para un estudio." In G. Figueroa (ed.), *Derecho y sociedad*. Santiago: Corporación de Promoción Universitaria. (Article originally published in 1971.)

Vallenilla Lanz, Laureano. 1929. *Cesarismo democrático* (2nd ed.). Caracas: Tipografia Universal.

Van Caenegem, R. C. 1987. *Judges, legislators and professors*. Cambridge: Cambridge University Press.

Van Puymbroeck, Rudolf (ed.). 2001. *Comprehensive legal and judicial development*. Washington, D.C.: World Bank.

Varela, David F. 1999. "El Banco Mundial y la reforma judicial en América Latina." Paper presented at the 2a Conferencia Sobre la Efectividad y Coste de la Justicia, Centro de Investigaciones en Derecho y Economía, Universidad Complutense, Madrid.

Vargas, Juan Enrique, C. Peña, and J. Correa. 2001. *El rol del estado y del mercado en la justicia*. Santiago: Universidad Diego Portales.

Vega, Wenceslao. 1986. *Historia del derecho dominicano*. Santo Domingo.

Véliz, Claudio. 1980. *The centralist tradition of Latin America*. Princeton, N.J.: Princeton University Press.

Venâncio Filho, Alberto. 1977. *Das arcadas ao bachalerismo: 150 anos de ensino jurídico no Brasil*. São Paulo: Perspectiva.

Ves Losada, Alfredo. 1990. "Current sociology of law in Argentina." In V. Ferrari (ed.), *Developing sociology of law*. Milan: Giuffrè.

Villey, Michel. 1964. *Le droit romain* (5th ed.). Paris: Presses Universitaires de France.

Villey, Michel. 1968. *La formation de la pensée juridique moderne.* Paris: Montchrestien.

Vitoria, Francisco de. 1917. *Relecciones teológicas.* Madrid: Librería Religiosa Hernández. (Originally published 1557.)

Walker, Charles. 2001. "Crime in the time of the great fear: Indians and the state in the Peruvian southern Andes." In R. Salvatore, C. Aguirre, and G. Joseph (eds.), *Crime and punishment in Latin America: Law and society since late colonial times.* Durham, N.C.: Duke University Press.

Watson, Alan. 1977. *Society and legal change.* Edinburgh: Scottish Academic Press.

Watson, Alan. 1993. *Legal transplants: An approach to comparative law* (2nd ed.). Athens: University of Georgia Press.

Watson, Alan. 2000. *Law out of context.* Athens: University of Georgia Press.

Wehling, Arno. 2000. "O direito brasileiro nos séculos XIX e XX." Unpublished paper.

Weiler, J.H.H. 2001. "The rule of lawyers and the ethos of diplomats: Reflections on WTO dispute settlements." In R. B. Porter et al. (eds.), *Efficiency, equity, legitimacy: The multilateral trading system at the millennium.* Washington, D.C.: Brookings Institution Press.

Whigham, Thomas. 1994. "Trade and conflict on the rivers: Corrientes, 1780–1840." In M. Szuchman and J. Brown (eds.), *Revolution and restoration: The rearrangement of power in Argentina, 1776–1860.* Lincoln: University of Nebraska Press.

Wieacker, Franz. 1957. *Historia del derecho privado de la Edad Moderna.* Madrid: Aguilar.

Wilson, Richard. 1989. "The new legal education in North and South America." *Stanford Journal of International Law* 25.

Witker, Jorge. 1978. *Antología de estudios sobre la enseñanza del derecho.* Mexico City: Universidad Nacional Autónoma de México.

Wolkmer, Antonio Carlos. 1998. *Historia do direito no Brasil.* Rio de Janeiro: Forense.

Zaffaroni, Eugenio Raúl. 1995. *Poder Judiciário: Crise, acertos e desacertos.* São Paulo: Editora Revista dos Tribunais.

Zatz, Marjorie S. 1994. *Producing legality: Law and socialism in Cuba.* New York: Routledge.

Zavala, Silvio. 1988. *Las instituciones jurídicas de la conquista de América* (3rd ed.). Mexico City: Porrúa.

Zimmermann, Eduardo. 1998. "Poder Judicial, la construcción del estado, y el federalismo: Argentina, 1860–1898." In E. Posada-Carbó (ed.), *In search of a new order: Essays on the politics and society of nineteenth-century Latin America.* London: Institute of Latin American Studies.

Zimmermann, Eduardo. 1999. "The education of lawyers and judges in Argentina's Organización Nacional." In E. Zimmermann (ed.), *Judicial institutions in nineteenth-century Latin America.* London: Institute of Latin American Studies.

Zolezzi Ibárcena, Lorenzo. 1982. *La profesión de abogado en Lima (una aproximación empírica).* Lima: Pontificia Universidad Católica del Perú.

Zolezzi Ibárcena, Lorenzo. 1993. "Informe sobre Perú." In J. Correa (ed.), *Situación y políticas judiciales en América Latina.* Santiago: Universidad Diego Portales.

Zweigert, Konrad, and H. Kötz. 1998. *Comparative law* (3rd ed.). Oxford: Clarendon Press.

The authorized representative in the EU for product safety and compliance is:
Mare Nostrum Group
B.V Doelen 72
4831 GR Breda
The Netherlands

www.ingramcontent.com/pod-product-compliance
Lightning Source LLC
LaVergne TN
LVHW102013210926
848483LV00014B/429/J